W0006062

Missing, Presumed Murdered

Also by DICK KIRBY:

Rough Justice: Memoirs of a Flying Squad Officer

The Real Sweeney

You're Nicked!

Villains

The Guv'nors: Ten of Scotland Yard's Finest Detectives

The Sweeney: The First Sixty Years of Scotland Yard's Crimebusting Flying Squad 1919–1978

Scotland Yard's Ghost Squad: The Secret Weapon against Post-War Crime

The Brave Blue Line: 100 Years of Metropolitan Police Gallantry

Death on the Beat: Police Officers Killed in the Line of Duty

The Scourge of Soho: The Controversial Career of SAS Hero Harry Challenor MM

Whitechapel's Sherlock Holmes: The Casebook of Fred Wensley OBE, KPM, Victorian Crimebuster

The Wrong Man: The Shooting of Steven Waldorf and the Hunt for David Martin

Laid Bare: The Nude Murders and the Hunt for 'Jack the Stripper'

London's Gangs at War

Operation Countryman: The Flawed Enquiry into London Police Corruption

Scotland Yard's Gangbuster: Bert Wickstead's Most Celebrated Cases

The Mayfair Mafia: The Lives and Crimes of the Messina Brothers

Scotland Yard's Flying Squad: 100 Years of Crime Fighting

Scotland Yard's Murder Squad

The Racetrack Gangs: Four Decades of Doping, Intimidation and Violent Crime

IRA Terror on Britain's Streets 1939-1940: the Wartime Bombing Campaign and Hitler Connection

Scotland Yard's Casebook of Serious Crimes: 75 Years of No-Nonsense Policing

The Brighton Police Scandal: A Story of Corruption, Intimidation & Violence

Missing, Presumed Murdered

The McKay Case and Other Convictions without a Corpse

DICK KIRBY

First published in Great Britain in 2022 by
Pen & Sword True Crime
An imprint of
Pen & Sword Books Ltd
Yorkshire – Philadelphia

ISBN 978 1 39909 344 6

A CIP catalogue record for this book is available from the British Library.

Printed and bound in the UK by CPI Group (UK) Ltd, Croydon, CR0 4YY.

Pen & Sword Books Limited incorporates the imprints of Atlas, Archaeology, Aviation, Discovery, Family History, Fiction, History, Maritime, Military, Military Classics, Politics, Select, Transport, True Crime, Air World, Frontline Publishing, Leo Cooper, Remember When, Seaforth Publishing, The Praetorian Press, Wharncliffe Local History, Wharncliffe Transport, Wharncliffe True Crime and White Owl.

For a complete list of Pen & Sword titles please contact

PEN & SWORD BOOKS LIMITED
47 Church Street, Barnsley, South Yorkshire, S70 2AS, England
E-mail: enquiries@pen-and-sword.co.uk
Website: www.pen-and-sword.co.uk

Or
PEN AND SWORD BOOKS
1950 Lawrence Rd, Havertown, PA 19083, USA
E-mail: Uspen-and-sword@casematepublishers.com
Website: www.penandswordbooks.com

This book is dedicated to the memory of
former Detective Superintendent, Metropolitan Police,
Edwin Williams BA (Joint Hons), PGCE,
MBPsS, Dip.NEBSS.

'He was a friend who lost his way'
Ann Kirby

Praise for Dick Kirby's Books

'He treats criminals the only way they understand. His language is often shocking, his methods unorthodox.' **NATIONAL ASSOCIATION OF RETIRED POLICE OFFICERS' MAGAZINE**

'The continuing increase in violent crime will make many readers yearn for yesteryear and officers of Dick Kirby's calibre.' **POLICE MAGAZINE**

'His reflections on the political aspect of law enforcement will ring true for cops, everywhere.' **AMERICAN POLICE BEAT**

'Its no-nonsense portrayal of life in the police will give readers a memorable literary experience.' **SUFFOLK JOURNAL**

'A great read with fascinating stories and amusing anecdotes from a man who experienced it all.' **SUFFOLK AND NORFOLK LIFE MAGAZINE.**

'A gritty series of episodes from his time in the Met – laced with black humour and humanity.' **EAST ANGLIAN DAILY TIMES**

'This is magic. The artfulness of these anti-heroes has you pining for the bad old days.' **DAILY SPORT**

'Crammed with vivid descriptions of long-forgotten police operations, races along like an Invicta tourer at full throttle.' **DAILY EXPRESS**

'Rarely, if ever, have I been so captivated and moved by a book . . . the way in which Mr Kirby has gone about it is exceptional.' **POLICE MEMORABILIA COLLECTORS CLUB**

'Dick Kirby has chosen his fascinating subject well.' **LAW SOCIETY GAZETTE**

'Thrilling stories of gang-busting, murder and insurrection . . .' **BERTRAMS BOOKS**

‘A scrupulously honest and detailed account of the unfortunate events leading to police shooting an innocent man . . . nobody is better qualified to write an account of this story than Dick Kirby.’ **THE LONDON POLICE PENSIONER MAGAZINE**

‘Dick Kirby knows his stuff!’ **SURREY-CONSTABULARY.COM**

‘Kirby looks to untangle facts from speculation and questions everything.’ **GET WEST LONDON**

‘Murder, torture and extortion all feature prominently as Mr Kirby investigates some of the most famous incidents of the post-war era.’ **MAIL ONLINE**

‘Only an insider with the engaging style of Dick Kirby could have produced this nakedly forthright page-turner.’ **JOSEPH WAMBAUGH, AUTHOR OF THE CHOIRBOYS**

‘Kirby’s wit and extremely dry humour comes on straight away as early as the prologue which, of course, makes heavy reading subjects easier and creates a relationship between the author (narrator) and the reader.’ **THE LOVE OF BOOKS**

‘Dick Kirby’s book gives precious insight into its exploits for over a century.’ **PAUL MILLEN, AUTHOR OF CRIME SCENE INVESTIGATOR**

‘Dick Kirby has written a book that all crime aficionados will want to read.’ **THE WASHINGTON TIMES**

‘Kirby does not hold back in detailing the grisly parts, bringing home to the reader the harsh reality that these ruthless killers had no boundaries.’ **LONDON POLICE PENSIONER MAGAZINE**

Contents

About the Author

Dick Kirby was born in 1943 in the East End of London and joined the Metropolitan Police in 1967. Half of his twenty-six years' service as a detective was spent with the Yard's Serious Crime Squad and the Flying Squad.

Before being discharged with an injury award and pension in 1993, Kirby was commended by Commissioners, Judges and Magistrates on forty occasions for displaying 'courage, determination and detective ability'.

Married, with four children and five grandchildren, Kirby lives in a Suffolk village with his wife. He appears on television and radio and can be relied upon to provide forthright views on spineless, supine senior police officers (and other politicians) with their insipid, uninformed, absurd and mendacious claims on how they intend to defeat serious crime and claim the streets.

He contributes regularly to newspapers and magazines, reviews books, films and music and is employed by a television company as a consultant and researcher. He also writes memoirs, biographies and true crime books which are widely quoted – this is his twenty-fourth.

Kirby can be visited on his website: www.dickkirby.com

Acknowledgements

My thanks, as always, go to the indefatigable Brigadier Henry Wilson of Pen & Sword Books for his encouragement, as well as support from others at P&S, including Matt Jones, Tara Moran and my editor, George Chamier, together with Jon Wilkinson for his splendid and imaginative jacket designs.

Additionally, great assistance was provided by Jackie Eggleton and Sioban Clarke of the Metropolitan Women's Police Association; Bob Fenton QGM, Ex-CID Officers' Association; Alan Moss of History by the Yard; Julia Mullan, NARPO Magazine and Susi Rogol, editor of the *London Police Pensioner*.

The following gave unstintingly of their time and I am much obliged to them: John Baldwin; Rod Bellis; Dave Bowen; Di Burgess; Jackie Cole; Tony Collinson: Tony Craighill: Ken German; Valerie Grantham; Graham Howard; Garry Jones; Martyn Jones; David Kerney; Colin Kinnaird; Peter Lines; Dave McEnhill; John 'Jock' McNeil; Roy Medcalf; Michael Stuart Moore QC; Robert Needham BA; Brian Norris; Gary Purser: Martin Reeves; Peter Rimmer; Keith Robinson; Peter Ryan; Jim Smith BEM; Janice Stephens; the late Tony Stevens; Roy Thornton; Geoff Walker; John Weeks; Wally Whyte: Rodger Williams; Steve Williams; Trevor Wilson MBE; Edgar Withers; John Wright; Ken Wright.

Rod Bellis and Ken German kindly supplied some of the photos, others are from the author's collection, and whilst every effort has been made to trace copyright holders of other photographs, Pen & Sword and I apologise for any inadvertent omissions.

I could not let these acknowledgements pass by without reference to my friend of 50-plus years, Ed Williams, to whom this book is dedicated and who suffered a horrific death in March 2021. Ed had a multiplicity of problems but never failed to encourage my literary efforts and I think of him every day. God give him peace; during his last few years he experienced little enough of it.

As always, I have received the utmost support from my family: Suzanne and Steve Cowper, their children Emma Cowper B. Mus, Jessica Cowper B. Mus and Harry Cowper MTheatre; Barbara and Rich Jerreat, their children Samuel and Annie Grace; and my two sons, Mark & Robert.

Most of all, my thanks go to Ann, my uncomplaining wife and dear companion for sixty years who has been the candle that lights my way.

Dick Kirby
Suffolk, 2021

Author's Note

Many people are under the impression that a criminal investigation is rather like a jigsaw puzzle. Jack Warner, in his role as Detective Inspector Fred Fellows in Val Guest's 1962 film *Jigsaw*, certainly intimated that to be the case during his fictional murder investigation, and to a limited extent, he was right. But, you see, when one purchases a jigsaw puzzle of anything up to 5,000 pieces and opens the box, one would expect all the pieces to be there. If – as is usually the case – they are, then it's up to the player; and though it may be quite difficult and time-consuming, in the fullness of time a perfect picture will result, with all the pieces in the right place. If only criminal detection were that simple.

When a criminal investigation is launched, some parts of the jigsaw might already be apparent, so they're gathered together and then the hunt begins for the rest. Sometimes they're found, but if they're not – and providing there's a sufficiency of evidence upon which to proceed, once an arrest has been made – then the detective has to go ahead with what he's got. If he's lucky, evidence will continue to accrue as he goes along, and in some cases even when the trial is underway. But, believe me, nothing is cut and dried. (I appreciate that the foregoing paragraph should have been expressed in the past tense; I'm referring to those halcyon days when detectives actually detected and took their cases to court, prior to the present, unhappy time when the contemptible CPS – 'Couldn't Prosecute Satan' – coupled with the pernicious Police and Criminal Evidence Act, 1984 have brought investigations and criminal proceedings to a shuddering halt.)

A classic successful case was that of the murder in 1947 of Alec d'Antiquis, a brave man who was shot dead when he tried to stop three gunmen who had held up a jeweller's in London's West End. There were twenty-seven witnesses to the shooting; all of them gave different descriptions of the perpetrators. When they attended the witness albums at the Yard, even though all of the witnesses claimed that they would be able to identify the murderers, no one was picked out, even though their photographs were contained in the albums. A revolver was recovered from the scene; so was the stolen getaway car. Neither revealed any fingerprints, and none were found in the jeweller's shop. The main suspect was brought in; of the original twenty-seven witnesses, twenty-two attended the suspect's identification parade – none of them picked him out.

With that paucity of information it seems slightly amazing that within twenty days of non-stop work the investigators had arrested and charged the three men responsible (as well as charging two other men with a further jeweller's robbery) and later saw them convicted.

However . . . at least the enquiry team had a corpse to start with; that always helps.

* * *

Many people still believe that to prove a murder there has to be a dead body. John George Haigh, aka 'The Acid Bath Murderer' (someone that we'll be focusing on a little later) obviously thought so – in fact, he said so: 'How can you prove murder if there is no body?'

But as that noted pathologist Professor Cedric Keith Simpson accurately remarked, 'The Crown has to prove a crime, not produce a dead body.'

It's difficult to obtain a conviction for murder without a body – but not impossible.

Introduction

All cases of murder without a body have some sense of bizarreness about them; none more so than that of William Harrison, a 70-year-old manager for Viscountess Campden who, on 16 August 1660, set out from his home in Chipping Campden, Gloucestershire to walk to Charingworth, a village two miles away, in order to collect rent money from some of his employer's tenants. He failed to come home at the expected time, so his wife sent his manservant, John Perry, to look for him; but by the following morning, neither of the men had returned.

Harrison's son Edward set out to look for the two and on the way to Charingworth he met Perry, who told him he had been unable to find Harrison. It appeared that Harrison had obtained £23 in rent from a tenant in Charingworth; he had also gone to Ebrington, where he had seen one of the tenants there the previous night. But after an abortive visit to the village of Paxford, to the south and midway between Charingworth and Chipping Campden, they discovered that heavily bloodstained clothing belonging to William Harrison had been found on the road between Chipping Campden and Ebrington; but there was no sign of his body.

It certainly appeared that there had been foul play; and since John Perry had been out all night, allegedly looking for his master, the finger of suspicion was well and truly pointed at him and he was interviewed by the local Justice of the Peace.

I mentioned the bizarreness which often surrounds these cases; here's curious aspect No.1.

John Perry – who possibly wasn't the sharpest knife in the drawer – after a series of contradictory stories stated that, whilst he was innocent of any involvement, he had witnessed Harrison being murdered for his money by his (John's) mother Joan and his brother Richard, who had strangled Harrison and dumped the body in a nearby cesspool by Wallington's Mill. Mother and brother denied it, and the cesspool was drained and found to be empty of a corpse; other ponds in the locality were dragged and local ruins searched, all to no avail.

John stated that he had no reason to invent the story, although he also admitted suggesting the robbery to his brother. He additionally admitted lying when he said that he had been attacked by robbers a few weeks prior to Harrison's murder, but he stated that in 1659 his mother and brother had stolen £140 from Harrison's house. That was quite a tidy sum. Apart from being worth something like £20,000 at today's values, in 1659 it would have been sufficient to purchase twenty-one horses, twenty-five cows and pay the wages of five shillings per week to a skilled tradesman for five and a half years. The money had been buried in Richard's garden, said John, the idea being that it would be dug up and divided the following September. Consequently, the garden was excavated; not a trace of the money was found.

The trio appeared at court charged with stealing the £140 from William Harrison's house, as well as murdering and robbing him, all of which they denied.

The judge had refused to try them for murder because there was no body; however, the three changed their pleas to guilty to stealing the £140 because fortuitously, thirteen days after Harrison's disappearance, the Indemnity and Oblivion Act of 1660 was placed on the statute books. It provided that, with the exception of certain crimes (including murder), a general pardon would be granted to people who had committed crimes during the Civil War and Interregnum (i.e. the eleven years between the reigns of Charles I and II).

On to peculiar aspect No.2.

In the spring of 1661, the court now decided to hear the charge of murder. Since they had previously pleaded guilty to the robbery plot, the trio were now considered to be criminals, but to this charge the Perry family *definitely* pleaded not guilty, with John telling the court that his previous evidence was as the result of insanity. It did no good at all; found guilty, they were sentenced to death.

Richard and John, on the scaffold at Broadway Hill in Gloucestershire, earnestly reiterated their innocence but were hanged simultaneously. In murder trials with more than one defendant it was normal practice for all of them to be hanged together. An exception was made in this case; Joan Perry was suspected of being a witch, so she was hanged first, in case she was impudent enough to bewitch her sons and prevent them confessing.

All well and good. Three despicable characters had paid the supreme penalty for, to all intents and purposes, callously murdering a well-loved and highly respectable member of the community. Except that they hadn't, which brings us on to grotesque aspect No.3.

In 1662, William Harrison reappeared.

After the population of Chipping Campden and the surrounding countryside had recovered from their shock, Harrison stated that having set out and collected the £23 he had been accosted and attacked by two men, one of whom had stabbed him in the side with a sword, whilst the other stabbed him in the leg. He had been robbed of his money, which was then returned to him. He had then been taken on horseback to the port of Deal in Kent, sold for the sum of £7 and put on board a ship, where his wounds were dressed. While at sea, he was abducted by Barbary pirates and then taken to Turkey, where he was sold as a slave to an 87-year-old doctor in Smyrna. After some twenty-seven months of slavery, his master had died, and Harrison had gone to a port where, with a silver bowl given to him by his master, he bribed his way on a Hamburg-registered ship bound for Lisbon. From there he had returned to England.

Let's take a closer look at this, shall we? The distance from Chipping Campden to Deal is 198 miles. Did Harrison do that on one horse, or were remounts provided? Did he call out for help at any point during the journey (during which, one would have thought, due to his sword wounds, he might surely have bled to death) and if not, why not? Why did his kidnappers stuff his money back into his pockets? Having wounded him in the leg and side with a sword, why did they have him nursed back to health? Why sell him into slavery at all? Who – Barbary pirates or not – would want a 70-year-old man as a slave? Most men taken captive by the pirates were destined to be oar-pulling galley slaves for the rest of their lives, and a 70-year-old could not be seen as particularly productive in that department. Harrison said that his master put him to work gathering cotton and referred to him as 'Boll' (a seed-bearing capsule of cotton) – but why should he do that when the Turkish word for boll is *tohum kabuğu*?

But that was the account that Harrison wrote to a knight of the realm referred to only as 'Sir T.O.' and a Justice of the Peace, which he concluded with the words:

> So, honoured sir, I have given you a true account of my great sufferings and fortunate deliverance, by the mercy and goodness of God my most gracious Father, in Jesus Christ my saviour and redeemer to whose name be ascribed all honour, praise and glory, I conclude and remain . . .

Who could accept that sanctimonious bullshit as being the plain, unvarnished truth?

Well, just about everybody in high office, especially Sir Thomas Overbury, who was almost certainly the Justice of the Peace who initially examined the case of the Perry family, was certainly the knight of the realm to whom Harrison rendered the story of his adventures and who, fifteen years after the event, sent an account of the whole strange business (which he described as being 'one of the most remarkable occurrences which hath happened in the memory of man') to 'a Doctor of Physick' in London.

After all, Harrison was a well-respected man, employed by the wife of a peer of the realm. Who were the Perrys? A perjuror, a woman who was quite possibly a witch – oh, and brother Richard. He may not have been as unfortunate as previously thought. On his way to church, his two children came out of the house and hugged him – both then suffered nosebleeds. That, you know, was considered in the superstitious local neighbourhood to be a bad sign, so he was plainly guilty . . .

* * *

Some thirty-seven years after the odd happenings in Chipping Campden came the next case of murder without a body.

William Kidd had been born in Greenock, Scotland in 1655 and by the age of thirty-four he was a member of a band of mixed French and English pirates. Led by Kidd, the crew mutinied, the captain became surplus to requirements and, renaming the ship, Kidd became its captain. Then, since England was at war with France, he went on to destroy towns on French islands and attack French ships.

By 1695 the now self-styled Captain Kidd had acquired a new ship, *Adventure Galley*, attacked more ships and later, in New York, recruited a crew villainous even by pirate standards. He set sail for Madagascar, where he hoped to engage pirates off that island's coast, but the voyage was beset with difficulties. One third of his crew died from cholera, more deserted and, unusually for a new ship, the *Adventure Galley* developed serious leaks. When Kidd declined to attack ships flying the American or Dutch flags, what remained of the crew grew restless and there was open talk of mutiny.

All of this understandably put Kidd into an ill humour; and on 30 October 1697, when he refused to attack a Dutch ship in the Indian Ocean, one of his gunners, a William Moore, who had urged him to do so, took exception to his captain referring to him as 'a dirty dog'.

'If I am a dirty dog, you have made me so', said Moore, adding, 'you have brought me to ruin, and many more.'

Picking up an ironbound bucket, Kidd heaved it at Moore, who fell to the deck, his skull well and truly fractured. He died the following day, not that that caused Kidd much concern. As he remarked to the ship's surgeon as Moore was chucked overboard, 'I have good friends in England that will bring me off for that.'

Kidd was well aware that he was wanted for acts of piracy, as was a Bostonian associate; and fearing that if arrested, Kidd could implicate him, the Bostonian lured him to Boston, Massachusetts, where Kidd was arrested in 1699 and a year later was sent to England in chains.

He appeared at the High Court of Admiralty in London charged with five counts of piracy, plus the murder of William Moore. Two of his former crew – Joseph Palmer and Robert Bradinham – provided evidence of the murder in exchange for pardons, and despite being represented by two lawyers, Kidd was found guilty of all charges and sentenced to death.

Whoever the 'good friends he had in England' were, they failed to materialize, and whatever letters he wrote begging for clemency to King William III – 'William of Orange' – failed. Perhaps Kidd stressed the number of Dutch merchant vessels he had spared, in order to excite the Dutch-born monarch's sympathy, but the leniency that Kidd had extended to the crews of those vessels did not provoke the sympathy he desired from the ruler of England.

On 23 May 1701, at Execution Dock, Wapping, Kidd was hanged; but the rope broke and Kidd survived. The idiot, baying mob of onlookers who, seconds before, had been hungrily anticipating seeing a pirate captain kicking at the end of a rope, now decided that the snapped rope was an Act of God and demanded his release. Not so; within minutes, the hangman obtained a fresh rope of greater sturdiness, and this time, Kidd was successfully dispatched.

The authorities had not quite finished with Kidd. His lifeless body was taken to Tilbury Point, where it was gibbeted – bound in chains and suspended from a gallows-type structure – and there it stayed for a period of three years.

This was done to act as a deterrent to anybody similarly minded to take up a piratical occupation. There was a school of thought that sights such as this would be offensive to foreign visitors. Not a bit of it.

Gibbets became a popular, if gruesome tourist attraction, particularly amongst the French, who would have to wait for another eighty-eight years for their Revolution. Gibbeting, for them, was a sort of *hors-d'oeuvres* to the horrors yet to come.

Chapter 1

The Prolific Letter-Writer

Three innocent people had been hanged for a murder that no one had committed, and the outspoken William Moore had been consigned to Davy Jones' locker. Time passed, and people continued to bludgeon, stab, throttle, poison, shoot or, in any possible way, murder one another. Most were sufficiently considerate to leave their victims' bodies where they might be found; one who was not was an American homeopath named Dr Hawley Harvey Crippen. In 1910, tiring of his wife Cora Henrietta Crippen, he murdered her and buried her body under the brick floor of the basement in their address at 39 Hilldrop Crescent, Holloway, North London. He and his girlfriend then fled on the SS *Montrose*, which sailed for Canada, but the captain grew suspicious of them and telegraphed the Yard. Chief Inspector Walter Dew, who had made a complete arse of the original investigation, boarded the faster SS *Laurentic* and pursued, overtook and apprehended Crippen, who was returned to England and duly hanged. So this was a spirited attempt by Crippen to dispose of his victim which didn't quite come off.

That was followed by the First World War, which claimed the lives of 885,138 British military personnel, plus 109,000 civilians worldwide, but since the Articles of War prevailed, these deaths – according to one's principles – could not be legally seen as murder.

But the next recorded case of a murder without a body involved a little boy as the victim, a boy who died as the result of having a father who was arguably deranged but who was also definitely cunning, controlling, manipulative – and highly dangerous.

* * *

Thomas Joseph Davidson was born in 1899 and had he really exerted himself he could not have been a more worthless character. Lazy, feckless and shiftless, he absented himself from the army on several occasions and each time made whining excuses which were obviously sufficiently convincing for him to escape being shot for desertion. In the light of what was going to happen, some readers will regard the lack of expenditure on military ammunition for use on Davidson to have been a downright shame.

In 1923 he was sentenced to one month's imprisonment for failing to pay arrears on a bastardy order, and two years later, found to be sleeping rough and having no visible means of subsistence, he received one day's imprisonment. By now he was married, but five months later, he was arrested for two cases of snatching handbags. At the time he was circulated as being wanted in a case of false pretences, so he was sentenced to three months' hard labour. When he was found guilty on the same day of indecently assaulting a 12-year-old girl he received a further three months, consecutive.

Within a few months of his release he was sentenced to another three months' hard labour, this time for stealing a purse from his brother. By April 1929 he had actually obtained honest employment, but he rewarded his employer's trust with embezzlement and stealing 1½ tons of coal; and this time, he was sentenced to six months' hard labour.

His unhappy marriage had produced a son, then aged seven, whose name was John Desmond Davidson and who was known to his parents as 'Jackie'.

By the beginning of December 1933 the marriage had deteriorated to such a degree that Jackie was sent to live with a Mrs Clark at Greenford Avenue, Hanwell and was last seen by his mother at Mrs Clark's home on 17 December.

It was hardly surprising that, given her husband's repellent behaviour, Olive Squire Davidson had sought solace in the arms of a greengrocer, one Herbert Norman Rose. On 18 December, this *ménage à trois* erupted into conflict, with Davidson demanding to know what Rose wanted, and Rose replying that 'he wanted to see fair play'. What was clear was that Davidson desperately wanted his wife back but that she, in turn, was terrified of him.

Since October, Thomas Davidson had been working in a piggery at Stockley, Middlesex and living alone in a hut supplied by his employer, Mr Hezekiah Amer. On 19 December Davidson discovered where his wife was living and he brought her to the hut; she stayed there the following night (she would later say that she was too scared to leave) but departed on the morning of Thursday, 21 December. It was clear that the couple did not part on the best of terms. It was then that

Davidson went to Mrs Clark's house and took the boy away, saying that he would return the child the following day. In fact, Mrs Clark had never met Davidson before, but was content to let the boy go, since it appeared that Olive Davidson had previously told her that she would have no objection to him taking the child out. He brought the boy back to the hut and informed his employer that the child was his son; that was the one and only time that Amer saw the boy.

The following day, Davidson returned to Mrs Clark's address to tell her that Jackie had been knocked down by a motor lorry and was dead.

On 24 December, Amer asked Davidson if he wanted breakfast, which he declined. He then said, 'Jackie is dead.'

Oddly, Amer asked, 'Did he get knocked down by a motor lorry?' so it appears that what Davidson had told Mrs Clark two days previously had reached Amer's ears.

'No', replied Davidson. 'He was following me across the dump on Thursday and would not go back. He fell into the dock and got drowned.'

'You did that, Jack?' said Amer, and Davidson replied, No.'

Amer asked, 'Whatever were you thinking about?' and according to him, Davidson 'looked wild' and asked, 'Shall I go and give myself up?'

'Yes', replied Amer. 'Go straight away.'

Illogically, Davidson replied, 'Give me one more chance; it was not my fault. I shall get hung. I done it. I took him away and drowned him.'

Amer, not surprisingly, told Davidson to 'clear out', and he left eventually on 27 December. But even more surprisingly, Amer made no mention to anybody of Davidson's astonishing and incriminating statement.

There was one other person who claimed to have seen the boy alive. A woman who owned a café on the Uxbridge Road stated that she saw Davidson and the boy on two consecutive days. Since Davidson had not taken Jackie from Mrs Clark's address until 21 December, this meant that the couple must have been seen on 22 and 23 December – but since 21 December the boy's concerned mother and other people had been searching for him, without success.

So despite Davidson telling several people that his son was dead – he was certainly missing – the police at Ealing seemed to be carrying out very little proactive work regarding investigation of the matter.

It was high time something was done, especially when Olive Davidson received a letter from her husband which had been posted in Hanwell in March 1934 and which read:

> Once more, you have betrayed my trust in you. I never would have thought it of you. I am sleeping with our darling child tonight. Love, I will give you one more chance to prove your trust in me. I am bringing Jackie tomorrow evening by the bridge by the public house, 8.30 Tuesday night where we stayed those two nights. It is no good you bringing the police because I have my friends on the look-out. Of course, they don't know my intention but on the first sign of any suspicious person, I shall know and they will not take either of us alive, for according to the way you behaved you wish us both dead, otherwise you would have come.
>
> Jackie sends his love, although he was shivering with cold. I put him under my coat. I shall be there, 8.30 Tuesday night and on the stroke of 8.30, failing your arrival, or if anyone else comes, bye-bye to both of us.
>
> You know what I said I would do, for neither of us will be wanted in this world. I have the means of doing it; if anyone gets within one yard of me they cannot save us. As true as God is my Judge, that will happen.
>
> You told me you were your own mistress. That is a lie, otherwise you would have seen me, and girl, I had the shock of my life this morning for you never looked so rough in your life, not even when we had no home. Come without fail; everything depends upon it. I will help you out of the hole you have got into.
>
> *—Brokenhearted Jackie and Jack.*

It was time to call in the big guns, which arrived from Scotland Yard in the form of Detective Inspector Albert E. Greenacre.

Aged twenty-three, this former gamekeeper from Great Yarmouth was either lucky or pretty astute; he joined the Metropolitan Police four months before the outbreak of the First World War and completed his twenty-five years' service four months before the start of the Second. He walked the beat around Bow Street as Police Constable 714 'E' and, being appointed to the CID, distinguished himself by being commended seventeen times for smart police work, as well as receiving monetary rewards of between 7s 6d and £1 on eleven occasions.

Prior to the arranged meeting between the Davidsons, information was received that Thomas Davidson might well be in possession of a firearm. Greenacre had had quite enough excitement with regard to firearms; in 1929, together with

Detective Sergeant Bob Fabian ('of the Yard'), he had arrested fraudsman Reginald Wallace at Mayfair's Connaught Hotel. As well as being a conman with a string of convictions, having served two terms of penal servitude, Wallace was a nasty piece of work. Upon their arrival at Vine Street police station, Wallace suddenly produced a fully loaded six-chambered revolver, and it took all of Fabian's and Greenacre's combined efforts to relieve him of it. So, although that was five years ago and Wallace had been packed off to quod with a combination of penal servitude and preventative detention amounting to eleven years, Greenacre at the age of forty-three undoubtedly and prudently thought that tackling a gunman was a task best left to younger officers.[1]

Therefore, on the evening of 3 April 1934 it was youthful Detectives Castle, Macey and Kimber who set off in a police car, and at 8.35 they first saw Davidson and his wife walking along Somerset Road, Southall. Davidson was wearing an overcoat and had his hands in its pockets. The officers drove past them, stopped and got out of the car. Then, when the couple reached the junction of Allenby Road and with a complete lack of ceremony, Detective William Macey flung his arms around Davidson, pinning his arms to his sides.

'I'm a police officer', said Macey. 'Have you got a shooter on you?'

'No, what do I want with a shooter?' replied Davidson.

The other officers restrained Davidson, who still had his right hand inside his pocket. Macey felt the outline of what appeared to be a pistol in Davidson's pocket and told Davidson, who was by now struggling furiously, 'Let go what you're holding in your jacket and take your hand out.'

With the assistance of Detective Kimber, Macey pulled Davidson's hand from his pocket, from which he then extracted a double-barrelled smooth-bore pistol; Davidson's reaction was, 'You bastard – you were too quick for me!'

Macey broke the gun, revealing it to be fully loaded, and said, 'I'm going to take you to Southall police station for carrying this loaded pistol with intent to do bodily harm to some person or persons.'

'You bastard!' exclaimed Davidson. 'I would have had you!'

Placed in the police car and driven to the station, Davidson attempted to put his hand in his right-hand jacket pocket but

---

1 For further details of that exciting case, see *Scotland Yard's Casebook of Serious Crimes: 75 Years of No-Nonsense Policing*, Pen & Sword Books, 2021

was restrained by Detectives Kimber and Macey. Upon their arrival, Davidson was searched. In that pocket was found a bottle of spirit of salts marked 'poison' and a total of fifty cartridges, all of which fitted the gun. Additionally, a book was found with ruled pages exactly like the paper used for the incriminating letter Davidson had sent to his wife.

'The letter is in Davidson's handwriting', Greenacre later told the bench at Ealing Police Court, and in those days, when a detective asserted he was a handwriting expert, his statement was accepted, as it was by the chairman without reservation.

Whilst he was at the police station, Greenacre had asked Davidson about the whereabouts of his son; Davidson replied that he was staying with friends, to keep the boy away from his mother. In July, at a court appearance, Greenacre again questioned Davidson, who told him that the boy was staying with friends in Essex.

But on 21 July, Greenacre received a letter from Davidson which read:

> Dear Sir, with reference to the enquiries as to the whereabouts of my son, Jackie, which have been going on for the past seven months, my son is dead. I killed him. I think it is best to make a clean sweep of things and get things squared up. I do not intend to give any explanation as to why or how it happened in this letter or where he is buried.
>
> If my wife is brought along to see me, I will explain everything. He will be found in a very few hours.
>
> Otherwise you will dig for hours and then find nothing. I do not expect her or wish her to see me on my own. She can be accompanied by anyone she wishes.

On 26 July Greenacre, together with Olive Davidson, saw the prisoner.

'I've brought your wife along at your request', said Greenacre, and Davidson, turning to his wife, said, 'See what you have brought me to?'

'I've read your letter', said Greenacre, 'and I gather that you want to tell me something further.'

'Yes', replied Davidson. 'I'll tell you all about it.'

After being cautioned, Davidson elected to make a statement, which read:

> I have seen you, in order to make a voluntary statement concerning the disappearance of my son, Jackie. I have tried in every possible way to get my wife to come back, so

> that I could make a clean breast. She has failed to fulfil her promise or return. I have no further interest in life . . .
>
> On Thursday, December 21st, I took the boy to where I was staying at Stockley, where there is a piggery near the canal. Jackie stayed with me on the Friday, Saturday and Sunday. On the Saturday night, I made another effort to get my wife to come back to me and Jackie.
>
> [There then followed, in great detail, a description of how Davidson had endeavoured to get his wife, who was staying with friends, to come back to him, without success.]

The statement continued:

> I rode back to Stockley. Jackie was in bed with my dog looking after him. I was so upset by the other affair that I was determined not to linger any longer. I woke Jackie up and made him some tea and sat talking until three o'clock on Sunday morning. I went to bed, got up at 6.30, and fed the animals, as usual.
>
> At about 10.30, the owner [of the piggery] came round and told me that I would have to clear out. I continued with my usual work and in the evening, I went back to the shed and sat with Jackie. I went to bed but could not sleep and walked about outside until the early morning [of the 25th].
>
> I took Jackie and went to the canal dock and jumped in myself with him. I recovered myself on the opposite side of the canal. I got up and hunted for Jackie and found he was a good distance away, and was dead. I took him out and tried to pump the water out of his stomach, but it was hopeless.
>
> I went to the piggery for a blanket and took him [Jackie] to the edge of the dump. He was fully dressed and had gloves on. Between that time and January 10th I went back to where I had left Jackie's body but he had been covered by refuse and I could not find it.
>
> After I put the body down, I pulled some straw and rubbish over the body. I did not go back to my shed but hung around. When I jumped into the canal with Jackie, it was my intention to drown both of us.

After signing the statement, Davidson went with Greenacre to the dump and pointed out the spot at Sabey's Dock where he said that he and Jackie had gone into the water.

Returning to Ealing police station, Davidson said, 'I don't blame my wife for what has happened. I blame the dirty toe-rags she has got mixed up with. They have led her away. I am prepared to take my punishment. I am content to think the boy is dead and gone. He would never have done any good in the world.'

Davidson was an interminable writer of letters. On 30 July, his wife received another (very long) letter from him, which contained the following:

> You are not the Olive I used to know. You are only the shadow of a skeleton and you are as cruel as you used to be kind. I am looking forward to my end, although it is not a cheerful one. But I shall walk to it with the consolation that I died for the honour of my darling child and in an endless attempt to regain my wife.

Appearing at Uxbridge Police Court on 27 August, Davidson was charged with his son's murder, and although he declined legal aid, it was provided for him.

The respected pathologist Sir Bernard Spilsbury visited the site of the burning refuse dump and came to the conclusion that the body would have been roasted before disappearing completely. Possibly the odd bone might have been found (although none was), but identification would have been impossible.

Davidson was tried before Mr Justice Atkinson at the Old Bailey, where he pleaded not guilty to his son's murder.

The evidence for the prosecution, led by Mr Eustace Fulton, was pretty damning – especially when Olive Davidson's lover, Herbert Rose, stated that Davidson had told him to tell his wife that Jackie had been killed by being knocked off his bicycle. But that was not all: between 22 and 24 December 1933, Davidson had told three persons on separate occasions that his son had been killed by a lorry, and on two other occasions during the same period he had told two different persons that his son had died by drowning. So there was all that, plus the letters to his wife and Inspector Greenacre as well as his detailed, written confession given to the police in the presence of his wife.

However, the defence had a few tricks up their sleeve.

In the witness box, Davidson described taking his son to the piggery after asking, 'Do you want to come with me?' and Jackie replying, 'Yes, Dad.' After being given some tea, the child started crying and asked, 'Are you going to take me back to my Mummy?'

In his evidence, Davidson said:

> I said 'No', and he continually cried. I could not comfort him so I took him out and went towards Amer's house. I realised if I took him there my wife might realise where he was so I started back and took the towpath along the side of the canal and left while I went to collect a sackful of metal . . . I hunted for him

> with a torch, I found him in the water, about 2.30 the following morning. He was in amongst the reeds. I carried him to a fire near the dump.

To this, his counsel, Mr Wallace, asked, 'What was your state of mind?' and was told, 'I was heartbroken. I got the wind up and naturally thought I should be charged with deliberately doing it. I covered him with a blanket and then covered him over with some clean refuse.'

Davidson added that when he subsequently went back he was unable to find the body.

'Were you responsible for the death of the boy?' asked his barrister, to which Davidson replied, 'No, Sir.'

'Is it true you jumped into the water with him?'

'No.'

'Why did you go to Inspector Greenacre?'

'To get the matter thrashed out by law whether I had done anything wrong or not. I wanted to clear myself.'

This was a matter that everybody wanted to clear up, so not unnaturally Mr Justice Atkinson asked, 'If you wanted to clear yourself, why write a detailed letter in which you charged yourself explicitly with killing the boy?'

Davidson probably astonished everybody in court by giving the following reply: 'On previous occasions I told the truth and it got me into serious trouble, and this time, I thought I would do the reverse. I thought I would say I did it and let the truth come out.'

Davidson agreed with an incredulous prosecutor, Mr L.A. Byrne, that he wanted to be charged with murder and stand his trial in order to defend himself.

Summing up, Mr Justice Atkinson pointed out to the jury that Davidson had taken none of the usual steps that would normally be taken following a child's death, such as informing the police or the Registrar. There was also no doubt that he had made untrue statements at the time. He went on to say:

> No one but the prisoner knows what happened. No one else was there. No one saw that body. It has never, as far as we know, been found by anyone.
>
> If you are satisfied that what he told the police and his wife in those letters was true, then he is guilty. But if you think that what he has said today may be the truth, then he is not guilty.

It took the jury all of ten minutes on 18 September 1934 to come to the conclusion that Davidson's courtroom testimony was complete and utter cock and find him guilty, with a recommendation for mercy on account of the state of his mind at the time. Having been told that the jury's recommendation would be passed on to the proper quarters, Davidson showed no emotion as the Judge sentenced him to death.

As was usual in a case which resulted in the death penalty, there was an appeal before the Lord Chief Justice, Lord Hewart, Mr Justice Avory and Mr Justice du Parcq, but inevitably it was dismissed, with the Lord Chief Justice saying in judgement:

> In our opinion, it was perfectly open to the jury, upon the evidence which was given, to hold that the boy was dead and, after hearing the evidence of the appellant, to disbelieve the retraction of his confessions which he made, and to accept the statement which he had previously made, namely, that he was the cause of his son's death. As Mr Eustace Fulton has said, all his conduct was inconsistent with the view that this child had come by his death in a way not involving guilt upon the part of the appellant.

But Davidson did not hang. The Home Secretary recommended clemency to the King, and as a result, Davidson's death sentence was commuted to penal servitude for life.

Four years later, Albert Greenacre received his promotion to divisional detective inspector, just in time, after twenty-five years service, to miss the Second World War, collect his annual pension of £281 9s 1d and toddle off to spend his retirement at his Norfolk farm.

The case was reported in Jamaica in the *Kingston Gleaner*'s 16 November 1934 edition, not that there was anything unusual in that, (a) because in those days there were far fewer murders in the United Kingdom than there are now, and (b) because this was a pretty unusual case, a murder conviction without a body. So the *Gleaner* reported the case, as did many other newspapers around the world, and then everybody largely forgot about it – except in Jamaica, when it briefly resurfaced, seventy-eight years later.

* * *

A certain Raphael Masters was convicted on 8 February 2010 of murdering Donald Muirhead on 13 June 2005 in the island's parish of Westmoreland. His appeal against conviction was heard between 16 May and 15 June 2012 in Jamaica's Supreme Court.

The question was whether the partly decomposed body which had been found hanging between branches over a cliff was indeed that of Donald Muirhead.

The appellant's girlfriend, a lady named Kadian, had implicated Masters in the murder, and when he was confronted with her statement at Savannah-la-Mar police station, his response was:

> Weh Kadian seh in har statement a lie. A she get mi involved, and a mi chop the man. Stafford, weh she call Harry, and Denton neva down weh mi chop di man.

Well, that was pretty conclusive, and Masters went on to make a rather longer written statement in much the same vein, in the presence of Mr Rupert McDonald, an attorney-at-law, his 'duty counsel'. It was this statement that the prosecution relied upon to secure a conviction. However, by the time of the trial, Mr McDonald had unfortunately died.

During the intervening five years, between confession and trial, it appeared that Mr Masters had acquired a more comprehensive grasp of correct English, because in a very brief, unsworn statement to the jury, he said:

> My name is Raphael Masters. I live in Cambridge, St James. And I work at Chung's wholesale, in Montego Bay. I don't know nothing about what they are talking about.

Amazingly, this failed to sway the jury, who took just five minutes longer than the jury took in Davidson's trial to find Masters guilty.

The defence appealed on the grounds of insufficient evidence, that there was a lack of evidence regarding the identification of the deceased and that in Masters' confession references to 'di man' or 'di person' did not correctly identify the deceased.

Not that it did any good. The Crown cited the appeal rulings of both Davidson and Onufrejczyk (about whom, more later) and kicked the appeal into touch.

In a way, Davidson was fortunate. Given a life sentence of penal servitude, he would have been released after about twelve years.

Not so Mr Masters, who came off rather worse, because in sentencing him, the trial Judge told him that he would serve 'a mere thirty years at hard labour'. The appeal court varied this, for the sentence to commence three months *after* the original sentencing date.

Chapter 2

Lost at Sea

The Second World War arrived, and as a result of heavy German bombing, 29,890 Londoners were killed. Harry Dobkin, employed as a firewatcher, decided that the bomb damage would act as a convincing cover to get rid of his troublesome wife. On Good Friday 1941, he strangled, then dismembered her, set fire to the body parts and buried them under a stone slab in the ruins of a bombed Baptist church in Vauxhall Road, South London. The bones were discovered over a year later, by workmen in July 1942. Initially, it was thought that this was a body blown apart by the force of an enemy bomb, but a post mortem revealed that (a) her limbs had been sawn (as opposed to blown) off and (b) the thyroid bone in her throat had been fractured. The workmen's tools could not have caused this; there was a blood clot around the bone, so it had been broken in life – and that only happens in cases of strangulation.

It took six weeks' hard work, but eventually Rachel Dobkin was identified by her teeth and dentures, and husband Harry was arrested, tried and hanged. The defence attempted to prove that the body found was not that of Mrs Dobkin, but it was not just the odontological aspect of the investigation which identified her. The pathologist took a photograph of the skull, obtained a full-face photograph of Mrs Dobkin which he enlarged to the same size, and superimposed them. They were an exact match.

Like Crippen, Harry Dobkin tried to be clever – but he wasn't clever enough.

* * *

Open promiscuity is the norm nowadays – in 1947, it wasn't. Middle-class morality – and morality among the working classes who aspired to 'genteel' behaviour – was strict. Pregnancies in single women were treated with haughty contempt. A girl was expected to slip between the sheets on the night of her honeymoon still a virgin. Divorce retained a stigma; indeed, in the Metropolitan Police it was a block to promotion, and heaven help the police officer who was found to be in a relationship with a woman 'not his wife' – that was a sacking offence.

Terminology has changed, too; in the 1940s, if a girl told her heterosexual boyfriend that she wanted to go out and 'have a gay time', he would undoubtedly have hoped to participate in such festivities. Similarly, if the expression 'slag' was used, it would be assumed to relate to a heap containing rock and mud, the result of a mining enterprise, rather than to a lady of dubious morals frequenting the 'Queen Vic'.

So when Mrs Ellen Victoria Gibson described her daughter as being 'one of the finest types of English womanhood, physically, mentally and morally', she was only saying what many mothers of that era would have said. However, others would have disagreed with her.

The daughter referred to was 21-year-old Eileen Isabella Ronnie Gibson, who used the stage name 'Gay Gibson'. Seeing service with the Auxiliary Territorial Service in the last stages of the Second World War, she joined 'Stars in Battledress' and thus began her short-lived career on the stage. In 1947 she travelled to South Africa, joined a repertory company and, after appearing in Sidney Howard's *The Silver Cord*, went on to star in Clifford Odets' *Golden Boy*. Rouben Mamoulian had directed this very popular boxing film in 1939, and now the part of the slinky Lorna Moon, originally played by Barbara Stanwyck, was taken by Gay Gibson. The part of Joe Bonaparte, the 'Golden Boy' of the title, which brought William Holden overnight success was taken by the celebrated British lightweight boxer, Eric Boon, who had been fighting in South Africa since 1946. Sadly, Boon lost on points to Giel de Roode at Wembley Stadium, Johannesburg on 8 September 1947, but he rallied sufficiently, two nights later, to appear in his role on the opening night at the Standard Theatre in that city and be well received.

It was decided to move the play to Pretoria, but Gay Gibson had decided that she wanted to return to England to pursue her acting career there. On 10 October 1947, she boarded the Union Castle liner *Durban Castle* to set sail for Southampton. At 17,388 tons, the British-registered liner had been launched in 1938 for the 'Round Africa' service.

Gay Gibson was 5 feet 5 inches tall, an auburn-haired, extremely attractive young woman, described as being polite and well-behaved. She was also said to be extremely flirtatious and had had several affaires. Her behaviour was said to have changed when she started acting; she became temperamental and made scenes, fainting and displaying concerns about her health as well as telling exaggerated stories about her background; perhaps performing in the same way that some other actresses carry on, or maybe the way in which her character Lorna Moon was supposed to behave. It is also possible that she was pregnant; but by the same token, she may have said that to draw attention to herself.

Whether she was pregnant or not will never be known. Within just over a week of sailing, what remained of her body would be reposing seven miles below the surface of the shark-infested Indian Ocean, about 90 miles off the coast of West Africa.

* * *

The author of her demise was James Camb, a 30-year-old first-class deck steward, who had first served with the Union Castle line in 1933 and then continuously since 1945. His duties were to minister to the needs of passengers in the saloons and lounges and on deck, as well as to prepare trays to be taken to the passengers' cabins. However, he had no duties inside the cabins, for passengers of either sex.

Married, with a 3-year-old daughter, Camb was a native of Lancashire. Good-looking, with dark, swept-back hair, he was what was then popularly described as 'a ladies' man'. Some of his shipmates disliked him but that, Camb would say, was 'because they were jealous of me'. Others admired him, dubbing him 'Don Jimmy', after Don Juan, the seventeenth century Spanish libertine. In popular legend, it was the father of his sweetheart Doña Ana whom the Don killed; on this occasion, his Lancastrian counterpart settled for the unfortunate Miss Gibson.

For James Camb was not a charming suitor who scaled balconies for romantic encounters; he was a predatory, drooling pervert. It was his proud claim that he had 'had' a woman passenger on every voyage.

On the *Durban Castle*'s outward journey to South Africa, he attempted to justify his boast on at least four occasions.

On the evening of 18 September 1947, Camb had invited a young woman passenger to have a drink with him in the ship's deckchair cabin. When he had tried to kiss her and she had twice refused, Camb forced her to her knees and began throttling her. When he released her, there was blood in her mouth, her eyes were badly bloodshot – the ship's surgeon told her the condition would not improve for a month – and she later told a friend what had happened, naming Camb as her attacker.

But a few hours prior to that attack in the deckchair cabin, another young woman travelling to South Africa with her aunt complained to the assistant purser that Camb had followed her into her cabin and tried to grab hold of her, whereupon she pushed him away.

Some four days later, the same woman decided to take an afternoon nap in her cabin. She awoke to find Camb kneeling beside her bunk, and he got on top of her, kissed her, tried to pull down her shorts and squeezed her breasts. It was only when she banged on the wall to alert her aunt in the next cabin that Camb desisted. The woman did complain to two men, one of them a crew member, but asked that the captain should not be informed.

On 7 October, a third woman went to her cabin following a dinner/dance, undressed and went to bed. She did not lock her door and awoke at about 12.30 am to find Camb standing next to her bunk. She told him that he should not be there, but he refused to leave and during the following 20 minutes he kissed her three or four times but did not attempt any further sexual advances and eventually left.

No formal complaint was lodged to anyone in authority at the time by any of the three women. In the light of what was to occur, that was a great pity, and so the scene was set for tragedy as the *Durban Castle* set sail from Cape Town on the 5,985-mile return journey to Southampton.

Miss Gibson was one of the sixty first-class passengers out of a total of 250 on board and she was berthed in cabin No.126. There were four decks, and Miss Gibson's cabin was on 'B' Deck (also known as 'The Shade Deck'); her outside cabin, which had a porthole, was on the port side of the ship.

Camb was certainly interested in Gay Gibson, and it's possible she reciprocated that interest. They had several conversations during the first week of the voyage and then, on the evening of 17 October, she attended a dinner/dance on deck with two male companions, both older than herself. She had three or four dances with the men before going to the smoking room on the top deck, where she remained until 12.40 am, at which time one of her dining companions escorted her to her cabin and then left. About 20 minutes later, Miss Gibson left her cabin, still wearing the black evening dress she had worn at the dance and stood on the promenade deck at the ship's rail smoking a cigarette. She was seen by William Allan Conway, a boatswain's mate who was swabbing down the deck. Noticing that she was wearing dainty, silver-coloured dance shoes, Conway realised that they and she would get wet if she stayed where she was, so he suggested she move to the midships on the port side. She told him that she found it too warm on her deck, so Conway suggested she sit in one of the deckchairs. She said, 'Goodnight', left – and Conway was the last person to see her alive.

At 2.58 that morning, two night-watchmen – Frederick Dennis Steer and James Alfred Murray – were on duty in the first-class pantry on 'A' Deck, one deck below Miss Gibson's cabin. Suddenly, two bells were rung from 'B' Deck: a green one requesting the presence of a stewardess and a red one for a steward – it was highly unusual for the buttons to be pressed simultaneously.

Steer went up to 'B' Deck, checked the indicator board and saw that both calls had originated from Cabin 126. He went straight to the cabin and knocked on the door; it opened, and the light was on in the cabin, but then a man's hand appeared on the door from inside the cabin and prevented Steer from entering. The man said, 'It's all right' and shut the door, but not before Steer had recognised him as James Camb.

Steer went and reported to Murray, the senior of the two night-watchmen, but when a report was then made to the officer on the bridge, the two night-watchmen, out of misplaced loyalty, did not mention Camb's name.

When both men returned to the cabin, the interior light was still on. They left, but when they returned at about 3.30 am, the cabin was in darkness. No further attempt was made to open the cabin door.

Steer next saw Camb two days later, and Camb asked if he had mentioned to anyone that it had been him in Miss Gibson's cabin. By now, Steer had been given specific instructions on how he should answer that question if it was asked: he replied, 'No.'

'Thank goodness I have not been with her homeward bound this trip', replied Camb, adding, 'I'm in a tight jam.'

That was one of five denials he would make in respect of Gay Gibson's disappearance; because when Eileen Elizabeth Field, a stewardess, went to Miss Gibson's cabin at 7.30 am on the morning of 18 October, the door was unlocked; this, for Miss Gibson, was unusual, and of the occupant there was no sign at all. The porthole was open – quite usual when the ship was in the tropics – and the bed sheets were disarranged. There were marks on the pillow and the sheets. Miss Gibson's black evening gown was hanging behind the door, but two items were missing: her pyjamas and her dressing gown.

Miss Field tidied up the cabin, but when she discovered that Gay Gibson had not had her bath and that nobody appeared to have seen her, she became alarmed and submitted a report.

Some time had now elapsed, and by the time news of Miss Gibson's disappearance reached the ears of the ship's Captain, Arthur Victor George Patey, it was 9.57 am. He broadcast to the whole of the ship that Miss Gibson was missing, and when no one came forward with any information as to her whereabouts, he reversed the ship's course at 10.20 and sent a message to all nearby ships asking them to keep a look-out. However, seven hours had passed since Miss Gibson's disappearance and, with the ship cruising at 17.9 knots, Captain Patey realized after an hour that it was no use continuing the search and he resumed the homeward-bound course.

But by now, Captain Patey had been informed that it was Camb who had been seen in Miss Gibson's cabin.

'Was it you?' asked the Captain, and Camb denied it, saying that he had gone to bed at 12.45 am and had stayed there until gone six. However, an assistant smoke-room steward named William Pott said that he had seen Camb on 'D' Deck at 12.45 – and there was something else. Pott shared a cabin with Camb, and later that morning, he saw that instead of being dressed in a singlet (usual in the tropics when cleaning up and preparing for the day), Camb was wearing a white jacket with long sleeves.

In the meantime, Captain Patey locked the door of cabin 126, added a further lock and placed both keys in his safe. Clearly unhappy with Camb, especially his unusual wearing of a long-sleeved jacket, he wanted the steward medically examined.

When Camb asked why, the Captain replied, 'You're suspected in connection with the disappearance of Miss Gibson, and it's in your own interests that you should be examined.'

As he left the Captain's cabin Camb was heard to mutter, 'Why all this suspicion? Let's get down to bedrock.'

On 19 October, Camb was medically examined by the ship's surgeon, Dr Anthony Griffiths. He found marks on three parts of Camb's body: on the right and rear side of his neck several abrasions and 6–9 scratches about one inch in length, together with scratches of the same length on his collar bone. There were scratches and abrasions on Camb's left wrist, and on the front of his right wrist were 9–12 scratches; they were between half and three-quarters of an inch in length and some extended up the arm. Camb's explanation was that he had woken in the night and, due to a heat rash, had scratched himself. While some of the marks were not considered to be suspicious, the ones on his right wrist and arm were; they appeared to be recently inflicted scratches, and as to Camb's assertion that he had suffered from heat rash, the doctor found no evidence of that.

On the same day, Camb submitted a letter to the Captain, this time stating that shortly after 1.00 am he had gone to bed and had fallen asleep an hour later. Following his medical examination, he prepared a second letter, mentioning 'some slight scratches' and 'also a few on my right wrist'. These, he said, were self-inflicted, due to having scratched himself three or four nights previously.

The ship docked at Cowes Road, Southampton, and the police, already alerted by radio from Captain Patey, boarded her at 1.25 am on 25 October.

At that time, Scotland Yard detectives, members of C1 Department colloquially known as the Murder Squad, were on standby to investigate murder anywhere in the British Empire, including murders committed on British-registered ships on the high seas. That had been the case since 1906, and this was something that every chief constable was aware of.[1]

When the *Durban Castle* docked at Southampton, the Chief Constable merely had to inform Scotland Yard, and a detective chief inspector and his first-class sergeant would be dispatched to commence the investigation. These chief inspectors were highly experienced; as former first-class sergeants they would have gained enormous experience working with chief inspectors, so that when they reached that rank themselves there was little they could be told about murder investigation.

So all that Charles George Box OBE, the newly appointed Chief Constable of Southampton, had to do was lift his telephone, and Fabian, Capstick or any of the other chief inspectors from C1 Department would have been on the next train to Southampton. But his force would have been responsible for paying the wages and expenses of those visiting officers; so he didn't.

Instead, he appointed two detectives from Southampton County Borough Police Force, a sergeant and a constable, to investigate an allegation of murder committed on the high seas. The constable, who had joined the force six years previously, had already acquired a reputation for dodgy behaviour. During the three months which remained of his service as a police officer, that poor reputation would be enhanced.

* * *

1 For further details of this unit, see *Scotland Yard's Murder Squad*, Pen & Sword Books, 2020

Detective Sergeant Quinlan was handed the keys to cabin 126 and the two statements that Camb had given to Captain Patey. At 5.25 am the Sergeant, together with Detective Constable Minden Plumley, saw Camb and told him, 'I have been making enquiries into the disappearance of a first-class passenger from this ship, Miss Gibson', to which Camb replied, 'Should I know anything about it?'

Camb admitting knowing Miss Gibson but denied ever going to her cabin and stated that on the night in question he had been asleep by 2.00 am. Quinlan then asked to see Camb's wrists, and while he thought the scratches on the left wrist were faint and difficult to see, those on the right wrist were more pronounced. Camb said he had 'nearly scratched himself to death'.

'These marks on your wrists appear to be of too serious a nature to be self-inflicted', said Quinlan and he then added, 'I have good reason to believe that you can give me further information regarding this matter; I have also reason to believe that you were in Miss Gibson's cabin at about 3.00 am in the early hours of the morning of 18 October.'

'That puts me in a tight spot', replied Camb (as indeed it did), and he was taken to Southampton's police headquarters.

Quinlan and other officers returned to the ship and took samples, photographs and items from Cabin 126, some of which were handed over to the Hendon Police Laboratory.

Later that day, Camb was interviewed once more and admitted a little more about seeing Miss Gibson, the evening prior to her disappearance.

Detective Sergeant Herbert Gibbons was at that time an acting inspector and had discussed the matter with Quinlan; now, at about 6.30 pm he confronted Camb with these words:

> Let's review the circumstances and see what your position is. You have said that you did not see Miss Gibson after 11.30 pm on the night of 17–18 October, but that you went to her cabin at 1.00 am and she was not there. If it can be proved conclusively that not only were you in the cabin at 3.00 am, but that she was there also, and evidence to show that Miss Gibson disappeared from that cabin while you were there, and there is scientific evidence that the disappearance of Miss Gibson was through the porthole, you will realise the importance of a flat denial of your presence there. There are also scratch marks on your wrists which have a certain significance. You must realise that the time is fast approaching when a decision will have to be made regarding you. You are being given an opportunity to

> make any explanation you may care to do about this, and that explanation, so far, has been a categorical denial that you know anything about the disappearance of Miss Gibson. If we are in a position to show that you were the last person with Miss Gibson, and you were in her cabin at three o'clock in the morning, and that Miss Gibson disappeared while you were there, you may find that such a complete denial will be difficult to explain if later you are called upon to explain it.

Gibbons' statement was sufficiently forceful for Camb to reply, 'Does that mean that I murdered her and that I shall be charged with murder?'

Gibbons replied that he could not say whether Camb would be charged or not but he stressed that if Camb could give a reasonable explanation for Miss Gibson's disappearance he should say so – and Camb said this: 'You mean that Miss Gibson might have died from some cause other than being murdered; she might have had a heart attack or something?'

Gibbons suggested to Camb that he and he alone could give an explanation of her death and disappearance and left him with Sergeant Quinlan to decide what course of action he should take.

'Are you in the habit of visiting female passengers in their cabins?' asked Quinlan, and Camb replied, 'Well, yes; some of them like us better than the passengers. I've been with them several times on other trips.'

'Was that at night?'

'Yes, I've been with several; of course, if I was found out, I would get the sack.'

After some further conversation, Quinlan told him flatly, 'I have no doubt in my mind that you were the last person to see Miss Gibson.'

There was a pause before Camb decided to make a statement, and after he had been cautioned, the following statement was taken down by Plumley on a typewriter:

> I have been cautioned by Detective Sergeant Quinlan that I need not say anything and that everything I do say will be taken down in writing and may be given in evidence, signed James Camb. I have already stated to you that I went to Miss Gibson's cabin at about 11 o'clock on Friday, 17 October 1947 and during the course of conversation with her, I made an appointment to meet her that night. I knocked at the door after I had finished work about one o'clock, but there was no answer. I opened the door of her cabin and found it was

> empty. I then went forward to the well deck, where I sat for about half an hour, smoking. I then returned to Miss Gibson's cabin at about two o'clock and found her there. After a short conversation, I got into bed with her consent. Intimacy took place. Whilst in the act of sexual intercourse she suddenly clutched at me, foaming at the mouth. I immediately ceased the act, but she was very still. I felt for her heartbeats but could not find any. She was at this time very still and I cannot offer any explanation as to how the bells came to be rung, as I most definitely did not touch them myself. Thinking she had fainted, I tried artificial respiration on her. Whilst doing this, the night watchman knocked at the door and attempted to open it. I shut the door again, saying it was all right. Then I panicked, as I thought he had gone to the bridge to report to the officer of the watch and I did not want to be found in such a compromising position. I bolted the door and again tried respiration. After a few minutes, I could not find any sign of life. After a struggle with the limp body – by the way, she was still wearing her dressing gown – I managed to lift her up to the port-hole and push her through. I am fairly certain that at that time she was dead, but I was terribly frightened. I then went forward and turned in. The time would be about 3.30 am. I have read this statement over and it is true, signed James Camb.

As Quinlan was about to leave the room, Camb said, 'What will happen about this? My wife must not know about this. If she does, I will do away with myself.'

The following day, Sunday, 26 October, at 1.30 pm, Quinlan cautioned Camb, saying, 'I'm going to charge you with the murder of Miss Eileen Gibson', and he replied, 'My God, I did not think it would be as serious as this.'

Some six hours later, Quinlan asked Camb to give formal consent to have photographs taken of the scratch marks and to provide a blood sample, a request to which Camb agreed. The consent form was signed by Camb in the police cell; the only person present was Detective Constable Plumley, and according to him, Camb said this:

> I did not think it would be as serious as this. All I am worried about is my wife. I have not had any sleep since this thing happened. I can't understand why the officer of the watch did not hear something. It was a hell of a splash when she hit the water. She struggled. I had my hands around her neck and when I was trying to pull them away, she scratched me. I panicked and threw her out of the port-hole.

It would be a statement that would be the subject of some lively discussion, firstly at the committal proceedings at Southampton Magistrates' Court by Mr T. J. Molony, barrister for the defence, who suggested that Plumley had made the suggestion to Camb 'that there had been a hell of a splash' when the body hit the water.

Plumley replied, 'I made no suggestion at all to Camb. I was so astonished at Camb's remark that I made immediate notes in longhand, after leaving him.'

'Did you ask him to sign any record of why he said that?'

'No, Sir. I did not consider it necessary.'

'If he said what was said he did, it might be very important?'

'Yes, Sir.'

'Did that strike you as a police officer?'

'Not until after leaving him, sir. I was so astounded by the remark.'

'Did you think as a police officer that there would be any objection to asking him to sign an accurate statement of what he said?'

'No, Sir.'

'Can you give any explanation as to why you did not attempt to get a signature?'

'To my knowledge, it is not in accordance with the usual procedure to obtain a signature from a prisoner for every remark he makes.'

Well, there you have it. To the disbelieving lawyer, it appeared that skulduggery had gone on, but that was not necessarily so, and there are three reasons why. First, when a suspect has been charged with a serious offence and has been left alone to ruminate over deeply disturbing matters (as Camb had been, for six hours), it is certainly not unknown for such a person, when confronted with a police officer, to suddenly blurt out an incriminating statement. Next, should Plumley have requested Camb to authenticate his notes with a signature? The answer nowadays would be 'yes', but in 1947 the answer was 'no'; a police officer's notebook was for the use of the officer only. And finally, if a prisoner wished to make a statement he should be permitted to do so – but not in this case. He had already been formally charged, and therefore no further questioning would be permitted.

There was a declaration read in court from Dr Walter Eric Montgomery of the Metropolitan Laboratory at Hendon to say that blood spots were found on the cabin's bed sheet; they were classified as Group 'O' – Camb's blood group was 'A'.

Asked if he had anything to say, Camb read quietly from a folded sheet of notepaper: 'I am not guilty of this charge. I did not kill Miss Gibson. She died in the way I have described. My mistake was trying to conceal what had happened. Witnesses already called could, I am sure, have told much that would help in this case, and witnesses in South Africa know about the state of her health.' He then added in a whisper, 'That is all.'

And with that, on 24 November 1947, Camb was committed to stand his trial at Hampshire Assizes.

Camb was quite right. There were witnesses from South Africa who would provide testimony regarding Gay Gibson, and some fairly unpleasant details would be recounted. They were free to say what they liked; Gay Gibson was not around to rebut them.

When Camb had told the police that he had entertained women passengers on board ship he was quick to say that this had happened 'before the war'. He was not being entirely frank. There were the four other encounters – that are known about – which happened on the outward voyage of the *Durban Castle*, less than one month before Miss Gibson's demise and have already been recounted. The three witnesses, aged between sixteen and nineteen, had sworn affidavits to a Commissioner for Oaths in Cape Town on 5 November 1947. These were the unfortunate young women who had encountered Camb on the outward voyage of the *Durban Castle* and who were able to provide graphic details of his behaviour. The affidavits were forwarded to the police at Southampton; they would never see light of day during the forthcoming trial. It was not that the prosecution felt that the three women's evidence was unsafe or unsatisfactory; it was because the evidence was considered far too prejudicial and might have prevented the murdering pervert in the dock from getting a fair trial.

* * *

The case opened at the Hampshire Assizes, held at The Castle, Winchester on 18 March 1948.

The Judge was a hard-liner, Mr Justice Hilbery; he had presided over what became known as 'The Battle of Lewes Racetrack' at Sussex Assizes in 1936 and handed out such swingeing sentences that they effectively broke the power of the racetrack gangs.[2]

2 For further details of this incident, see *The Racetrack Gangs: Four Decades of Doping, Intimidation & Violent Crime*, Pen & Sword Books, 2020

Furthermore, when Robert Edward O'Brien, the proprietor of the 'Chez Nous Bottle Party Club', sued the *Daily Telegraph* in 1937 for damaging his reputation, Mr Justice Hilbery curtly told him that he and his club had no reputation to damage, dismissed the action and left O'Brien in prison, where he was serving a sentence for debt.

Leading the prosecution was a heavyweight, in every sense of the word. Geoffrey Dorling Roberts KC – always known as 'Khaki' – had been capped three times by England in 1907, before winning the first of his two Oxford Blues for rugby. During the First World War, serving with the 8th Devonshire Regiment, he was Mentioned in Dispatches on five occasions. Described as 'a tremendous tank of a man', he had been one of the counsel for the prosecution during the Nuremberg war crimes trials; his cross-examination was said to be 'devastating'.

His junior was 45-year-old Henry Elam, a formidable advocate who at the time of the trial had just been appointed Recorder of Exeter.

Camb was represented by Joshua David Casswell KC, MA; his junior, Mr T. J. Molony, had appeared for Camb during the Magistrates' Court proceedings.

Onlookers – many of them women – had been queuing since 5.30 that morning for what would prove to be an interesting spectacle.

Camb having pleaded 'Not Guilty', the trial got underway. When it came to the cause of the scratch marks on Camb's wrist, the ship's surgeon, Dr Griffiths, told the court, 'They are entirely consistent with scratches that are caused by fingernails. I put them each at between 12 to 48 hours old previous to my examination at midday on the 19th.' Asked if he had seen anything in the area of those scratches that would have caused skin irritation, the doctor replied, 'No.'

The detective sergeants, Quinlan and Gibbons, were cross-examined, with little effect; not so Detective Constable Minden Plumley, because he was a detective constable no longer. He was not even a police officer. After seven years' service he had, he said, voluntarily resigned on 18 January 1948. He said he had considered it to be to his advantage that he should leave the force; but if he was suggesting that the advantage might have been of a pecuniary nature, it had not blossomed into a lucrative profession, because at the time of giving evidence he was unemployed.

Casswell for the defence tore into him, suggesting that far from Camb blurting out a highly incriminating statement, Plumley had told Camb that the written statement he had made was untrue; Plumley denied saying to him, 'You probably strangled her unintentionally and that's when you panicked.' Plumley similarly rejected having said, 'Did you have your hands round her neck, or what?'; but Casswell was really saving himself up for an all-out attack on Plumley's character.

There had been a piece in the 26 October edition of the *Sunday Chronicle* to the effect that Camb had strangled Miss Gibson, then pushed her through the porthole. Had Plumley provided that information to the press? asked Casswell. No, replied Plumley, he had not.

Was the Chief Constable perfectly satisfied with Plumley's performance as a police officer? Plumley replied that he was not in a position to say.

There had been a case in July 1947 at Southampton Quarter Sessions during which Plumley admitted giving a man beer to drink in a pub before taking him to the police station to make a statement.

'Were the jury directed by the Recorder not to convict?' asked Casswell.

'I do not remember the summing-up by the Recorder', replied Plumley, but it did not sound particularly convincing, any more than after admitting that he and another officer had smashed up a car together – and although the chief constable complained about his conduct – he did not think that had anything to do with his resignation.

Plumley told the court that he did not remember being involved in a fight just before Christmas 1947; a man who had been arrested had 'made no accusations' about being assaulted at the police station; and when property belonging to a prisoner, which should have been entered in the Property Record Book, was found in Plumley's locker, his response was, 'It may have happened, but I have no recollection of it.'

It was not just a lacklustre performance, it was a terrible one, which could have caused immeasurable damage to the prosecution's case; and although Chief Constable Box may have rejoiced at Plumley's departure he must have rued the day the previous October when he failed to pick up his telephone and say, 'Get me Scotland Yard, please.'

* * *

Evidence was given that Camb's palm-print was found inside the cabin's door – in case he repudiated his statement and said he had not been there – and fibres had been found around the rim of the porthole which were probably from Miss Gibson's dressing gown, which Camb had said she was wearing when he pushed her through. It took matters no further forward.

Various army personnel gave evidence of Miss Gibson's health during her period of service; she had experienced an infection in her right ear and had suffered a slight cold. Apart from that, her medical form was marked NAD – Nothing Abnormal Detected.

Gay Gibson's mother took the stand and was extremely outspoken in protection of her daughter's morality, despite the defence suggesting otherwise. In fact, it caused 'Khaki' Roberts to rise to object, saying, 'How an attempt to blacken the character of this girl who is dead and cannot answer for herself can be relevant to any issue which the jury have to try, I fail to see . . .', but the Judge permitted this line of questioning.

Dr Montgomery of the Metropolitan Laboratory at Hendon, who had a statement tendered at the Magistrates' Court hearing, now appeared at court to give evidence, pointing out the blood spots and confirming that they could not have come from Camb. But apart from that, his evidence was pretty useless. There was lipstick and perspiration on the pillow, as well as a hair which matched hairs found in Miss Gibson's hairbrush. There were also stains on the sheets; one was similar to brown boot polish; there was a black stain but he was unable to determine its nature, and the same applied to a yellow stain.

But it was a different matter when the noted pathologist Dr Robert Donald Teare MB, MRCP was called. He was asked if, in a case of strangulation, there would be likely to be any discharge of blood from the victim. This was his reply:

> Yes. It sometimes occurs as a result of the tongue being forced against or between the teeth; it sometimes occurs as the result of scratch marks by the victim in attempts to release herself or himself; it sometimes occurs as part of the general picture of death from asphyxia which is characterised by small haemorrhages in the more delicate lining of the body, the gums, the back of the throat, the lungs, the lining of the nose and occasionally, the ears.

This was good evidence for the prosecution, but more was to come – from the defence. Experts for the defence had examined the bed sheets and had found quite a lot of dried urine; and how Dr Montgomery missed that – if it was the yellow stain of which he was unable to determine the nature – beggars belief. Dr Teare not only agreed that urination was likely to be the last act of a person before death but also agreed with the Judge that that was likely to be the case in an act of strangulation.

This cross-examination over, Dr Teare was re-examined by Roberts.

'When you were asked to approach this case first, one of the questions you asked was whether urine had been found?'

'I did.'

'You have told the jury that in cases of strangulation the involuntary discharge of urine at the moment of death is common. You did not have that information until you were cross-examined by my learned friend?'

'I did not.'

'Now that you know that the defence have ascertained the presence of urine on one of the sheets of this bed, does that strengthen your view as to whether death in this case was from strangulation?'

'It does, considerably.'

'Does it follow from that, that in cases of strangulation it is common to find the victim scratches the assailant in the death agony?

'Yes.'

'And that feature is present here – or may be?'

'Yes.'

And that was the case for the prosecution.

* * *

Camb took the stand and was led through his evidence; he was at pains to explain that prior to her disappearance, he and Miss Gibson had been on friendly, if not flirtatious terms. On the night of her disappearance, Camb stated that he had gone to her cabin; she let him in and was wearing a yellow dressing gown, under which she was naked. They had consensual sex on the bunk, whereupon she gave a gasp, her body suddenly stiffened and then went limp. There was bloodstained froth on her lips, and Camb said that he spent 20–25 minutes attempting to revive her.

But with regard to the two bells being simultaneously pressed, he could give no explanation. That the bells had been pressed when he was in the cabin, there was no dispute. He could not say that when, according to him, Miss Gibson had collapsed, he had pressed them in a panic, wanting to summon assistance;

had that been the case, why then would he have refused admittance to Steer when he appeared under a minute later and told him, 'It's all right'?

No, the only inference that could be drawn was that it had been Miss Gibson who, panic-stricken, had rung for assistance after Camb had forced himself on her; and that when Steer arrived, she could not call out because she was unconscious – or dead.

Camb asserted, as he had done all along, that the marks on his body had been caused by him scratching himself.

Questioned regarding the conversation he had had with Plumley, Camb said:

> He opened by saying, 'Now look, this is off the record; you went into that cabin with one intention and because she would not let you have your own way you throttled her and slung her through the porthole. That is what happened, isn't it?' I said, 'No. I have already made my statement and I have nothing further to say.' He said, 'My God, man! There must have been a hell of a splash. Weren't you afraid of the officer of the watch hearing something?' I didn't answer that because, being a seaman, I knew the impossibility of such a remark.

Although Camb admitted signing the consent form regarding the taking of blood samples, he denied that Sergeant Quinlan had asked his permission to do so; but when Quinlan gave evidence, it was not a matter that he was challenged about.

Asked in cross-examination by Roberts if he would describe himself as a truthful man, Camb replied, 'I think so'; but when he was asked, given that for the next eight days following Miss Gibson's disappearance he had made at least six untrue statements, how that fitted his self-description as truthful, Camb replied, 'I would say that that description arose from the predicament I found myself in.'

He admitted that he had exhibited 'beastly conduct' and also that if his first version of events was as false as the second, when he had pushed Miss Gibson's body through the porthole he had destroyed the most deadly evidence against him.

The main thrust of his defence was that if the ship's authorities had known that he had been in Miss Gibson's cabin, this would have constituted a sacking offence.

There followed a series of witnesses for the defence, two from Miss Gibson's army days, one of whom said she had seen her undergo a seizure with her tongue at the back of her throat which was considered so serious that she was admitted to hospital and detained overnight – yet there was no medical record of it.

The second witness described Miss Gibson as being hysterical and neurotic and having had an affair with a driver named Pierre; but this witness was quite adamant that at the time the previous witness had said Miss Gibson was admitted to hospital she had never been absent.

Mike Abel, who had appeared in *Golden Boy*, came from South Africa to give evidence; Gay Gibson's mother had described him during her testimony as 'a gangster'. He certainly appeared to be pretty shifty when he told the court about what he described as Gibson's hysterical behaviour: bouts of laughing and sobbing, and declarations of love for him, interspersed with kicking, slapping, then kissing him. There were, he said, fainting attacks, chest complaints and saliva at the corners of her mouth. She had told him, he said, that both her parents had been killed by a V2 rocket and that both her brothers were killed while serving in the navy; she also mentioned that she was pregnant and needed £200 for a termination.

An actor-producer agreed with the kicking, slapping and kissing incident and described Gay Gibson as being 'often distraught and highly strung'. His wife – who said she was a fully qualified medical practitioner, although no mention of her could be found in the 1947 Medical Register for Johannesburg – stated that Miss Gibson had spoken to her about her concerns that she might be pregnant and suggested that she should be fitted with a Dutch Cap; one such item was found in Miss Gibson's luggage.

It was Dr Frederick Dennison Maurice Hocking who had examined the bed sheets and had come to the conclusion that the smears of blood and the urine were consistent with a violent strangling; equally, he said, it could be attributed to natural causes of death in certain circumstances and therefore the account given by Camb was a perfectly possible one.

'You say that the marks on the right forearm could have been made by digging nails into the flesh?' asked Roberts, and was told, 'Yes.'

'You have heard Camb say that they were caused by scratching?'

'They did not appear to me to be scratch marks; they were far too deep.'

Professor James Mathewson Webster had been shown the depositions and photographs, prior to Dr Hocking being retained by the defence. After he had submitted his report to the Director of Public Prosecutions, the Director had decided that he would not be called for the prosecution, and his evidence was made available for the defence, who called him now.

He said straight away that the account given by Camb of the girl's death could have been a true one. He accepted that the blood, saliva and lipstick had come from the girl's mouth, that the urine on the bed sheet was evidence of a terminal act and that consequently the girl was dead before she went into the water.

But like the other medical experts who had been called, he could not and would not exclude the possibility of strangulation as the cause of death.

In his closing speech to the jury, Casswell placed great emphasis on the remarks of the scientists – it might be strangulation, but then again, it might not – as well as the background information given by some of Miss Gibson's contemporaries.

During his closing speech, Roberts concentrated on the bells which were used to try to summon assistance and were situated right next to one side of the bunk and within easy reach of Miss Gibson's right hand. These were not bells which could mistakenly respond to a mere touch; they had to be depressed with a certain amount of force. And how did Camb come by those scratches on his body – scratches which he stated were self-inflicted because of a heat rash of which there was no evidence whatsoever?

Where were her black pyjamas? She must have been wearing them when Camb entered her cabin, despite Camb's assertion that she was waiting to have sex with him, wearing a dressing gown under which she was naked – but without the contraceptive diaphragm which she had in her possession. And it was those pyjamas that Miss Gibson was wearing – as well as the dressing gown, to dispose of any evidence which might accompany it – when she was pushed through the porthole.

Why did Camb dispose of the body? Had she died from natural causes, as Camb claimed, why not leave her body there to be found in the morning? The reason was because as well as Camb's skin particles being lodged under her nails, there would have been evidence of her strangulation.

(There would have been, for example, burst blood vessels in her eyes; something that Camb knew about from experience, as did Roberts from one of the South Africa affidavits. The young woman whom Camb had tried to throttle less than a month earlier had shown Camb the state of her eyes following the ship's doctor's examination. He had said, 'Good God! I did not think your eyes would come up like that!' and had begged her not to tell anybody. So Roberts was aware of this; but it was not a matter that he could disclose to the jury.)

'You will remember that the prisoner has said – and in my submission it is for you to say whether truthfully or not – that

"Miss Gibson did not cause me any injury at all; I did not suffer any injury at all",' said Roberts to the jury.

At that, Casswell got to his feet. 'He said that some of the marks may have been caused by Miss Gibson.'

Mr Justice Hilbery quoted from Camb's testimony. 'I received no injury from Miss Gibson.'

But Casswell persisted: 'I understood him to say, "Some of the marks may have been caused by Miss Gibson".'

'He certainly said twice, "I received no injury when with Miss Gibson; I told the truth that I had made these scratches",' said the Judge firmly, and while that should have brought home to Casswell the folly of making interruptions, there was more to come from 'Khaki' Roberts, who now demonstrated his cleverness in capitalizing on mistakes made by an opponent, when he said:

> Members of the jury, I invite my friend's interruptions because they may help you to see the more clearly where the truth lies in this case. If you consider I am not doing the evidence full justice, and if my friend thinks I am wrong, let him interrupt me. Did the prisoner not say, 'My hands and right wrist I scratched those myself; I received no injury of any sort while in the company of Miss Gibson; no blood came from my body'? My suggestion to you, members of the jury, is that it is rather an astonishing thing when you have expert evidence explaining to you in one way marks on the body of that prisoner, and in a way which is entirely contrary to the evidence which the prisoner has given himself about it. The experts can explain evidence, they can give you a theoretical suggestion for you to accept, but they cannot contradict the evidence of the person for whom they are appearing, the evidence which he himself has given, and it was put very clearly to Camb over and over again. And you will remember that Dr Hocking said that these indentations in the flesh of the prisoner would have hurt, *must* have hurt. We all know that if the human nail is driven deeply into the flesh it certainly *can* hurt. But he says, 'No, I had no injury at all . . .'

During the summings-up for both the defence and the prosecution, Plumley was mentioned; Casswell suggested to the jury that they would not convict upon his evidence; Roberts merely said that the prosecution did not depend in it. During his summing-up, Mr Justice Hilbery did not mention him at all. He did stop for 20 minutes when a woman juror became distressed, and he mentioned in passing the fact that Dr Montgomery (who came out of the proceedings with even less credibility than Plumley) had failed to notice the dried patch of urine that measured fifteen inches by six on the bed sheet.

Telling the jury to consider their verdict, he was interrupted by Casswell, who said, 'With respect, my lord, you did not mention the bolting of the door.'

This was the third time Casswell had interrupted during his summing-up, and by now Mr Justice Hilbery must have been getting more than a little brassed-off with it, because he replied, rather snappily:

> I have not attempted to mention all the points in this case. My duty is to point out the salient features of the case, or those which I think may be a guide to you. There are others which no doubt you will think useful, in fact, there are many other matters and if you think they are useful give them all the weight you think is right. I have not attempted to mention everything and I am not bound to do so.

After a four-day trial, the jury were out for 45 minutes before returning with a verdict of guilty of murder. Asked by the Clerk of Assize if he had anything to say, Camb replied, 'My lord, at the opening of this case I was asked to plead guilty or not guilty; I pleaded not guilty and I repeat that statement now.'

Camb was then sentenced to death. His appeal took place on 26 April 1948 before Lord Goddard, the Lord Chief Justice, together with Mr Justice Humphreys and Mr Justice Pritchard. The grounds of the appeal were that the Judge's summing-up did not put the defence fairly to the jury. Giving judgement and dismissing the appeal, the pro-prosecution and hard-line Lord Goddard said, 'Undoubtedly the learned judge's summing-up was not favourable to the prisoner; no one would contend that it was', but he felt that 'the prisoner had the advantage of an able and sustained defence. There was abundant evidence on which the jury could find as they did, and there was no misdirection by the learned Judge.'

But Camb did not hang. Even before his appeal, the House of Commons had suspended the death penalty for five years, and four days after Camb's unsuccessful appeal, the Home Secretary commuted his sentence to one of life imprisonment. Winston Churchill, who was one of the dissenters, thundered, 'The House of Commons has, by its vote, saved the life of the brutal, lascivious murderer who thrust the poor girl he had raped and assaulted through the porthole of a ship to the sharks.'

Camb was fortunate; on 10 June 1948, during Lord Goddard's maiden speech in the House of Lords, a proposal to abolish the death penalty had been defeated by 181 votes to 28.

Camb's wife divorced him, and after serving eleven years, he was released on a life licence from Wakefield Prison. Within four weeks he had sold his 'true story' to the *Sunday Pictorial.* It was serialized over four weeks, and in it he once more asserted his innocence; he also married again.

By 1965 the death penalty had been suspended once more for a period of five years; the decision aroused considerable controversy in the pro- and anti-hanging lobbies. It attracted the attention of one Jane Hitchcock of Branch Hill, NW3 who supported the death penalty in a letter to the 27 October 1967 edition of the *Chelsea News and General Advertiser*, proposing that the case of 'Mr James Camb (sex murderer) has proved that in some cases Broadmoor or prison is not the answer.'

Perhaps Ms Hitchcock was aware that Camb (who by now had changed his name by deed poll to James Clarke) had five months previously pleaded guilty to indecently assaulting an 8-year-old girl in Bishop's Stortford. Incredibly, he had been placed on probation for two years. His life licence could have been revoked; it wasn't.

I previously described Camb as being 'a drooling, predatory pervert', and there may be some who have come to the conclusion that I was being overly censorious. I wasn't.

On 26 April 1971, Camb was working as a head waiter at the Waverley Castle Hotel, Melrose, when he broke into a room containing three young girls, two aged eleven and another ten, and subjected them to what the Scots refer to as 'lewd and libidinous practices' – in other words, he committed indecent assaults on girls under the age of puberty. He pleaded guilty at Jedburgh Sheriff Court and was committed to Edinburgh's High Court on 28 May 1971 for sentence before the Lord Justice Clerk, Lord Grant. The offences were recounted in detail by Mr John H. McClusky QC, the Advocate Depute, and Camb was sentenced to three years' imprisonment – in addition to his life licence being finally revoked on 18 May.

He remained at Wakefield Prison until 1978, and he died in Leeds on 7 July 1979, following a heart attack. He was said to be 'a shadow of his former self'. His second wife had left him. Despite being described as 'a model prisoner' and having 'the highest references' from his post-prison workplaces, there were few people left to mourn his passing.

Certainly not me.

Chapter 3

The Acid Bath Murderer

So thanks to Samuel Sydney Silverman and a number of other drippy Members of Parliament, James Camb was rescued from the hangman's noose; nor was he alone.

On 13 February 1948, Donald Thomas, a thief and army deserter who had already carried out sixteen burglaries in North London's Southgate area, was just about to commence his seventeenth when he was stopped by Police Constable 807 'Y' Nathaniel Edgar, who had the impudence to question him. Thomas then shot him three times in the back, mortally wounding him, and escaped before being tracked to a Brixton boarding house, where 16-stone Inspector William Moody provided him with an early-morning wake-up call by landing on top of him. Divesting Thomas of a Luger pistol, Inspector Moody asked if it was loaded, to be told, 'Yes, full up – and they were all for you!'

When Thomas was found guilty of capital murder on 20 April 1948, it was Mr Justice Hilbery, once more, who pronounced the death sentence; Donald's initial gun-toting resolution had deserted him and he whimpered piteously to the warders, 'What do you think? They won't hang me, will they?' But, as with Camb, there was never any chance that 'they' would.[1]

Fortunately, as has already been mentioned, Rayner Goddard in his maiden House of Lords speech restored sanity to judicial proceedings, and it was just as well, because Lewes Assizes was going to be treated to the trial of a serial murderer utterly motivated by greed and arguably as mad as a bag of bollocks.

* * *

Mrs Olive Henrietta Helen Olivia Robarts Durand-Deacon was a 69-year-old widow possessed not only of an imposing collection of names; her late husband had left her comfortably provided for,

---

1 For further details of this disturbing case, see *Death on the Beat: Police Officers Killed in the Line of Duty*, Pen & Sword Books, 2012

and in consequence, she was able to lead a pleasant existence in Room 115 at the prestigious Onslow Court Hotel at 108 Queen's Gate, South Kensington.

Mrs Durand-Deacon had lived at the hotel for six years and was on friendly terms with a fellow resident who was personable and well-dressed. He had been in residence for four years, occupying Room 404; without knowing too much about him, other than that he was an engineer who patented inventions, Mrs Durand-Deacon obviously thought he was a man of means, because the hotel charged him the rate of £5 15s 6d per week, plus a 10 per cent service charge.

She was quite unaware that the man who sat at the dining room table next to hers – 39-year-old John George Haigh – was not quite as well-heeled as she might have thought. He was heavily in debt; his bank account was overdrawn by £83, his cheques appeared to be made of rubber and by now – Valentine's Day 1949 – he had not paid his hotel bill for six weeks. On 3 February, the cheque he had presented to the hotel's manageress for £33 had been returned marked up 'refer to drawer'. He had no income whatsoever – but when Mrs Durand-Deacon told him that she had an idea about manufacturing plastic fingernails and asked for his advice on both the production and marketing of such items, Haigh could see a lifeline being tossed in his direction. Unfortunately, his thought processes on how that might be achieved differed quite considerably from Mrs Durand-Deacon's. They had nothing to do with his manufacturing skills and everything to do with the furs and jewellery belonging to the lady who was shortly to become his unwitting benefactress.

On 15 February, Haigh drove his very smart (and very expensive) 20 hp Alvis sports saloon down to Giles Yard, at 2 Leopold Road, Crawley, Sussex, where he had the use of a workshop. He asked a Mr Davies, a business acquaintance, if he could obtain a carboy (approximately 10 gallons) of sulphuric acid for him. Mr Davies had done so before, and when he returned two days later, Haigh would find three carboys full of acid waiting for him. Additionally, Haigh saw Mr Edward Charles Jones, another business acquaintance, and borrowed £50 from him, promising that it would be repaid within a week.

To the relief of the Onslow Court Hotel's manageress, Miss Alicia Robbie – who had been making polite but insistent demands – Haigh paid off his outstanding bill of £49 in cash the following day. By Wednesday, 16 February, he was solvent to the tune of 4s 11d.

The next day, Haigh acquired from a wharf at Barking a 45-gallon drum specially designed to withstand corrosive acids. In addition, he had invited Mrs Durand-Deacon to his Crawley workshop on the Friday, since he told her that he felt sure her idea of artificial fingernails could be a viable and profitable article.

With Haigh driving his Alvis, they left the Onslow Court Hotel just after lunch at 2.30 on Friday, 18 February for the journey down to Crawley. For a lady eager to invest a decent sum of money in a non-existent business enterprise, there was much that Mrs Durand-Deacon did not know about her companion. She was quite ignorant of the fact that he was a consummate conman and forger who had served several prison terms, including one of hard labour and another of penal servitude. She would have been horrified to discover that he had murdered at least five people for their money and had, reputedly, a penchant for drinking their blood. And had she noticed the leather hatbox on the back seat of the Alvis, she might have admired it, blissfully unaware that it contained a stolen .38 Enfield revolver and eight rounds of ammunition.

The artificial fingernails enterprise was a blind; Mrs Durand-Deacon was going to her death.

* * *

Haigh had been born in 1909 in Lincolnshire and raised in the West Riding of Yorkshire; his parents were both members of the Plymouth Brethren, an ultra-conservative Protestant sect also known as 'The Peculiar People'. It is quite possible that his parents and the sect had laid the foundations for the shape his life would take. No entertainments or amusements of any kind were permitted in the Haigh household; no outside influences such as radio or newspapers containing their impious views were allowed. Like many children blessed with half-deranged parents – his father had a scar in the shape of a cross on his forehead which he told his son was the mark of Satan, who had personally branded him for being a sinner – Haigh became a polished liar in order to avoid punishment. However – according to Haigh – punishment was still doled out by his mother, who hit his hands with a hairbrush, drawing blood, which he licked off. Before long, he was cutting his own finger in order to draw blood. He seemed obsessed with all matters concerned with phlebotomy; as an altar boy, he dreamed of the crucified Christ dripping blood.

Nevertheless, he became a proficient pianist, playing the works of Mendelssohn, Tchaikovsky and Vivaldi, and won scholarships to the Queen Elizabeth Grammar School and later, Wakefield Cathedral, where he was the assistant organist. He worked in motor engineering, insurance and advertising, although in 1930 he was dismissed after being suspected of stealing from a cash box.

From 1933 Haigh was employed by an insurance company, but was dismissed after a year when his conduct was found to be 'unsatisfactory'. It was about this time that he married Beatrice Hamer, but the marriage floundered almost immediately, after Haigh was arrested for conspiracy to defraud.

With two partners, a man and a girl, he had systematically carried out car-deal frauds on hire-purchase companies. Haigh obtained headed notepaper from a garage that was for sale and wrote to hire-purchase companies stating that people from that area had bought cars from him and that he was applying for loans on their behalf; in this way they obtained £110. Moreover, Haigh admitted other offences, including obtaining £420 from a hire-purchase corporation by means of a forged receipt. None of the three accused had any previous convictions, and the man and the girl both had employers willing to take them back, so the judge bound the man over, fined him £25 and ordered him to pay £35 in prosecution costs. The girl who, the Judge felt, had been led on by Haigh, was similarly bound over and ordered to pay £5 prosecution costs.

Unfortunately for Haigh, the Judge at Leeds Assizes happened to be Mr Justice Goddard, who appears not once but on several occasions within these pages, and telling him that he seemed set on a career of forgery and only his youth had saved him from penal servitude, on 22 November 1934, he sentenced 25-year-old Haigh to fifteen months' imprisonment in the second division.

Released on 8 December 1935, Haigh moved to London where, after working as a chauffeur for a wealthy businessman named William McSwan, he purported to be a solicitor named William Cato Adamson with offices in Chancery Lane, Guildford and Hastings. By posing as a solicitor winding up estates for deceased clients, he told his victims he was in a position to sell them shares on very cheap terms in exchange for a 25 per cent deposit. The shares were, of course, non-existent, but using this ruse, he obtained £2,934 1s 3d, and it was likely that he would have obtained even more, had not one of his clients noticed that on his letter-headings he had misspelled Guildford as 'Guilford'. It led him to the dock of Surrey Assizes, where in November 1937 he admitted eight charges and Mr Justice Goddard's gloomy prediction came true: he was sentenced to four years' penal servitude.

The Second World War was underway when Haigh was released in August 1940, but he did not remain at liberty for long; in June 1941 at the London Sessions, for stealing furnishings and household goods, he received twenty-one months' hard labour. The licence from his sentence of penal servitude was revoked, and he was not released until 17 September 1943.

Purely by chance, he happened to bump into his pre-war employer, William McSwan, in The Goat public house in Kensington. McSwan introduced Haigh to his parents, Donald and Amy, wealthy people who had an apartment at Claverton Street, SW1. William McSwan worked for them, collecting rents on their London properties; it was money that Haigh wanted for himself.

He lured McSwan into a basement he had rented at 79 Gloucester Road, SW7 on 6 September 1944 and, using the leg of a pinball table, killed him with a blow to the head. Whilst he had been in working in the tinsmith's shop at Lincoln prison, Haigh had experimented with dropping field mice into acid and found that it took only thirty minutes for them to dissolve. Could the same be done with a human body? The French murderer, Georges-Alexandre Sarret, claimed he had done just that in 1925, so now was the perfect time for Haigh to put this theory to the test. Putting McSwan's body into a 40-gallon drum, Haigh poured concentrated sulphuric acid into it and waited two days to see if this would have the desired effect. It did; the body had turned into sludge, and all the contents of the drum were poured down a manhole.

His diary for 9 September was marked with a sign of the cross in red crayon, and this he later explained in the following words:

> I got the feeling I must get blood somewhere. I was meeting McSwan and the idea came to me to kill him and take some blood. I hit him over the head . . . got a mug and took some blood from his neck and drank it. At Gloucester Road I had acid and sheet metal for pickling. I found a water butt on a disused site and took it on a cart and put McSwan in acid. I put the body in the tub and poured the acid on it. I went to see McSwan's parents and told them he had gone away because of his call-up.

(Haigh would later say that it was a 40-gallon drum that was used, which certainly seems more likely than a disused water butt which would be highly unsuitable for use with sulphuric acid.)

When McSwan's parents queried his disappearance, Haigh told them that their son had gone to Scotland to avoid military service. He now took over McSwan's house and, forging letters purporting to be from their son, asked the parents to send their son's friend – Haigh – money. He also started collecting the rents from the parents' properties; during that year, he paid £347 into his bank account. However, he wanted rather more than that.

With the war at an end, McSwan's parents were concerned that their son had not returned. Haigh lured them to Gloucester Road on 2 July 1945, telling them that their son intended to meet them there on a surprise visit from Scotland. He then murdered them in the basement with blows to the head and disposed of their bodies, also in a drum filled with sulphuric acid. He stole William McSwan's pension cheques and forged a power of attorney to dispose of the couple's properties: a toyshop in Fulham as well as freehold properties in Raynes Park, Wimbledon and Beckenham. There also were gilt-edged securities, furniture and personal belongings which would realize £6,866, and Haigh moved straight in to the Onslow Court Hotel.

The money did not last long; Haigh was an inveterate gambler and by 1947 he was looking for fresh victims to rob and kill. He found them in the persons of Dr Archibald Henderson and his wife Rosalie. Pretending an interest in a property that they had for sale, Haigh was invited to their flat, and while he was there he stole Dr Henderson's revolver. He had acquired the use of the workshop at Leopold Road; now, he moved the 40-gallon drum and the acid from Gloucester Road to the workshop. On 12 February 1948, while the Hendersons were staying at Brighton's Metropole Hotel, Haigh lured Dr Henderson to Leopold Road on the pretext of showing him an invention. Upon their arrival, he shot Henderson in the back of his head with the stolen revolver. Telling Rosalie Henderson that her husband had fallen ill, Haigh shot her too, as soon as she entered the workshop. Both of their bodies were disposed of in acid, Haigh paid their bill at the Metropole and left with their luggage, dog and car. He sold the car and Mrs Henderson's jewellery, forged letters from them and sold their house in Fulham. For a time he kept their red setter and he was able to pay more than £7,000 into his bank account.

One year later, the money had been dissipated, once more through gambling; it was time for a fresh victim, and her name was Mrs Durand-Deacon.

She, too, was shot in the back of the head, and Haigh allegedly made an incision with a penknife into the side of her throat, collected her blood in a glass and drank it. (In fact, a bloodstained penknife was later found in his car.) He then stripped her of her valuables: rings, necklace, earrings and a cruciform, and also a black Persian Lamb coat which she was wearing, before putting her into the tank. Additionally, he took a fountain pen and about 30 shillings from her handbag; the cruciform and some keys were pushed into the ground in a lane at Buxted – they would later be recovered, on 8 March, by officers using a metal detector.

Haigh then went to Ye Old Ancient Prior's Restaurant, where he consumed a lightly poached egg and a cup of tea. After chatting to the proprietor, he returned to the workshop and filled the 45-gallon drum with acid; and if any evidence of malice aforethought was required, it was this. Mrs Durand-Deacon was a hefty 14 stone; and although he possessed a 40-gallon drum, Haigh obviously felt that that would not be sufficient to accommodate her body, hence he had acquired the larger drum a few days prior to her murder. As the acid-filled container consumed Mrs Durand-Deacon's body, Haigh was ready for a three-course dinner at a nearby coaching inn, and he returned to the Onslow Court Hotel by 11.00 pm.

But unlike Haigh's other victims, Mrs Durand-Deacon had a number of friends who wished to know her whereabouts. She had been seen to leave the Onslow Court Hotel with Haigh. And the day after her disappearance, questions – a lot of them – started to be asked . . .

One of the waitresses was concerned that Mrs Durand-Deacon had not dined the previous night, and Mrs Constance Lane, a close friend, discovered that her room had not been slept in. She asked Haigh, 'Do you know where she is? Is she ill? I haven't seen her – I don't know where she is. I understand from her that you wanted to take her to your factory in Crawley?'

'Yes', replied Haigh. 'But I wasn't ready. I had not had lunch and she said she wanted to go to the Army & Navy Stores and she asked me to pick her up there. I waited an hour for her but she never arrived.'

So on Saturday, 19 February, Haigh left Mrs Lane in a very worried state; but he had important business to attend to. First, he went to Putney, where he sold the dead woman's ruby and diamond wristwatch to a jeweller for £10 and signed the receipt with a false name and address. Then on to Crawley, where the process in the tank had not been satisfactorily completed, so he drove to Bull's the Jewellers at Horsham. This was to get a valuation for the jewellery, but the owner was not there, so he went to Cottage Cleaners in Reigate, where Mrs Durant-Deacon's expensive coat was valued at £50.

The following morning, Haigh asked Mrs Lane if she had received any news; of course, she had not and she mentioned that she intended to go to report her friend's disappearance at Chelsea police station. Haigh, with his usual conman's bluff, said he would accompany her, and at 2.15 pm they saw 37-year-old Woman Police Sergeant 11 'B' Alexandra Maud Lambourne.

During 1949, 1,241 people disappeared from the streets of England, but most of them reappeared, and by the end of that year just twenty men and six women were still missing, for a variety of reasons: illness, loss of memory, romance, debt or simply because they wanted to vanish. Once a report had been lodged, details of the missing person would be entered into the confidential publication *Police Gazette*, to be circulated to all police stations in the United Kingdom, and it was one of the tasks allocated to women police to follow up and make all the necessary enquiries.

Miss Lambourne – she preferred to be called 'Maudie' rather than Alexandra, which she considered pretentious – after seven years service had been promoted to sergeant at Paddington Green. Now attached to Chelsea, the former dressmaker had been commended by the commissioner on four occasions, all for her investigations into cases of illegal abortions. She was a very astute officer and she did not take to Haigh who, she thought, possessed very shifty, hard eyes over his moustache. Haigh, who was inordinately vain, thought his facial appendage gave him a close resemblance to the film star, Ronald Colman; Miss Lambourne's opinion was that the moustache was more reminiscent of Adolf Hitler.

Haigh told her of the missed appointment to pick Mrs Durand-Deacon up at the Army & Navy Stores in Victoria Street and was asked where he went thereafter. 'I returned to the hotel', replied Haigh, and although Miss Lambourne was not to know it, that was another of Haigh's several lies to the police. It would later be established that at 4.00 pm on the afternoon of her disappearance, Mrs Durand-Deacon and Haigh had been seen at the George Hotel in Crawley.

On the morning of Monday, 21 February, Haigh was off on his travels again, first to the Crawley workshop, where he found that fat and bone still adhered to the sludge in the tank, something he found intensely irritating. He emptied off the sludge with a bucket and tipped it on to the ground opposite the shed, then pumped more acid into the tank to dissolve the remaining tissues. Then on to Horsham, where he had the jewellery valued at £130, before returning to London.

Meanwhile, Sergeant Lambourne had been making enquiries at the hotel, and what she discovered from the manageress – that until very recently, Haigh had been indebted to the hotel for a considerable sum – only confirmed her suspicions that the previous day, she had been speaking to a very dodgy character.

Sergeant Lambourne established that Mrs Durand-Deacon was a lady of conventional habits; she had not obviously intended to be away for very long, since a meal had been prepared for her expected return.

She traced Mrs Durand-Deacon's relatives through her bank and solicitors, made several other pertinent enquiries to eliminate any possibility of her being elsewhere and came to the following conclusions:

a. Haigh did not appear to be unduly concerned.
b. He was relatively young and was seeing a woman who was elderly and rich.
c. There was no reason at all for her disappearance.
d. Haigh's explanation did not ring true, and she felt that the appointment that had been mentioned had, in fact, been kept.

A check at Criminal Records Office at the Yard revealed Haigh's chequered past, and now Sergeant Lambourne prepared a report for the head of Chelsea's CID. In part, it read:

> Apart from the fact that I do not like the man Haigh with his mannerisms, I have a sense that he is 'wrong' and there may be a case behind the whole business.

Consequently, when Haigh walked into the hotel, he found Divisional Detective Inspector Shelley Symes and Detective Inspector Albert Webb waiting to speak to him.

Symes habitually wore a lugubrious look on his jowly face but he was a shrewd officer who had joined the police twenty-two years previously, and as he ascended the ranks in the CID he had been repeatedly commended for his ability in cases as diverse as robbery with violence, larceny, housebreaking, false pretences and murder.

Now he was in charge of Chelsea's Criminal Investigation Department and he told Haigh, 'I'm making enquiries with respect to a lady named Mrs Olive Durand-Deacon who is missing from the hotel.'

'Yes, I thought you would see me as I went with her friend Mrs Lane to the police station to report her missing', replied Haigh. 'I'll tell you all I know about it.'

DI Webb then took a written statement from him, in which he stated he was a director of Hurstlea Products Ltd of Leopold Road, Crawley and outlined his appointment to see Mrs Durand-Deacon at the Army & Navy Stores and her failure to arrive, followed by his lone trip to Crawley. And that, for the time being, was that.

On Tuesday, the following morning, Haigh returned to Bull's the Jewellers at Horsham where, giving the jeweller the name of J. McLean of St George's Drive, SW, he sold Mrs Durand-Deacon's five rings, a paste necklet and clip, earrings, an opal tie-pin in a red case, a double row of cultured pearls and an emerald and diamond snap. For that, he received £100, collecting £60 then, the balance to be given to him the following day. On to Crawley, where he repaid Mr Jones £36 of the £50 debt and then emptied the drum and its contents into the yard. Haigh had tried to dissolve Mrs Durand-Deacon's plastic handbag, but without success, so that he stuffed it behind some bricks beside a fence.

The next day, Haigh collected the remaining £40 from the jeweller's in Horsham, put £5 into his bank account in Crawley and then saw Mr Jones to repay him the remaining £14 of the debt – but he found Jones gravely concerned.

The previous day, at the request of Chelsea CID, Detective Sergeant Patrick Heslin from Horsham CID, West Sussex Police had visited Leopold Road, where he spoke to Mr Jones, who denied that Haigh was a director of Hurstlea Products and said he was merely a business associate. Jones permitted Heslin and four constables to search the workshop but he was worried in case Haigh had been storing illegal goods there. His fears were groundless; despite a meticulous search, nothing untoward was found. Nevertheless, Jones did not care for the police to come snooping around.

'I hope you're not in any trouble', he told Haigh, who laughed and replied, 'No.'

'Because if there is any trouble', persisted Jones, 'I'd prefer you not to come to the works', adding, 'I'd prefer you to stay away.'

Haigh took him at his word; he left, and the £14 debt remained outstanding.

On the afternoon ofThursday, 24 February, the police returned to the hotel, where Haigh was questioned once more; he provided them with a second statement which was much the same as his previous one, although he added a little more detail.

Matters were now hotting up. On the Saturday, again at the request of Chelsea police, Detective Sergeant Heslin made a return trip to the yard and was taken by Jones to Haigh's storeroom, where the padlock had to be forced.

Inside were three carboys, a stirrup pump, a rubber apron and gloves, a mackintosh, a gas mask, an attaché case and a locked leather hatbox. A key from the attaché case fitted the hatbox; inside was the revolver, ammunition and, most importantly, there was a ration book, a receipt from Cottage Cleaners for a black Persian Lamb coat. There were also papers in the names of Mrs Rosalie May Henderson, Dr Archibald Henderson, Donald McSwan, William Donald McSwan and Amy B. S. McSwan. These names meant nothing to the police at the time; in addition, in the attaché case were more papers in the names of the McSwans and a contract note in Haigh's name.

The next two days kept DDI Symes fully occupied, as he visited Crawley, Horsham and Reigate, took possession of various items and made many enquiries.

As a result, when Haigh drew up in his Alvis outside the Onslow Court Hotel at 4.15 pm on Monday, 28 February, DI Albert Webb was waiting for him. Now there were no polite requests for assistance and information. 'I want you to come to Chelsea police station at once and see Superintendent Barratt and Detective Inspector Symes', Webb told him, and Haigh, apparently unperturbed, replied, 'Certainly. I'll do anything to help you, as you know.'

He was seated in the divisional detective inspector's office, where he smoked and dozed off. At 6 o'clock he was given a cup of tea, and there he stayed until 7.30 that evening. Haigh was then seen by Symes and Barratt, who questioned him about the Persian Lamb coat (which Haigh said belonged to a Mrs Henderson, whose affairs he was managing while she was on vacation in South Africa) and asked how many times he had been to Horsham.

'I used to go to Horsham a lot', replied Haigh, 'but lately I've only been there once in the evening, to the pictures.'

'You've been there in the morning recently on no less than four occasions', stated Symes.

'Ah!' replied Haigh. 'I can see you know what you're talking about. I admit the coat belonged to Mrs Durand-Deacon and that I sold her jewellery, as you know, to Bull's in Horsham.'

Symes showed him the cleaner's ticket, and Haigh said, 'Yes, I wondered if you'd got it when you started.'

'How did you come by this property?' asked Symes, adding, 'and where is Mrs Durand-Deacon?' He then cautioned Haigh.

There was a pause. And then Haigh replied, 'It's a long story. It's one of blackmail and I shall have to implicate many others. How do I stand about that?'

'What you have to say', replied Symes, 'is entirely a matter for you.'

Just then, he and Barratt were called from the room to answer a telephone call, leaving Haigh with DI Webb.

Haigh suddenly asked, 'Tell me frankly, what are the chances of anyone being released from Broadmoor?'

Webb, obviously mystified, replied, 'I can't discuss that sort of thing with you.'

'Well, if I told you the truth, you would not believe me', said Haigh. 'It sounds too fantastic for belief.'

Knowing that something highly incriminating, fantastic or not, was coming his way, Webb started to say, 'I must caution you . . .', but Haigh interrupted him, saying, 'I understand all that. Mrs Durand-Deacon no longer exists. She has disappeared completely and no trace of her can ever be found.'

'What's happened to her?' asked Webb, to be told, 'I have destroyed her with acid. You will find the sludge that remains, at Crawley. I did the same with the Hendersons and the McSwans. Every trace has gone. How can you prove murder if there is no body?'

Webb, understandably startled, summoned Barratt and Symes and told them, 'He's just told me that Mrs Durand-Deacon doesn't exist and that he's destroyed her by acid.'

'It's perfectly true', replied Haigh. 'But it's a very long story and it'll take hours to tell.'

'I am', replied Symes with masterly understatement, 'prepared to listen.'

While DI Webb took down Haigh's statement, which took 2½ hours to write, Barratt and Symes listened in stunned silence to the most incredible criminal revelations they had ever heard and the like of which they would never hear again:

> I have already made some statements to you about the disappearance of Mrs Durand-Deacon. I have been worried about the matter and fenced about in the hope that you would not find out about it. The truth is, however, that we left the hotel together and went to Crawley in my car. She was inveigled into going to Crawley by me in view of her interest in artificial fingernails. Having taken her into the storeroom at Leopold Road, I shot her in the back of the head whilst

she was examining some paper for use as fingernails. Then I went out to the car and fetched in a drinking glass and made an incision, I think with a penknife, in the side of the throat which I then drank. Following that, I removed the coat she was wearing, a Persian lamb, and the jewellery, rings, necklace, earrings and cruciform and put her in a forty-five gallon tank. I then filled the tank up with sulphuric acid by means of a stirrup-pump from a carboy. I then left it to react. I should have said that in between putting her in the tank and pumping in the acid, I went round to the Ancient Priors for a cup of tea. Having left the tank to react, I brought the jewellery and the revolver into the car and left the coat on the bench. I went to the George for dinner and I remember I was late, about nine-ish. I then came back to town and returned to the hotel about half-past ten.

The following morning, I had breakfast and discussed the disappearance of Mrs Durand-Deacon with the waitress and Mrs Lane . . . The ration books and clothing coupon books and other documents in the names of McSwan and Henderson are the subject of another story. This is covered very briefly by the fact that in 1944, I disposed of William Donald McSwan in a similar manner to the above, in the basement of 79 Gloucester Road, SW7 and of Donald McSwan and Amy McSwan in 1946 at the same address, and in 1948 of Dr Archibald Henderson and his wife Rosalie Henderson also in a similar manner at Leopold Road, Crawley.

Going back to the McSwans, William Donald, the son, whose address at that particular time I can't remember, met me at The Goat public house, Kensington High Street and from there, we went to No. 79 Gloucester Road, where, in the basement which I had rented, I hit him on the head with a cosh, withdrew a glass of blood from his throat as before and drank it. He was dead within five minutes or so. I put him in a forty-gallon tank and disposed of him with acid as in the case of Mrs Durand-Deacon, disposing of the sludge down a manhole in the basement. I took his watch and odds and ends, including an identity card before putting him into the tank. I had known this McSwan and his mother and father for some time, and on seeing his mother and father, explained that he had gone off to avoid his army call-up. I wrote a number of letters in due course to his mother and father, purporting to come from him and posted in, I think, Glasgow and Edinburgh, explaining various details of the disposition of properties, which were to follow. In the following year, I took separately to the same basement, the father, Donald and the mother, Amy, disposing of them in exactly the same way as the son. The files of the McSwans are at my hotel and will give details of the properties which I disposed of, after their deaths. I have since

> got additional ration books by producing their identity cards in the usual way.
>
> I met the Hendersons by answering an advertisement offering for sale their property at 22 Ladbroke Square. I did not purchase 22 Ladbroke Square. They sold it and moved to 16 Dawes Road, Fulham. This runs in a period from November 1947 to February 1948. In February 1948, the Hendersons were staying at Kingsgate Castle, Kent. I visited them there and went with them to Brighton, where they stayed at the Metropole. From there, I took Dr Henderson to Crawley and disposed of him in the storeroom at Leopold Road, by shooting him in the head with his own revolver, which I had taken from his property at Dawes Road. I put him in a tank of acid, as in the other cases. This was in the morning and I went back to Brighton and brought up Mrs Henderson on the pretext that her husband was ill. I shot her in the storeroom and put her in another tank and disposed of her with acid. In each of the last four cases, I had my glass of blood, as before. In the case of Dr Henderson I removed his gold cigarette case, his gold pocket watch and chain and from his wife, her wedding ring and diamond ring and disposed of all this to Bull's at Horsham for about £300. I paid their bill at the Hotel Metropole, collected their luggage and their red setter and took the luggage to Dawes Road. The dog I kept for a period at the hotel and later at Gatwick Hall until I had to send him to Professor Sorsby's Kennels in the country on account of night blindness. By means of letters, purporting to come from the Hendersons, I kept the relatives quiet, by sending letters to Mrs Henderson's brother, Arnold Burlin, who lives in Manchester.

The following day, Symes obtained various pieces of documentation from Haigh's room; now it was imperative to authenticate his claims. The jewellery was identified by Mrs Durand-Deacon's sister, Mrs Esmé Rose Fargus, who also identified the Persian Lamb coat, as did Mrs Lane and Miss Robbie, the hotel's manageress. Pieces of material found in Room 108 also exactly matched fabric used in repairs to the coat, which had traces of human blood on the collar.

The Chief Constable of Sussex requested that Scotland Yard take over the investigation since the offences had taken place in their area, and Detective Chief Inspector Guy Mahon was deputed to oversee the investigation.

It was just as well that the bulk of the investigation had already taken place. Mahon had been appointed chief inspector less than six weeks previously and since joining the force twenty-four years earlier, he had spent the minimum time in various divisions and departments. Now he was in C1 Department (colloquially known as the 'Murder Squad'), a department in which he had served twice before, once for a period of three months and once for six. He was what was termed 'a high-flyer', spending time in different postings in the hope that they would provide him with experience when he reached the highest echelons. Before we leave the lacklustre Mr Mahon – he would contribute little to this investigation – it remains to say that during the rest of his sanitized career he would serve in the Research and Planning Department twice, for seven and thirteen months respectively, and that when he took command of the Flying Squad, his tenure lasted just five months.

So when Mahon, plus the eminent pathologist Professor Keith Simpson, together with Dr G. E. Turfitt, the Deputy Director of the Metropolitan Police Laboratory, were sent to Crawley, DDI Symes went as well to provide a proper police presence. Detective Superintendent Eagles, the representative of the West Sussex Constabulary, was also in attendance.

Specks of blood were found on the whitewashed wall above the workshop bench, and a hat-pin was found in the bottom of a green drum.

Next, Simpson examined an area in the yard covering six feet by four feet – and three or four inches deep. Over a period of three days, 475lbs of earth soaked with a yellow, greasy residue was lifted from the yard at Leopold Road into five wooden crates and transported to Dr Turfitt's laboratory, where it was spread out on steel trays and sifted.

There was found 28lbs of animal fat, three faceted human gallstones and part of a left foot eroded by acid. A plastic cast was made of the foot by Superintendent Cyril Cuthbert, and a compelling comparison was made with one of Mrs Durand-Deacon's left shoes. Eighteen fragments of human bone indicated that they belonged to a female (the pelvic bone proved that) and came from one body, and the presence of osteoarthritis indicated late adult age. A full set of upper and lower dentures were positively identified by Miss Helen Mayo, the dentist who supplied them to Mrs Durand-Deacon, and the handle of a red plastic handbag was found, similar to one belonging to her, as was the cap of a lipstick.

Any of the remains of the McSwans at Gloucester Road and the Hendersons at Leopold Road were, of course, long gone. But it was estimated that had the sludge not been sifted from Leopold Road when it was, within a month the acid would have dissolved everything, including the dentures – although not the gallstones. But they alone could not have identified Mrs Durand-Deacon as the victim, and Haigh would have made good his assertion that that unfortunate lady's body had indeed vanished.

On 1 March, Haigh's room was searched; he identified a blue shirt in there as his and admitted that the bloodstains on the cuffs must have come from Mrs Durand-Deacon.

Haigh was charged with Mrs Durand-Deacon's murder on 2 March at Horsham police station and, following his appearance at the Magistrates' Court, was remanded in custody at Lewes prison – but within two days he asked to see DI Webb. He now made a further statement, in which he admitted murdering three more people, all of whom had been coshed and disposed of in acid. He had stolen whatever they possessed – it was not much, he said – and drunk their blood. One was a woman whom he met in Hammersmith in February 1945, and the next was a man named Max, whom he had met in The Goat public house seven months later; those two, he said, had been disposed of in the basement of Gloucester Road. The third was a girl named Mary; he had met her in Eastbourne in 1948 and disposed of her at Crawley.

Despite the most searching enquiries, none of these victims could be identified, and it's possible that none of them existed; they might well have been invented by Haigh, since he was going all-out for a plea of insanity.

On remand, Haigh was eager to tell the doctors and psychiatrists who visited him of his recurring dreams. They consisted of a forest of crucifixes which turned into trees and whose branches dripped blood. Then one of the trees turned into a man who collected blood in a bowl from another tree. This second tree grew paler and Haigh felt that he was losing strength; but when the man approached him and invited him to drink from the bowl of blood, he was unable to, the man gradually faded and Haigh woke up. After that, said Haigh, he felt persecuted for days, but when he killed again, the dream would occur once more and on this occasion the man did not recede and Haigh could drink from the bowl and thus satisfy his thirst. He also confessed to drinking his own urine from the age of eleven.

Apart from Haigh professing that he was as bonkers as conkers (thereby attempting to evade the hangman's noose), something else happened that could possibly have nullified any chance of a successful prosecution.

On 4 March, the *Daily Mirror* published lurid reports of 'The Vampire Killer' which mentioned Mrs Durand-Deacon's murder and the murder of several others, with references to blood-drinking and 'acid cremations'. Members of the public protested, and other newspapers contacted the Yard asking them to confirm or deny the story. It was clear that the case against Haigh could become so hopelessly prejudiced that proceedings might well have to be dropped. The Yard's Public Information Officer, Mr P. H. Fearnley, sent out a confidential memorandum to the editors of all leading newspapers telling them that whatever had been contained in Haigh's statement was *sub judice* and that any reference to it could well become a matter for consideration by the trial court. It was. The *Daily Mirror*'s editor, Silvester Bolam, was charged with contempt of court and apologised for what he referred to as 'his grave error of judgement'. The apology was not accepted by the Lord Chief Justice, Lord Goddard, who thundered, 'It is not an error of judgement – it is a question of policy!'

The newspaper was fined £10,000 and ordered to pay costs, and Bolam was sentenced to three months' imprisonment.

Before Haigh's first appearance at Horsham Magistrates' Court, a hundred people appeared outside in the streets, and one hour prior to his second appearance, twenty-one women queued outside the court for admittance to the public gallery. By the time Haigh arrived, there was a stampede of two hundred people in the public square, and among those wanting admittance to the court, women outnumbered men by three to one; a hundred people had to be turned away. Following his brief appearance at court, Haigh was taken by car to the police station for a conference with his solicitors; before the car could leave, its way was blocked by a pram pushed by a young mother who wanted a better look at Haigh. Two police officers had to manhandle her – and her pram, containing an infant – out of the way. As the police car slowly made its way to the police station it was watched by women who had paid for window seats to observe Haigh.

On Haigh's fourth appearance, two hundred people were again in the Market Square, girls and office workers leaned out of windows to see him arrive and seventy people queued up for entry into the court. First in the queue was Mrs E. Field of New Street, Horsham. 'I've been to every hearing, so far', she said excitedly.

Haigh wrote to his parents, proudly boasting that 'It isn't everybody who can create more sensation than a film star' and adding, 'Only Princess Margaret or Mr Churchill could command such interest.' If his parents had continued to insulate themselves from the outside world, it was a waste of Haigh's self-aggrandisement, since that unbalanced couple had probably never heard of the former Prime Minister or the future Queen's younger sister and would have had difficulty in comprehending what a film star was.

Despite the proceedings against the *Daily Mirror*, Haigh's trial for the single murder, that of Mrs Durand-Deacon, to which he pleaded not guilty, went ahead on 18 July 1949 at Lewes Assizes before the 81-year-old Mr Justice Humphreys. The prosecution was conducted by the Attorney General, Sir Hartley Shawcross KC, MP, and the defence by Sir David Maxwell Fyfe KC, MP.

Hundreds of people waited outside the court, many bringing their children with them. One of the onlookers in the public gallery was the American film star Robert Montgomery; another was 21-year-old Miss Barbara Stephens of Crawley, who had had a platonic friendship with Haigh for several years.

The trial was short and sweet; out of thirty-three witnesses, only four were cross-examined. Nine doctors had examined Haigh in prison; only one, Dr Henry Yellowlees, had concluded that he suffered from paranoid insanity. The others were convinced Haigh was shamming madness, as did two further psychiatrists called by the defence who were immediately rejected after they came to the same conclusion. But when Yellowlees was cross-examined, he was obliged to admit that Haigh knew that what he had done was 'punishable by law', and the Attorney General did not call any evidence to rebut Yellowlees' evidence because, as he said, 'There is nothing to rebut.'

In fact, it was Yellowlees' evidence that had taken up most of the court's time, so that the trial went into a second day. Haigh, who had sat in the dock busy with the *Daily Telegraph* crossword, did not give evidence, and the jury of eleven men and one woman were out for just seventeen minutes, returning at 4.40 pm.

'Is the prisoner guilty of murder; or guilty but insane?' asked the Clerk of the Assizes.

'Guilty of murder', replied the white-haired foreman, adding, 'It is our unanimous verdict.'

Asked if he had anything to say, Haigh replied, 'Nothing at all', and smiled as he was sentenced to death. As Mr Justice Humphreys left the court, he was loudly applauded by a somewhat fickle crowd of 1,000 spectators.

There were a number of bizarre occurrences prior to Haigh's execution. He petitioned the prison governor for a dress rehearsal of his hanging, so that each man would know the part he had to play and the execution would 'go off smoothly'. This was refused, but he had more success with Madame Tussaud's, who agreed to clothe his waxwork, soon to appear in 'The Chamber of Horrors', in his green Lovat suit and paisley tie.

The public were either shocked or titillated by the case, which elicited much gallows humour ('"Time for your bath", said Haigh, acidly').

The distinguished (if rather peculiar) Swiss pianist Albert Ferber, who arrived in England in 1937, had written a score for the 1947 film, *The Hangman Waits*, in which the plot revolved around a sadistic killer working as a organist in an Eastbourne theatre. The film had been released some time prior to Haigh's arrest, although it appeared to coincide more or less with Haigh's claim of having murdered a girl from that seaside town. Ferber had previously met Haigh during his Wigmore Hall recitals and was convinced of his innocence. He visited Haigh while he awaited execution and asked to have a grand piano brought to the prison, in order that he might give a recital for the condemned man. This plea met with the same lack of success as Haigh's request for a dress rehearsal of his execution.

Haigh had an attentive audience in the shape of prison warders and police officers, to whom he remarked:

> All men who are freed from a sense of guilt are happy. I take the view that the world's a happy hunting-ground, full of mugs who were born to be exploited by blokes like me. They are rabbits on which we feed.

Haigh wrote an account of his life for the readers of the *News of the World* (who had paid for his defence) and just prior to being led to the gallows he was asked if he'd like a brandy. 'Better make it a large one, old boy', he replied.

He was hanged at Wandsworth Prison on 10 August 1949. The hangman, Albert Pierrepoint, bound Haigh's wrists with a strap made of pale calf leather; this was used on a small number of special occasions to indicate, as he said, that there was 'more than a formal interest in this particular execution'. Haigh's dispatch took the unfortunately long time of eleven seconds.

Much of the paraphernalia in the case – the gas mask, rubber gloves and apron, the revolver, Mrs Durand-Deacon's handbag, gallstones and foot bones, and a letter to DI Webb from Haigh asking for his green suit to be sent to him to wear for committal proceedings – made their way into the Yard's Black Museum. There, it still reposes, although hysterical political correctness has since renamed the venue 'The Crime Museum'.

In a curious footnote, some good came out of Haigh's life.

Ten days after his execution, Haigh's wife remarried at Bodmin Registry Office, Cornwall. After Haigh had been sent to prison on the first occasion, Beatrice Hamer – as she now styled herself – decided she wanted nothing more to do with him. But when he was released from prison they met, by coincidence, in the street, whereupon Haigh told her that he had no intention of supporting her because he already had a wife. 'Thank goodness for that!' exclaimed the lady and flung her wedding ring down in the gutter.

Believing she had not been legally married in the first place, she then married an RAF officer who was killed on active service in 1943. Whatever her marital status was before, she was now officially a widow – in fact, a widow and bar – and she married a farmer named Dennis Alan Neale who, like his bride was thirty-four years of age – and hopefully, they both found happiness.

Sadness entered Mr Justice Humphreys' life when his wife died in 1953. He sold their Ealing home and – obviously not a superstitious man – moved into the Onslow Court Hotel, where he remained until his death, three years later.

Haigh's misdeeds ended on a chilling note.

After Haigh's arrest, many more enquiries were carried out, and one of them centred around countless sheets of paper which had been found with the scrawled signature on them of 'Cyril Armstrong'.

This was the Revd Cyril Armstrong, the vicar of St Bride's Church in Fleet Street, who at one time had been Chaplain to the Royal Household. He had also been a curate at Wakefield Cathedral when Haigh had been a choirboy there. Following one of his prison sentences, Haigh had sought out the vicar, who had helped him financially and also in obtaining employment.

'I remembered him as a choirboy with a lovely voice, but I had no idea he was practising my signature', said the reverend gentleman, adding, 'and I would hate to think of the reason.'

* * *

That was the end of Haigh, immortalized in Madame Tussaud's wax museum, with his artefacts reposing at Scotland Yard's museum, but it was not quite the end of the case.

Sergeant Lambourne had acted with great acumen right at the commencement of the case, and it is fair to say that had she not followed her instincts, there might not have been an investigation at all. Would Mrs Durand-Deacon have simply been recorded as a missing person, with the authorities hoping that one day she might reappear? It would have left Haigh to go on murdering for profit – there appears to be no earthly reason why he would have stopped – and as has already been said, just a few more weeks and all traces of Mrs Durand-Deacon would have been forever consumed by the acid.

There was a great deal of press coverage of Sergeant Lambourne's expertise, with the *Star*'s reporter informing his readers that she

> is, I understand, among several officers concerned in the case who are likely to receive special commendation from the commissioner. If she gets it, it will be her fifth since she joined the force in 1940.

The uniform chief superintendent of 'B' Division certainly thought so, and two weeks after the *Star*'s announcement, he penned a compelling report to the Commander, No.1 Area recommending Sergeant Lambourne for a commissioner's commendation. However, this had to pass through the desk of the District Detective Superintendent, Tom Barratt.

Barratt was a good cop; as a detective sergeant in 1937 he had arrested James Hynes, a thoroughly dangerous American criminal wanted for a £20,000 Park Lane robbery. Hynes had been wounded in the Jack 'Legs' Diamond/Al Capone gang wars, and Barratt had traced him to an East End Turkish baths. Although Hynes' face was covered with a towel, Barratt had identified him from the indentations made by the four machine gun bullets in his stomach. So he was well versed in the ways of criminal investigation and what was needed to earn a commendation.

But perhaps Barratt disliked what he perceived as being dictated to by a uniform counterpart. It is quite possible that he took umbrage at the superintendent's perhaps tactless comments when he wrote:

> In my opinion, Sergeant Lambourne conducted this apparently routine matter with ability and intelligence, and but for her, the CID enquiry would not have been taken up quite as promptly as it was done.

Then again, maybe Barratt abjured the amount of press coverage that had been bestowed upon a woman police officer; and it could be that he was a tad misogynistic.

But at any event, in his minute to the Assistant Commissioner (Crime), through Commander 1 Area, Barratt recommended Inspector Webb for a commissioner's commendation (which was well deserved), and the same for Detective Sergeant John Du

Rose (which was not). Du Rose had contributed a large amount of bugger-all to the investigation, but like the film director Alfred Hitchcock, he filled a small walk-on part in a number of large productions.

Grudgingly, Barratt recommended that Sergeant Lambourne be commended by Commander 1 Area for 'promptitude and intelligence'. This meant that that minor commendation would not be entered on her Central Record of Service.

'Maudie' rose to the rank of chief inspector; she had joined the Metropolitan Police three years before I was born and retired three months after I joined. She was much liked and well-respected by her contemporaries – but I cannot help but feel that Barratt's decision was incredibly mean and small-minded.

Chapter 4

The Painter and the Pervert

All murders are, of course, quite dreadful; but the details of the murderer which follows are, I think – how shall I put it? – rather seedy. Is that the correct terminology? See what you think.

Malika Maria de Fernandez was a 32-year-old portrait painter who had apparently travelled the world, spoke several languages and, by 24 March 1959, was working as a waitress in the Zanzibar Coffee Bar, Manchester. Her Latin-American origins were vague – as was the whereabouts of her father who, she said, was named Benjamin Mendoza de Fernandez but who has never been traced. Miss de Fernandez was living in Prestwich, Manchester, and although she would say that the reason she was working as a waitress was to 'make a little extra cash' to supplement her earnings from painting, it's possible that working in the coffee bar was her main source of income.

She was certainly a striking-looking woman, and the man who walked into those premises at 6.15 that evening was also attractive; at least, Miss de Fernandez certainly thought so initially.

This was Peter Edwin Rainbird, a 32-year-old station officer employed by the British Overseas Airways Corporation (BOAC) at nearby Ringway Airport, who sat down and ordered a meal which, two minutes later, Miss de Fernandez brought to his table.

To all intents and purposes, what the French refer to as a *coup de foudre* – or in more prosaic terms, 'love at first sight' – smote the couple, because by 6.30 Rainbird had invited the waitress to his table, where they both devoured a Spanish omelette.

Matters moved on apace, because two hours after entering the coffee bar, Rainbird proposed, asking her, 'Where shall we spend our honeymoon?' to which the much-travelled lady immediately replied, 'Tehran'.

'I'm serious', said Rainbird. 'Are you?', and when Miss de Fernandez nodded, he called for champagne.

Paying forty-four shillings for a special licence, the couple were wed just four days after their initial meeting, on 28 March – Rainbird's thirty-third birthday.

Impetuous? Not a bit of it. As Rainbird told the readers of the *Daily Herald*, 'No, I'm not impulsive. I know what I want and, having made up my mind there seemed no point in waiting. I've known other girls, of course, but Malika has a kind of explosive charm which just swept me off my feet.'

Both liked to move in flamboyant social circles – and both loved the publicity that arose from their lightning courtship – but there was one facet of his personality that Rainbird had initially failed to disclose to his bride: tall, distinguished and personable Peter Rainbird was as gay as a fruit bat.

* * *

Nowadays, homosexuality is considered an inevitable feature of all private and public life, especially in the workplace, where to deny a gay person promotion on the grounds of their sexuality is more than sufficient to provoke a massively expensive lawsuit. But not in 1959. Then, if a homosexual man was arrested for 'importuning for immoral purposes' in the vicinity of public conveniences, it meant arrest and the possibility of a 40-shilling fine. Not, of course, that the size of such a fine deterred the old and the bold or the great and the good from what was known as 'cottaging' – it was fear of the public scorn and perhaps condemnation which was sure to follow. Noël Coward had a more exploratory view of convention ('Is your bum available this morning, dear boy?'), but Sir John Gielgud was one actor who was deeply remorseful about being thus caught and fined, although Dame Edith Evans did her best to console him ('Oh, Johnny, nobody cares – don't be such a silly bugger!'). Nevertheless, if a worker's predilection for 'batting for the other side' became known in the workplace, it could certainly lead to demotion, if not outright sacking.

In fact, Rainbird's sexuality was already the subject of comment with his employers, so this marriage of convenience provided the aura of respectability which he needed to keep his job. It was beneficial to his wife as well, because with his position at BOAC he could provide her with discounted air travel to enable her to jet off to all sorts of exotic locations.

But that was all. Theirs was an 'on-off' relationship which took her all over the world (and, so it was said, to many different affairs), and they moved from one flat to another in Manchester while their marriage disintegrated almost as fast as their courtship had advanced.

Rainbird soon moved into Heathfield Cottage, Saltersley Lane, Wilmslow, an affluent suburb of Manchester. The cottage was surrounded on two sides by woodland, and a peat bog was nearby. He shared the property with 25-year-old Phillip Clark, to whom he confessed that the marriage to Malika had never been consummated and described his wife as being 'a high-class prostitute'.

Clark was not at home when Malika returned several months later. In fact, neither was Rainbird. A neighbour saw her strolling around the property and never having met or even seen her before, he telephoned Rainbird at the airport to inform him of her presence. This was 27 October 1960, the last date that anyone would see Malika alive. Rainbird contacted Phillip Clark, told him his wife had returned and asked him to stay away 'until we've sorted things out'. The married couple had a tremendous row – it is quite possible that Malika had discovered that her husband was living with another man and threatened to expose him to his employers unless he paid up – and Rainbird strangled her. He dragged the body out to the patio and dismembered it with an axe used for chopping wood from one of the two garden sheds. The remains of the body he tried to dispose of by burning on a bonfire; when that was unsuccessful, he placed the body parts in sacks and buried them somewhere in the grounds of the cottage.

Rainbird and Clark remained at the cottage until 30 June 1961, then he left BOAC and moved away. Somewhere along the line, Rainbird changed his name to the rather affected 'Reyn-Bardt', setting up catering businesses, running a guest house, coffee bars and fish and chip shops, before settling in Portsmouth in 1963.

The Northcote Hotel at 35 Francis Avenue, Southsea, Hampshire is today a thriving, well-run and popular pub which puts on live music, but in 1975 it was in the hands of less reputable personages. Reyn-Bardt was then aged forty-nine and he had met up with an equally unsavoury character, 24-year-old Paul Russell Corrigan. The thriving cabaret club which they set up in the hotel was a success, so much so that Reyn-Bardt was able to purchase a flat in Malta.

But the Northcote Hotel was a cloak for their other activity, abducting young boys from the streets of Portsmouth for homosexual purposes, and both were caught and sentenced to seven years' imprisonment. Unwisely perhaps, they were confined in the same prison, where they were able to discuss their sick fantasy of abducting a young boy from the streets, then raping and murdering him. It was then, during these exciting conversations, that Reyn-Bardt disclosed to Corrigan that he had murdered his wife.

Both were released from prison in January 1981; and Corrigan acted out his fantasy. Together with a 16-year-old accomplice, he stalked and killed a 13-year old boy – a complete stranger riding his bike in Leicestershire – by repeatedly stabbing him with a hunting knife in what was described as 'satanic fury', leaving his naked body in a park.

Interviewed by police, Corrigan told them, 'I did it because I have wanted to for years. I have read about it, thought about it and written about it', and then the horrifying details of the ordeal that the boy had suffered in his final hours began to be recounted.

Corrigan was quite right; while he was serving his prison sentence he had written a 250-page dissertation on doing just that. It was passed around to the other drooling deviants encased in 'The Nonces' Wing' and, incredibly, the prison staff were aware of it. It might have been thought that the most sensible course of action would have been to have pushed Corrigan into Maidstone Prison's television room with some large, muscular armed robbers, the parents of young children, to see what they would make of the document and its author.

Fortunately for those who champion human rights, nothing of the kind happened, and Corrigan was freed after serving four years of his original sentence.

Despite that rather incriminating document, Corrigan was able to circumvent a conviction for murder, instead arguing that he was suffering from 'diminished responsibility' (as did his charmless 16-year-old apprentice), and after pleading guilty to manslaughter, on 16 June 1982 at Birmingham Crown Court, Corrigan was sentenced to life imprisonment and his little chum to seven years.

Unless one's a resident of Siberia, life imprisonment, as we know, does not necessarily mean life at all. The judge had declined to impose a minimum term, and Corrigan wanted to render his sentence as brief as possible; after all, he was only thirty years of age and there were lots more little boys in the outside world who needed abducting, raping and butchering – the detectives had found evidence of that when they inspected his gruesome hovel. So – what to do? Corrigan knew; he summoned detectives to his cell and grassed up his previous cell-mate, Peter Reyn-Bardt, for murdering his wife; so doing, he felt, had to contribute to a sizeable deduction in his sentence.

Reyn-Bardt was at that time living in Knightsbridge; questioned by the police, he denied everything. Searches were carried out and further enquiries were made, all of which took the matter no further forward. And that, for the time being, was that.

* * *

A few months later, on 13 May 1983, two commercial peat-cutters, Andy Mould and Stephen Dooley, were facing each other across the conveyor belt at a peat bog at Lindow Moss, which was about 300 yards from Heathfield Cottage. Suddenly, amongst the peat, a round object, which they jokingly thought might be an ostrich egg, bounced up. They took it to Ken Harewood, the manager of the peat works, who hazarded that the object might be a football; but when it was hosed down and freed of the adhesive remains of peat, they realized it was an incompletely preserved human head with attached remnants of soft tissue, brain, eye, optic nerve and hair. The police at Macclesfield were informed and they commenced a murder investigation.

A Home Office forensic scientist came to the conclusion that the head belonged to a recently deceased European female, probably aged thirty to fifty, and that, thought the police, was the breakthrough they had been looking for. Confronted with the news of their discovery, Reyn-Bardt cracked. 'Yes, you're right', he sighed. 'It's been so long. I thought I would never be found out. I may as well tell the truth, now. I did kill her.'

He made a written statement in which he admitted strangling his wife, saying, 'I thought she had gone forever, but there she was, back again. She was after money. She made my life a misery. She always wanted more.'

Arrested and charged with murder, he was committed to Chester Crown Court for trial.

But just to make sure, Detective Inspector George Abbott decided to double-check. He sent the head to Oxford University for further examination. Carbon dating revealed that whoever might claim ownership of that head, it was not Malika Maria Rainbird née de Fernandez. The head belonged to an unknown woman who had died 1,700 years previously.

At Chester Crown Court, Reyn-Bardt now immediately repudiated his confession, aided and abetted by his barrister, Victor Durand QC. Now aged seventy-five, Durand was perhaps getting past his sell-by date (although he soldiered on for another eleven years), and although he argued that the jury of six men and six women should return a verdict of manslaughter, the confessional and supporting evidence was too strong. The jury heard from Martin Thomas QC:

> No trace of her body has been found. But you will hear how she disappeared on or about 27 October 1960 and you will hear the full and detailed confession of the accused, how he strangled her, how he chopped up her body with an axe and how he disposed of her remains.

Reyn-Bardt claimed that his wife had attacked him, raking his face with her nails and demanding more money; he could remember shaking her by her shoulders but not how he had killed her. After a three-day trial and after three and a half hours of deliberations, on 15 December 1983 the jury, by a majority of 11–1, found him guilty of murder.

Mr Justice Leonard told him, 'I pass the only sentence which is permitted by law, which is one of life imprisonment.'

And that's exactly what it was; Reyn-Bardt died in prison.

And what of his chilling associate, Paul Russell Corrigan? Did he profit from a reduction in sentence as a reward from his spirited grassing-up of his fellow pervert?

Well, unfortunately not. For him, like Reyn-Bardt, life really did mean life. He served thirty-six years, five months and twenty-five days, before expiring in his cell at North Sea Camp Prison on 11 December 2018.

As for the remains of Mrs Rainbird's body, despite several excavations of the grounds of Heathcliff Cottage, the peat bog and the surrounding area, no traces of it have ever been found. The same applies to the remains of her 1,700 year predecessor, whose skull now rests in the basement of the British Museum.

Thus, Mrs Rainbird joins the ranks of those who are certainly dead but whose bodies have never been discovered.

Chapter 5

From Pole to Pole

Poland's history is a troubled one, no doubt about that.

During the First World War, Polish territory, which was then split between the Austro-Hungarian, German and Russian empires, became the scene of many bloody conflicts on the Great War's Eastern Front.

Following the war, Poland became an independent nation, but on 1 September 1939, the country was invaded by Nazi Germany, followed sixteen days later by Soviet Russia. Many Poles fled their country and they were wise to do so; during the following six years, 5½ million (half of them Jewish) died under Nazi rule, and Russia accounted for a further 150,000.

Many Poles served valiantly in the armed services of the Allies during the Second World War, but at the war's end a large number of them hesitated to return to their native country, it having been 'liberated' by the Soviets (who during the conflict had changed sides and were now, apparently, part of the Allied cause), and displaced Poles dispersed all over the western world. Britain passed the Polish Resettlement Act of 1947, and communities grew up all over the United Kingdom; by 1951, the UK census revealed that 162,339 residents named their birthplace as Poland.

One of these settlements was in Wales at Llandeilo, Carmarthenshire, a small rural community of farms, woodland and hills situated at the crossing of the River Towy by the A483 road on a nineteenth century stone bridge; it is an area where Welsh is widely spoken and, in the post-war years, so was Polish.

One of the inhabitants was 58-year-old Michial Onufrejczyk (pronounced 'Onofrayshic') who, due to his white beard, was known locally as 'Mr Whiskers'. Enlisting in the Polish Resettlement Corps in South Wales and with the aid of a loan from the Polish Army Funds, in 1949 he purchased the 129-acre Cefn Hendre Farm, situated a mile from the village of Cwymdu and about five miles from Llandeilo. He did little to integrate with the local community – which consisted of fourteen residents in half a dozen cottages – and his limited command of the English language precluded meaningful conversation.

Onufrejczyk was a veteran of the Polish army, in which he had served as a warrant officer during the First World War, been wounded twice and awarded the *Virtuti Militari*, the Polish equivalent of the Victoria Cross. During the second conflict, he had fought with the Allies in Libya and been awarded nine medals, all for gallantry.

However . . . no one by his name is shown in the Polish Order of Recipients, 1792–1992 as receiving the *Virtuti Militari* – and *nine* gallantry awards? I don't want to deviate from this tale, but let's just take a look at that, shall we? Gallantry awards and bullshit are matters I take really seriously.

On the subject of gallantry, let's focus on my chum, the late Nancy Wake, who was an intrepid member of the Second World War's Special Operations Executive. She possessed ten medals, four of which were campaign medals. The other six reflected her courage: a George Medal from England, four gallantry awards from France and the Medal of Freedom with Bronze Palm from the United States of which just 987 were ever issued. When one's the possessor of six well-earned gallantry awards, books are written about you, television shows and friendship with Prince Charles happen, as they did in Nancy's case, and a heritage pylon was erected to her memory in her native New Zealand.

And Onufrejczyk claimed to have *nine* awards for gallantry? My arse.

So if by now you've formed the opinion that I possess a slight antipathy towards this stalwart former soldier, you'd be right – and let's see why.

Michial Onufrejczyk was a blustering, domineering, grandstanding, violent bully. A complete stranger to the truth, he was a forger and an ace manipulator, coercing others into his schemes and able to turn himself into a victim when they refused. Oh, and by the way, he was also a cold-blooded murderer. This is how it all came about.

* * *

The farm had been run-down when Onufrejczyk first acquired it; in March 1953, he entered into a partnership with a fellow Pole, 58-year-old Stanislaw Sykut, who paid £719 18s 9d for a half-share and also took over a half-share of the farm's liabilities, including a mortgage held on the property by Barclays Bank. A partner in the enterprise was much needed; two other partners had preceded Sykut, who had come to the conclusion that far from being simply run-down, the property by now was quite dilapidated. The negotiations were carried out by a Llandeilo solicitor, John Vaughan-Roberts, who took steps to draw up a proper partnership agreement, which Onufrejczyk refused to sign. It was not a happy alliance; within two months Sykut had complained to the local police, displaying all the signs of having been physically assaulted. Upon being cautioned by a police sergeant for assault on a much smaller, weaker man, Onufrejczyk replied, 'Very sorry, very sorry. No do it again', although he would later say that he had acted in self-defence, alleging that Sykut had rushed at him with his fists raised.

But Sykut was plainly unhappy with the relationship and he had repeatedly asked his partner to sell the four-bedroom, 200-year-old farmhouse. Onufrejczyk had just as repeatedly refused. Finally Sykut, who wanted £700 to buy out of the partnership – and had advertised his proposed sale of the partnership in the press, including Polish newspapers – was obliged to threaten court action and gave notice to end the affiliation, which expired on 14 November 1953.

Onufrejczyk made desperate attempts to borrow money in order to buy out his partner; if the court action succeeded, there would have been a compulsory sale of the farm and stock and he would have lost practically everything. He would receive only a share of the assets after the sale and payment of liabilities.

On one occasion, both men were accompanied to the solicitor's office by Mrs Zbigniewa Julia Pawelec, the secretary of the Polish Farmers' Association, to act as interpreter. Afterwards, Sykut remained in Llandeilo and she and Onufrejczyk came home on the bus. He was furious about the proposed auction of the farm and told her, 'Sykut will rot in the hedges, even if I go to prison for it, and his daughter will die like a dog in the depths of Russia, by my making.'

Sykut was never seen again after 14 December 1953. Letters which he used to pick up from the local Post Office were not collected. He was last seen at the local blacksmith's on that date; later, Onufrejczyk went to see the blacksmith to ask him to say that it was on 17 December that he had last seen his partner.

On 18 December at 11.15 am, Benjamin Thomas Davies, a sheriff's officer, arrived at the farm to recover a debt of £215. This was because in 1950 Onufrejczyk had borrowed £200 from a close friend of Sykut's. It had not been repaid, and a High Court writ had been issued against him. Mr Davies, who was accompanied by Florian Busko to act as an interpreter, asked to see Sykut; he was told that he had gone to Llandeilo to see a doctor, but it later transpired that none of the medical practitioners in that town – Drs King Thomas, William Oldham, G. O. Morgan or P. M. Phillip – saw Sykut that day. Onufrejczyk was very reluctant to show the sheriff's officer into the farmhouse, saying that it was not very tidy; Davies practically had to force his way in. In fact, Busko thought that the kitchen was far cleaner than he had ever seen it before. He left a note for Sykut; when Busko saw Onufrejczyk on New Year's Eve, he asked if Sykut had received the note, since he was surprised that he had not heard from him. Onufrejczyk said that he had given the note to Sykut after Busko and the sheriff's officer had left. When he produced a document in Polish in which Sykut purported to sell Onufrejczyk his share of the farm for £600, Busko was able to say quite definitively, 'That is not Sykut's signature.'

Nevertheless, Onufrejczyk told half a dozen people that Sykut had gone to London for fourteen days; he told another half dozen that his partner had gone to Poland.

The story that he finally decided upon (and more or less stuck to) was that at 7 o'clock on the evening of 18 December a large car had arrived at the farm containing three Polish men, and Sykut had left with them. At least one of the men, he said, was armed with a pistol, and he stated that they were from the Polish embassy.

Two police officers called at the farm on 20 December; word had now spread with regard to Sykut's disappearance. Detective Sergeant E. J. Williams was one of those officers and he took a written statement from Onufrejczyk, who said that after going into partnership at the farm Sykut had complained that he was not in good health, that the work was too hard and that he wanted to terminate the partnership. Onufrejczyk told the officers that Sykut had gone to visit friends in London for fourteen days and that he had gone with two or three Poles on 18 December; what was more, he (Onufrejczyk) had bought Sykut's share of the farm.

Sykut, he said, had wanted to auction the farm and over a period of three months he (Onufrejczyk) had tried to borrow money from his niece, Mrs Pokara, telling her that if the farm was auctioned, he would lose everything. He went on to say:

> On or about December 17, 1953, I received a postal packet which I signed for at the Post Office at Cwm Du. The packet contained £450 in pound notes and a note from my niece. The money was loaned to me by my niece.

He went on to say that Sykut agreed to accept £450, saying that Onufrejczyk could pay a further £150 to his solicitor.

After dictating an agreement in Polish, Sykut and two other Poles got into a large green car. After the car had left, with a man named Jablonski saying that Sykut would be staying at the Polish Combatants' Club, Onufrejczyk said he was surprised to see a third man in the kitchen. Asked why he had not accompanied the others, the man replied enigmatically, 'I will walk down' and then proceeded to follow him 'with his hand in his pocket'.

It was high time for Onufrejczyk to try to authenticate his statement to the police, so the following day, 21 December, he arrived unexpectedly at Fortnam Road, Upper Holloway, London, the home of some friends, included his niece, Mrs Stanislawa Pokara. Telling her that he had come to London to meet his partner, he asked her to pretend that she had sent £450 to him, which she refused to do. However, the following day, he persuaded Mrs Pokara to draft three documents for him; two of these were agreements to sell a share in the farm for £450 cash and a promissory note for £150, and one was a letter to a solicitor in Llandeilo, purporting to come from Sykut and saying he was leaving the country to return to Poland because his wife was sick. He then dictated another letter purporting to come from Sykut to Piotr Biscup, a friend of Sykut's who had retained almost all of his personal possessions, saying:

> I sold the farm to Mr Onufrejczyk so please hand over all my personal belongings to Onufrejczyk, so that he can send them on to my family because I am leaving for Poland.

But Piotr and his wife Elena Biscup of Penrheolwen Cottage, just outside the village of Cwymdu, had received a visit from Sykut on 13 December – the day before his disappearance – and he had not told them that he was going away to Poland, London or anywhere else.

Onufrejczyk then told Mrs Pokara that he would get Sykut to sign these documents, but although they were signed in Sykut's name, the signatures were of course forgeries. He then took them to a Polish lawyer, Roman Bakalarczyk, who told him that the documents had not been properly prepared and were of no legal value. Returning to Mrs Pokara's house, Onufrejczyk told her of the lawyer's opinion and then dramatically told her, 'I will kill myself!' When Mrs Pokara – her suspicions now thoroughly aroused – demanded to know if he had killed Sykut, he burst into tears.

Properly prepared documents were now drawn up, and Onufrejczyk asked two people if they would forge Sykut's signature.

On 30 December, the sheriff's officer received a cheque in the sum of £15 from the joint account of Onufrejczyk and Sykut dated 18 December with two signatures. The one purporting to be Sykut's was a forgery.

* * *

By now, Carmarthenshire police had launched a full enquiry. Onufrejczyk basically stuck to his story: Sykut had left on 18 December taking two valises with him, he told them. Embellishments, however, were starting to creep in: Sykut had not said where he was going, nor had he heard from him since, and he did not know where he was. However, he said that he had paid Sykut £450 in notes for his share of the farm; one of the men had asked for £600 so he made out a promissory note for £150. Onufrejczyk said he had gone to Paddington on 21 December to meet them, but they had not shown up.

On 26 January 1954, police questioned the villagers of Cwymdu and also farmers of the region; Cefn Hendre was the only farm in that area owned by Poles, but Edminsford Mansion, a few miles away, had been taken over by Polish families and they too were questioned, without success. The fact remained that nobody could say they had seen Sykut since 14 December.

A man missing in mysterious circumstances; even more mysterious men purporting to be from the Polish Embassy and armed with pistols; Mrs Lizzie Jones, the blacksmith's wife, recalling hearing a car at 4.00 am 'just before Christmas' – but that was all. Then there was the missing man's business partner who was desperate for money and had given conflicting accounts of his partner's disappearance. High time, thought Mr T. Hubert Lewis, Chief Constable of Carmarthenshire, to call in Scotland Yard.

Lewis was highly respected as a senior officer who had started his career as a constable on the beat and, without any assistance, worked his way up the ranks, finding time, en route, to study law and become a barrister. He was certainly not averse to seeking assistance when it was necessary; following the murder of 78-year-old retired teacher Miss Elizabeth Thomas in January 1953, he had asked for the Yard's assistance. Detective Chief Inspector Reg Spooner was sent; he had his work cut out with the main suspect, who was deaf and dumb and unable to read or write, and who was inevitably acquitted.[1] Undismayed, Lewis called for the Yard

1 For further details of this case, see *The Guv'nors: Ten of Scotland Yard's Greatest Detectives*, Pen & Sword Books, 2010

again in October 1953, when two dairy farmers, Mr and Mrs John Harries, went missing. This time, Detective Chief Inspector Jack Capstick was sent who had far more success, arresting the Harries' nephew, who was executed for their murders the following year.

Now, following Lewis' latest request, 55-year-old John Pretsell Jamieson, whose promotion to Detective Superintendent had been announced three weeks previously, arrived at Ammanford police station. Jamieson was not a member of the Murder Squad – he was based at Paddington – but at that time there was a shortage of senior officers at the Yard and all were fully engaged. It was a good choice. With twenty-seven years' service, the hawk-faced, six-feet-tall native of Corstorphine, Edinburgh had served with the Flying Squad for over six years and had headed the secretive, post-war Ghost Squad; his expertise had resulted in him being commended by the commissioner on twenty-nine occasions – it would also be responsible, together with his expertise in managing murder investigations, for the award of the Queen's Police Medal for distinguished service.

Together with Detective Sergeant William Groom, Jamieson spent the last weekend of January sifting through the seventy statements which had already been obtained, as well as touring the area of the farm.

During the course of the investigations, it appeared that Sykut had been in the habit of writing on a weekly basis to his wife Janina and daughter Zana, who lived in Lublin, Poland. His one wish, said a friend, was to build up sufficient capital to provide for his family; but inexplicably, as he told his friend, he did not expect to see them again. Would recent events have impelled him to mention in those letters his present whereabouts? Jamieson called in Special Branch to assist.

A young Polish mother (who spoke fluent English) and a Polish former lieutenant, Mr J. Broida, had assisted Sykut with transactions over the farm; Sykut had been due to meet Broida on 16 December in Llandeilo in order to see a solicitor with the object of selling his share of the farm – but he had never arrived.

Meanwhile, a police search party carried out a minute inspection of the farmhouse, outbuildings and farm implements; forty officers, in two parties, under the watchful eye of the Chief Constable and Dr W. R. Harrison of the Cardiff Forensic Laboratory, started digging the area surrounding the farm, as well as examining fields, swamps, bog and woodlands for nine hours. But of Sykut there was not a trace.

The River Dulais which ran by the farm was now swollen with flood water; police concentrated their search on its banks.

Meanwhile, Chief Inspector L. D. Foster of Cardiff's Forensic Science laboratory carried out a minute examination, room by room, of the farmhouse. In the kitchen, 2,000 blood spots were found on a wall and around the fireplace; also a bloody handprint on the edge of a dresser. There was also a bloodstain which contained a tiny fragment of bone.

Dr Harrison found a piece of blood-spattered plasterboard; it had also been used as a blotter, because the signature 'S. Sykut' was found on it, in reverse.

* * *

On 9 February, Onufrejczyk was taken to Ammanford police station, where in the presence of his solicitor, Mr D. Stanley Glassbrook, and with Mrs Pawelec acting as an interpreter, he was interviewed by Jamieson. Onufrejczyk gave a 21-page statement. When questioned about the bloodspots, he told the police they had come from rabbits which had been hung from a hook – but it was pointed out to him that the blood was human. Asked about the handprint, he replied that Sykut had cut his hand on a hay machine.

He was asked once more to explain the bloodstains on the wall and around the fireplace, and to that he replied:

> I cannot explain where they came from because I cannot recollect anything that could explain it . . . I have done nothing wrong. I have been asked by the police if I will agree to have a small sample of my blood taken for comparison purposes with the blood found in the kitchen. I do not agree to this . . . I have taken no steps to find the three men as well as Sykut since 18 December. I have been asked if Sykut had been interested in politics. In my opinion, he was a Communist.

Onufrejczyk would remain there for 33 hours, before being released on bail.

By the following week Jamieson, pursuing enquiries in London, had been told by Arthur Cyril Clark, an executive officer at the Passport Office, that there was no record since 1948 of Sykut being granted or even applying for a passport. Similarly, Peter Conlan, an executive officer in the Aliens' Department of the Home Office, was able to say that no application for travel documents of any kind had ever been received from Sykut. Furthermore, Special Branch officer Detective Sergeant S. Watkins, who was stationed at Northolt Airport and who had checked the passenger lists, said that no one by that name had departed from the United Kingdom between 18 and 23 December. The evidence was coming together, and Jamieson had a conference with Carmarthenshire's Chief Constable.

Back in Llandeilo, Superintendent T. A. Jones from Ammanford police station had marshalled forty farmers and farm hands. Before they split into four parties to extend the search by five or six miles, he told them that he was sure that Sykut had not left the farm of his own free will and mentioned that a suggestion had been made that he had left the farm in the company of three men. 'How could anyone living in London or the Midlands find his way to Cefn Hendre Farm without asking his way?' he asked. 'We want your assistance and want to use your local knowledge.'

However, enquiries had progressed to such an extent that the superintendent was not really asking the assembled company for sightings of the car containing the three men; he was wanting confirmation that the car and the three men had *not* been seen by anybody, for the simple reason that he was in no doubt that they had never existed in the first place.

But in the event that this search proved fruitless – and it did – Mr John Evans of the Llandeilo Branch of the National Farmers' Union suggested that an appeal should be made to farmers from a wider area to come forward and organize a bigger search the following week.

Again, nothing was found. The farm was ailing. Three months had gone by since Sykut's disappearance and eleven cattle had died. The local mason, David Evans, gave his opinion: 'One day, they will find Stanislaw Sykut', he said, adding, 'and I think they will find him dead.' Many would agree with those sentiments; but they would be only half-right. Sykut *was* dead, but his body would never be found.

A full report compiled by Jamieson was submitted by Carmarthenshire's Chief Constable to the Director of Public Prosecutions, and as a result Onufrejczyk was arrested at the farm on 19 August by Detective Inspector Glynne Jones, head of the county's CID. Together with the officers from the Yard and in the presence of an interpreter, he said, 'We have been making enquiries for your missing partner, Stanislaw Sykut, whom you say left this farm on December 14, 1953. As a result of our enquiries, I am going to arrest you and charge you with the murder of Sykut.'

Before he could be cautioned, Onufrejczyk burst out in Polish, 'I deny this blame. I have not murdered Sykut. I didn't kill him and I haven't done him any harm.' And with that, the prisoner was taken to Ammanford police station.

When he appeared at Llandeilo Magistrates' Court, the three-man police presence of that town was insufficient to control the crowd of 200 who arrived; reinforcements from Ammanford had to be called in.

Mrs Stanislawa Pokara gave evidence and said she asked Onufrejczyk (whom she referred to as 'Uncle') why he could not write the letters instead of her; he replied he had forgotten his spectacles and told her that before he left the farm Sykut had told him, 'Michial, do everything in my name.' She added that Onufrejczyk had told her he was going to the Polish Combatants' Club, Queen's Gate Terrace to meet Sykut so that he could sign the papers; she offered to accompany him to act as a witness, but he had refused. When he returned he stated that Sykut had signed the documents, but Onufrejczyk had been told that the documents were not valid. He then asked when Mrs Pokara's husband would return; asked why, Onufrejczyk replied that he wanted her husband to accompany him to a solicitor's office in Llandeilo, purport to be Sykut and sign documents in his name; she refused. She had received a letter from Onufrejczyk on 28 December 1953 in which he thanked her for the loan of £450 – money which, she told the court, she had never lent him. On 2 January 1954, she received another letter in which he stated, 'If somebody asks you if you have written to me, please say you never wrote nothing for me . . . only that you gave me a loan for buying a home.'

Her husband, Stanislaw Pokara, told the bench he had first met Onufrejczyk in 1949, when he wanted a loan of £100 or £150; he did not part with any money to him. At the time of Onufrejczyk's visit to his house, Pokara was told by Onufrejczyk that he had paid Sykut £450 for his share of the farm on the occasion when the three men, with pistols arrived at the farm in 'the big black car'. Two days later, when he arrived home from work on 23 December, Pokara found three envelopes and a note asking that they be addressed to a solicitor and posted, 'but not until after Christmas'. He steamed the letters open, to find that they contained an authorization, an agreement and an inventory. One purported to be signed by Sykut, another was allegedly signed on the back by Sykut, and there were two witnesses' signatures.

The mother of Mrs Pokara, Mrs Felicja Nowacka, and her husband Josef both gave evidence of how Onufrejczyk came to their Crouch Hall Road, London address on 22 December; he asked Josef Nowacka to accompany him to a solicitor and pretend to be Sykut – Josef declined, as well as refusing to forge Sykut's signature. Swiftly transforming himself into a victim, Onufrejczyk dramatically announced, 'You are not willing to save my life', and adding, 'I am lost.'

That night, Onufrejczyk shared a room in a London hotel with a Karol Grausberg, who told him that he did not accept that Sykut had gone to Poland. Grausberg said he did not believe that Sykut could have obtained a passport from the Home Office in such a short space of time and that, even if he had succeeded in getting a visa, he would still have had to wait for months before the Polish government would agree to him entering the country – but Onufrejczyk insisted that Sykut had gone to Poland. During the night in the hotel Grausberg was woken up by his companion repeatedly moaning, 'My God, what have I done?' until at 3 o'clock in the morning he could stand it no longer and told Onufrejczyk to 'shut up'.

Evan Herbert Jones, a bank manager at Llandeilo, told the court that in September 1953 Onufrejczyk had asked for a £700 loan in order to buy out Sykut's share of the farm; since the joint account was £1,525 overdrawn, he had refused.

A friend of Sykut's, Joseph Wilczak, stayed at the farm for two nights in August 1953, at which time Sykut was 'looking like a frightened animal', his friend said. Two months later, Sykut was visited at the farm by his former company commander in the Polish army, who described him as looking like 'a sick man'. Roman Bakalarczyk, a Polish lawyer, told the court of the desperate straits that Onufrejczyk had found himself in since a request for a loan from the Agricultural Bank had been turned down. Several days after he had told the farmer that the documentation he had was worthless, and had tried to arrange a loan for him, Onufrejczyk had told him that he did not require a loan any longer since he had bought out Sykut's share of the farm; he showed Bakalarczyk a document in Polish to that effect. That document was shown to the previous witness, Wilczak, who had in the past received a number of letters from Sykut and who remarked, 'I do not think it is Sykut's signature.' That was also the opinion of Dr W .R. Harrison, Director of the Forensic Science Laboratory, Cardiff.

After fourteen days of evidence, each lasting six hours, and having heard evidence from sixty-five witnesses at the Shire Hall, the magistrates retired for 40 minutes before committing Onufrejczyk in custody to stand his trial for murder at the county's Assize Court – and the search continued around the farm . . .

Meanwhile, ever since Onufrejczyk had been held in custody, three neighbours had milked his cows twice daily. But on 23 September, between 700 and 800 men, women and children crowded into the farm when the livestock was put up for auction; this was necessary because of the lack of forage and the difficulty of obtaining labour. The auctioneer, Mr Dilwyn Thomas, assisted by Mr Howard Clee, dealt briskly with bids from the owners of 300 vehicles and the occupants of two coaches – they were cash-only transactions – and eventually, the twelve milking cows and the sixteen young stock were sold for a total of £542 15s 0d. A dark brown gelding, 'Boy', was sold to Mr G. A. Davies from Llanelly for £32 after Mr Clee helpfully pointed out that the animal understood English, Welsh and Polish.

The trial commenced at Glamorgan Assizes on 9 November 1954 before Mr Justice Oliver. Mr Elwyn Jones QC, MP defended, and the Welsh barrister William Mars-Jones MBE (Military Division) with Edmund Davies QC prosecuted. To the charge of murder, Onufrejczyk pleaded not guilty.

When Henryk Pawelec gave evidence that Onufrejczyk had told him that Sykut was 'a scoundrel' and that he wanted to 'end' him, saying, 'I am going to take a hatchet and finish with everything', it was suggested by Mr Jones that the expression about a hatchet used colloquially in Polish meant that a person was 'fed up'.

'It is not!' reported Mr Pawelec, adding that if someone used the expression to him, he would be gravely offended.

All of the other witnesses' testimony for the prosecution painted a grim picture as far as Onufrejczyk was concerned; it was evident that he had lied and lied, and when he gave evidence, this was put to him by Mr Edmund Davies: 'Will you agree that you are a man who will lie to get yourself out of any difficulty?'

This provoked the first of a number of histrionic responses. 'I do not lie!' Onufrejczyk roared. 'I am not scared of anything – I am innocent!'

Onufrejczyk went on to say that he was helpful to the police because he wanted to find Sykut to get his money back. 'Do you really mean, Onufrejczyk, that you were helpful to the police?' asked Davies, and at this the prisoner, loudly raising his voice, broke into rapid Polish, held two fingers above his head, drew his hands towards his chest and sobbed. Luckily, there was an interpreter on hand to say that what the prisoner wished to convey was, 'The only thing I want to retain is my honour and I never told any lies.'

But this was put to the test when Davies handed him a letter he had written to Mr and Mrs Pokara in Polish and asked him to read it out.

When he had done so, Davies asked, 'Is that letter a lie from beginning to end?'

'No, it is not a lie.'

'Is it not a lying letter to send thanks to people for £450 which they never sent you?'

'No.'

Onufrejczyk said that he had the money at home and that he had asked the Pokaras to send two parcels in order to avoid the 'grasp' of the income tax; in fact, he had explained this to the police.

'Is that letter a lie?'

'It was an attempt to conceal that money.'

Davies pointed out that in statements Onufrejczyk made to the police he said that he had received a parcel containing £450 from Mrs Pokara; but in the witness box he stated that he did not receive that money. 'Were you trying then to help the police?'

'Yes, because I was first to come to the police to say that Sykut had left.'

'Yet on 30 December when two policemen called at the farm and enquired where Sykut was, you had not been to the police before that date.'

'No. I was waiting fourteen days, and fourteen days had not lapsed yet.'

And then, quite out of the blue, Davies asked this: 'You have not told the jury anything about the robbery, have you?'

'What robbery? I don't know to what you're referring.'

'In January 1949, were you in the Polish camp near Chester?'

'Yes, I was chef in the kitchen.'

'While you were in that camp did you claim that you had been robbed of a large sum of money?'

'No.'

'Think again. Do you say that you never complained to anybody that you had been robbed of a large sum of money?'

'I can't remember such a thing.'

When Davies suggested that Onufrejczyk had embarked on 'a campaign of lies', he did not reply. He was asked why he visited the blacksmith on 29 December and insisted it was 17 December when the horse was taken in to be shod; and was asked to say in English the words he had used to the blacksmith.

'Look, sir, master . . .' began Onufrejczyk, before the rest became unintelligible. Seven hours after Davies had first put the question, he asked once more, 'Do you still claim to be a man who is not prepared to lie to get yourself out of any difficulties?'

'I don't want to tell lies!' exclaimed Onufrejczyk. 'I lied about as far as telling about the money was concerned.'

This could not come as a revelation to anyone listening to Onufrejczyk's testimony; it was clear that in Edmund Davies' words, he had 'lied and lied and lied'. However, more was to come.

He was questioned about the letters he had dictated to Mrs Pokara and in particular, the promissory note – 'What happened to that promissory note?'

'I have it here', replied Onufrejczyk, 'in my room, down below.'

This caused a raising of Davies' eyebrows. 'I called for that promissory note last week and it was not forthcoming.'

But the prisoner was given permission to go to the cells, accompanied by a warder and the interpreter, and returned holding a blank piece of paper with a stamp affixed to it.

The Judge examined it. So did Mr Elwyn Jones for the defence; evidently, it was the first time he'd seen it, because he looked at it carefully. Then it went back to the Judge. Finally, this remarkable document was handed to Edmund Davies, who asked, 'Is that the promissory note – a blank piece of paper? Where did you buy it?'

Onufrejczyk replied that he had bought it from a Post Office not far from Mrs Pokara's address; he had never filled one in before and he wanted a solicitor to fill it in.

It was the end of Onufrejczyk's examination, cross-examination and re-examination which had lasted fifteen hours spread over three days. His testimony had consisted almost exclusively of lies, bluster and contradictory gibberish.

Dr Alan Grant, a lecturer in the Forensic Department at the London Medical College, was called by the defence to say that the bloodstains on the walls of the kitchen had been caused by Sykut flicking his finger after cutting himself on a hay-making machine; and that in his opinion, an ordinary farmer, fearing lockjaw, would invariably try to stimulate rather than check the blood-flow from a cut. His initial reaction, said the doctor, would be to flick a cut finger, to get the blood to flow.

It really didn't sound right; a view shared by the judge during his summing-up when, referring to Dr Grant, he remarked scathingly, 'Do you think that really is acceptable from a man who knows as little as he, about the factual events?'

Advising the jury on the law, the Judge told them:

> In the trial of a person charged with murder, the fact of death is provable by circumstantial evidence, notwithstanding that neither the body nor any trace of the body has been found and that the accused has made no confession of any participation in the crime.
>
> Before he can be convicted, the fact of death must be proved by such circumstances as render the commission of the crime morally certain and leave no ground for reasonable doubt.
>
> The circumstantial evidence should be so cogent and compelling as to convince a jury that upon no rational hypotheses other than murder can the fact be accounted for.

After an absence of two and three quarter hours, the jury returned a verdict of guilty, and telling them, 'I am entirely in agreement with your verdict and I think it is entirely justified', the Judge exempted the jury from further service for life.

The interpreter, Wanda Poznanska, was not in court to inform Onufrejczyk of the verdict or the sentence of death, which Mr Justice Oliver pronounced without donning the customary black cap. This absence was immediately seized upon to make newspaper headlines. Was it due to some anomaly, some edict enshrined perhaps in the Magna Carta which forbade a Judge from wearing the black cap when pronouncing the sentence of death on a person incapable of comprehending what was being said? No, apparently not. Having consulted one of the finest legal brains in the country, the conclusion reached was that Mr Justice Oliver simply forgot to put it on.

This extraordinary trial – which had lasted twelve days and in which seventy witnesses were called – was over, and the crowd of 300 people who had gathered outside the court slowly drifted away.

Onufrejczyk's appeal was heard by the Lord Chief Justice, Lord Goddard, who sat with Mr Justice Cassels and Mr Justice Sellars on 11 January 1955. It was dismissed, with the Lord Chief Justice saying:

> It is equally clear that the fact of death, like any other fact, can be proved by circumstantial evidence, that is to say, evidence of facts which lead to one conclusion, provided the jury are satisfied and are warned that it must lead to one conclusion only.

Onufrejczyk's execution was set for 26 January at Swansea prison. The Attorney General refused his *fiat* for an appeal to the

House of Lords, and from his prison cell the condemned man petitioned the Home Secretary for a reprieve, as did his solicitor, with a second petition. Three days before he was due to hang, the petitions were successful and the death sentence was commuted to life imprisonment.

Almost five years to the day of Sykut's death, Onufrejczyk made another appearance in court, this time at London's Divorce Court. Branislawa Onufrejczyk was granted a degree nisi of nullity; when at the age of fifty-one she had married Onufrejczyk at Nottingham Registry Office in February 1951 she had been unaware that at the time he was still legally married to Irena Helena Onufrejczyk, a resident of Cracow, Poland.

Having added bigamy to his list of misdeeds, Onufrejczyk was released after serving ten years of his sentence; he was now seventy and he went to live in an old peoples' home in Bradford. He made one more journey to Llandeilo, plaintively asking passers-by if they had seen 'his old friend Sykut'; he died following a road accident one year later in 1966.

So what happened to Sykut's body? The Lord Chief Justice surmised that it might have been disposed of in a kiln at the farm; others felt that it could have been fed to pigs.

That was definitely the line of thought, sixteen years later, almost to the day and also at a farm, situated some 257 miles east of Llandeilo . . .

Chapter 6

Kidnap

Had he lived a century or so later, whoever said that there are 'Lies, damned lies and statistics' – variously attributed to Mark Twain, Benjamin Disraeli and Sir Charles Dilke – might have been thinking about the number of kidnappings, an offence which unctuous police chiefs claim 'are mercifully rare'. Actually, that was what I thought, too, until I checked the statistics: in the period of 2019/20, no fewer than 5,783 cases were recorded in England and Wales. Blimey, that's over fifteen a day! Can those figures be right? Probably not; it's more likely that some pasty-faced little twerp in the Office of National Statistics tripped over his algorithms and put a decimal point in the wrong place.

Actually, when I made the enquiry, what I had in mind was kidnapping which involves ransom demands and murder, and these cases are, indeed, mercifully rare.

The first that comes to mind is the case of 17-year-old Lesley Whittle, who was kidnapped from her home in Highley, Shropshire on 14 January 1975. A demand of £50,000 was made for her safe return, and eventually, over 400 police officers from West Mercia, Staffordshire and West Midlands police forces were deployed over an 11-month period. Two months after Miss Whittle's disappearance, her lifeless and naked body was found hanging in a drain shaft in Bathpool Park, Staffordshire. A complete arse was made of the investigation, with police chiefs from various forces squabbling for primacy, until the Home Office, embarrassed beyond compute, stepped in and sent Scotland Yard's Commander John Morrison OBE, QPM to take charge of the shambles. Morrison was the most senior officer in the history of the Murder Squad ever to be sent out on a provincial enquiry. In fact, the perpetrator, Donald Neilson (who had also murdered three men during Post Office robberies and seriously wounded two other people), was caught purely by chance by two police constables. He was convicted and died in prison in December 2011.

'Lessons', as white-faced police chiefs stutter, when matters for which they can be held accountable have turned to rat-shit, 'have been learnt', although they weren't prior to that fiasco. Scotland

Yard should have been called in at the earliest opportunity to coordinate matters. At least Lesley Whittle's family had the slight consolation of having her body to grieve over; it was more than could be said for the family of the unfortunate Muriel McKay, who vanished some five years earlier . . .

* * *

Wimbledon is an affluent district of London seven miles south-west of the city's centre. It is well-known, of course for holding championship lawn tennis events, as well as for its spacious common and rather smaller park. Following the Second World War, due to the amount of damage caused by enemy bombing, several large Victorian houses were converted into flats and others were demolished to make way for apartment blocks. The area is divided; the 'town' accommodates the retail section, and the 'village' contains the very smart, solid houses. They represent everything that Wimbledon has come to stand for: prosperity, prestige and respectability – property such as St Mary House, 20 Arthur Road, a neo-Georgian mansion situated opposite to St Mary's church and close to Home Park Road, which abuts Wimbledon Park.

In 1969, St Mary House had for thirteen years been the home of an Australian couple, newspaper magnate Alexander ('Alick') Benson McKay CBE and his wife, Muriel Freda. The property was then valued at £25,000, quite a respectable sum for that time.

The happily-married couple had three children, also married: Diane had three children and Jennifer had a son; all of these lived in Sussex. There was also a son, Ian, who had married and lived in Sydney, Australia. The 55-year-old Muriel, who was devoted to all her children, was looking forward to the possibility of visiting her son, whom she had not seen for over two years.

Although Muriel was troubled with menopausal problems and also arthritis, for which she was receiving medical treatment in the form of cortisone and vitamin injections, she was a happy, contented woman and much liked and admired in the area. Some three months prior to Christmas 1969, there had been a burglary at the family home and a television set, a record player, silver and some imitation jewellery, valued together at £3,000, were stolen. Naturally, this had unnerved Muriel, who had taken to carrying her more valuable items of jewellery in her handbag; this was not considered the most prudent course of action, but the crime rate in Wimbledon was reasonably low, and sensibly, a chain had been fitted to the property's front door.

Her husband, 60-year-old Alick, was in less good health than Muriel; he had sustained two heart attacks, a slight one in 1966 followed by a more serious one two years later, but now, on 29 December 1969, having left his position with the International Publishing Corporation (IPC) – the *Mirror* group of newspapers – (receiving a reputed golden handshake of £40,000), he had started a new job as deputy chairman of the *News of the World* with his old friend, Rupert Murdoch. In fact, ten days previously, Murdoch and his wife Anna, a tall, beautiful 25-year-old blonde, had left for a trip to Australia; and because he had no immediate need of it, Murdoch left his blue Rolls-Royce, registration number ULO 18F, in the care of McKay.

Six weeks prior to his departure, Murdoch and his wife had appeared on television, in *The David Frost Show*. Much of the programme had been devoted to the publicity generated by the publication of Christine Keeler's memoirs in the *News of the World*. She had been at the centre of a society scandal which had forced the resignation of John Profumo, Secretary of State for War, and the payment she had received for her story, a staggering £23,000, had attracted quite a lot of adverse reaction, against both her and the newspaper for paying it.

However, Murdoch's was a soaring story of success; the wealthy Australian business tycoon had not only purchased the *News of the World*, Britain's best-selling Sunday newspaper with a circulation of six million, but had swiftly also acquired the *Sun*, originally under the aegis of the *Mirror* group. The *Sun*'s circulation had been floundering; now, under new management, its circulation soared while its erstwhile owner's sales plummeted.

There was no doubt whatsoever in any viewers' minds that (a) Murdoch was married to a very beautiful young woman and (b) he was inordinately wealthy. This was certainly the impression gained by two greedy sets of eyes belonging to two greedy brothers watching television in a farm some 87 miles to the north of Wimbledon.

A plan was quickly hatched. One of the brothers went to the *News of the World*'s headquarters in Bouverie Street, London, EC4. There stood the blue Rolls-Royce. That must belong to the owner of the group – well, who else? And the brother was quite right, although he felt verification was needed.

Therefore, the licensing office for the Greater London Council in Black Horse Street, SE1 was the next port of call, where the brother explained that his vehicle, a Volvo estate, registration number XGO 994G, had been involved in a slight collision with a blue Rolls-Royce, registration number ULO 18F. Miss Maureen Callan was only too pleased to assist the polite young man and she confirmed that the vehicle was owned by the *News of the World*. The visitor then wished to know if the Rolls belonged to the company's chairman; Miss Callan did not possess that information but said she would be surprised if it did not. The young man thanked her and left, leaving the enquiry form that he had presented to her and upon which he had entered a false name and address. The date was 19 December, the day on which Mr and Mrs Murdoch had enjoyed a sumptuous luncheon at the Ritz hotel and had then left for Australia; but the young man – and his brother, who was deliriously happy at confirmation of the Roll-Royce's owner – was not to know that.

And so the blue Volvo estate started following the chauffeur-driven blue Rolls-Royce every evening when it left Bouverie Street, tailing it all the way to St Mary House, Wimbledon. Neither the chauffeur nor the passenger in the back – immersed in his study of business papers – was aware of the surveillance. There was no reason why they should have been.

And the brothers in the Volvo had no concerns, either. The Rolls belonged to Rupert Murdoch, right? And Murdoch was a very wealthy newspaper proprietor, right? And he had a very attractive wife, right? Therefore, when this expensive car, the property of a wealthy tycoon, arrived at St Mary House, 20 Arthur Road, Wimbledon, SW19 evening after evening, that was where this fabulously wealthy man and his beautiful bride lived, right?

Wrong.

The occupants of St Mary House with its four bedrooms, two bathrooms, lounge, dining room and study, Mr and Mrs Alick McKay, were undoubtedly comfortably off; but they were certainly not millionaires.

* * *

On 29 December 1969, Alick McKay arrived home at 7.45 pm. The chauffeur-driven Rolls swept into the 30ft long drive, its headlights illuminating the large redbrick house with its white windows. But as the car left, McKay had the feeling something was wrong. There was a rather tattered copy of the *People* newspaper dated 28 December on the driveway; he picked it up, then screwed it up and threw it away. He rang the doorbell, three short rings, followed by one long one, a code that he and his wife had devised following the burglary, but there was no reply. McKay tried the door handle; to his surprise, it opened immediately, and this really was odd, because the chain normally kept it in place. Inside were more sections of the *People* newspaper on the floor; there was also an ugly-looking rusty billhook on a table. The telephone appeared to be broken and the disc containing its number was missing. On the floor were Muriel's spectacles, and her shoes and handbag were on the first and third steps of the stairs respectively. There was a ball of string and some elastoplast on another table. McKay went from room to room, calling, 'Muriel! Muriel!' but there was no reply. He checked her belongings: her passport, chequebook and in the garage her car, a Ford Capri, were still there. The television in the sitting room was switched on, the fire was burning in the grate and Carl, the family dachshund, was evidently pleased to see him. But of Muriel there was no sign. Also missing was his wife's jewellery, which included a three-string choker of pearls, an emerald and platinum eternity ring with diamonds, a gold and pearl pendant, an emerald brooch, a gold wristwatch, a chain and a Victorian bangle. Cash – approximately £25 – was also missing from her handbag, and the total value of the property was later assessed at approximately £600.

In the kitchen were two steaks ready to be cooked; it appeared that Muriel had left in a great hurry.

There was more. Now, he could see the front door had been forced; the Yale lock was bent and the safety latch was hanging loose.

Mistakenly believing that the telephone was out of order, Alick McKay ran to a neighbour's house to telephone the police. The time was 8.00 pm.

The first to arrive as the result of an emergency call was Police Constable 591 'V' Peter Lines. 'The door was open', he told me. 'The place felt eerie; there was a rusty billhook on the floor.' (It had been left there by Alick McKay, who had taken it with him as a weapon, in case intruders were still in the house.)

Inspector William Anderson also arrived, and later the night-duty CID officer, Detective Sergeant Wally Whyte, who took details from Alick McKay; Whyte also spoke with the uniform superintendent at Wimbledon, Jack Newell ('A good bloke, who was clearly unhappy about the situation', as he told me), and as more officers arrived, there was – initially, at least – a plethora of possible explanations. Detective Sergeant Graham Birch thought it a publicity stunt; this was due to McKay's newly acquired newspaper, the *Sun*, which specialized in sensational headlines. However, having spoken to both Birch and Alick McKay, Whyte came to a very different conclusion. Several officers thought that Muriel McKay had left of her own volition, either alone or with a man friend, and there was also a line of thought that McKay himself could be implicated in his wife's disappearance. Perhaps there had been a family argument – or was she ill? McKay was asked to telephone his daughters, to see if his wife had gone to either of their addresses; she had not, and Diane arrived with her husband David Dyer, the other daughter, Jennifer, arriving with her husband Ian Burgess just after midnight. Also alerted by McKay was Larry Lamb, the editor of the *Sun*, who in turn told a reporter and a photographer to go to the house.

The police felt that it was wrong to involve the press at such an early stage, and Andrew Henderson, the District Liaison Officer for the Yard's Press Bureau, was informed. So was Detective Chief Superintendent Wilfred 'Bill' Smith, the head of 'V' Division's CID, and his deputy, Detective Inspector John Minors; neither initially made an appearance. Mrs Marjorie Nightingale, Mrs McKay's home help (and probably the last person to have seen her on 29 December), was asked to return to St Mary House, where she was closely questioned to see if she could recall any suspicious activity or any change in Mrs McKay's demeanour, before going into the kitchen to prepare tea and sandwiches for the ever-increasing numbers of police and reporters.

Alick McKay spoke to Stafford Somerfield, the editor of the *News of the World*, and informed him that he was not particularly impressed with the attitude of the police, since they were giving the impression that he had somehow been involved with his wife's disappearance. Somerfield had been a friend of the McKay family for years – he also had friends in high places, and he telephoned Deputy Assistant Commissioner John Du Rose OBE, who was asleep at his home at Daybrook Road, Merton Park, SW19. Although Du Rose had never heard of the McKays, Somerfield quickly pointed out Alick McKay's importance in the world of newspapers. Du Rose knew the value of publicity; he had recently been prominent in a group photograph of detectives outside Tintagel House following the successful conviction of the Kray brothers. What's more, he knew how negative publicity – *The Times* police corruption enquiry had just broken – could adversely affect the image of the police.

He made a number of terse telephone calls, and the police enquiry now very quickly gained momentum.

The McKays' telephone which was originally thought to have been broken, wasn't; its connection clicked back in, and the other phones in the house were working perfectly. In fact, they were ringing continuously, mainly with calls from the press, but at 1.15 am a telephone call was received that should have dramatically altered the police perspective on matters.

Chapter 7

Demand

David Dyer answered the telephone, believing it to be yet another newspaper enquiry. But the GPO telephone operator, Terry Underwood, had put the call through from a public telephone kiosk – Epping 4253X – situated at Bell Common, Epping, Essex, close to the A11 trunk road, after the caller had tried several times to get through to the McKay number – 946-2656 – unsuccessfully. The caller put one shilling in the slot, but at one stage Underwood thought the call had finished and, apologising if the caller had been cut off, asked if he wanted to be reconnected. To his astonishment, the caller said, 'Tell him the Mafia wants him', after which Underwood listened intently to the rest of the conversation.

The caller asked to speak to Mr McKay; he had an Asian-sounding voice, with a hint of an American drawl, and Sergeant Whyte, listening on an extension, hurriedly made notes in his pocketbook of the following conversation:

'This is the Mafia, Group Three. We are from America. Mafia. M3. We have your wife.'

'You have got my wife?'

'You will need a million pounds by Wednesday.'

'What are you talking about? I don't understand.'

'Mafia. Do you understand?'

'Yes, I do.'

'We have your wife. It will cost you a million pounds to get her back.'

'This is ridiculous. I haven't *got* a million. I haven't got anything like it. I don't know anyone who has.'

'You had better get it. You have friends. Get it from them. Get a million pounds by Wednesday or . . .'

'This is ridiculous. Who are you?'

'This is M3. The Mafia in England. We have taken your wife. We tried to get Rupert Murdoch's wife. We could not get her, so we took yours instead.'

'Rupert Murdoch?'

'I haven't much time. Don't waste it. You have a million pounds by Wednesday night or we will kill her. Do you understand?'

'Yes . . . what do I have to do?'

'All you have to do is wait for the contact. We will contact you on Wednesday. Just have the money. You will get your instructions.'

'But who are you?'

'The Mafia. Have the money. Or you won't have a wife. We will contact you again.'

The caller then replaced the receiver. When Terry Underwood was later interviewed, he stated that the caller had used the expression 'man' – in the context of 'Well, man, you try' – several times during the conversation.

A genuine kidnapping? A ransom? This was something unheard of in Britain. Instead, could it be a hoax, and a sick one at that?

But there was the forced entry, the suspicious objects, the missing jewellery. DCS Bill Smith was again telephoned at home. Apprised of the telephone call, he was roused from his bed, dressed in record time and was on his way to St Mary House.

* * *

In 1969, the 69-year-old Wimbledon police station at 15–23 Queen's Road was one of 184 police stations in the Metropolitan Police District. With its code sign 'VW', it was home to sixteen CID officers as well as an assortment of uniform officers, one of whom was 22-year-old Woman Police Constable Jackie Cole, who took a caustic view of the enquiry and who told me:

> In my opinion, if the matter had been dealt with correctly right at the start, and if those in charge at 'VW' had actually lowered the high opinion of themselves and listened to the fact that it was totally out of character for her to leave the home for no reason, then it may have been a different outcome.

She may not have been speaking as a result of hindsight; right from the start, the *Daily Mirror*'s headline on 30 December was, 'Hunt for Kidnappers as Wife Vanishes', but initial newspaper reports had the police commenting, 'It's probably a cruel hoax', followed by 'She may have lost her memory.' As late as 4 January, police were dismissing as 'ludicrous' reports that they were treating Mrs McKay's disappearance as murder.

Be that as it may, a major enquiry was set up.

Many people believe that when a major enquiry commences, a large empty incident room, ready, fully equipped and adequately staffed, miraculously appears in a police station. Leaving aside the obvious fact that nowadays, due to a calamitous Home Office/police decision, there are very few police stations left to provide such a room, this was simply not true. When a major incident arose, any existing room (preferably large but if not, of any size) would be seized up, the protesting incumbents pushed out and impolitely told where to go, and a large number of harassed-looking detectives would be moved in. So would desks, chairs, 'in' and 'out' trays, filing cabinets, index cards, typewriters and hordes of Metropolitan Police stationery. In each district there was an office, usually under the control of a lacklustre uniform chief inspector so utterly useless that he had been put in charge of shelves full of spare telephones. These were required for major incidents; the chief inspector parsimoniously guarded them as though they were his own property, until he was rudely disabused of that notion by a bad-tempered detective.

Now some of those telephones made their way to Wimbledon, to the newly-formed incident room on the first floor of the police station, recently vacated by temporary detective constables and situated next to Smith's and Minors' offices, where GPO engineers were hurriedly inserting fresh telephone lines to bolster Wimbledon's 946-1113 number.

Probably the most important officer in that room was the office manager, who during the McKay investigation was 41-year-old Detective Sergeant Jim Parker. Following National Service with the RAF, Parker had walked the beat in Paddington as Police Constable 134 'D' before being appointed to the CID. Half an inch under six feet, the bespectacled Parker had already been commended on several occasions, on one of which he had sustained injuries during the arrest of a violent garage-breaker. Nobody better could have been chosen as office manager; his abilities in this enquiry would eventually be recognized by commendations from the commissioner, the trial Judge, the Attorney General and the Director of Public Prosecutions.

These were the days before computers, so 'the system' was utilized. Index cards recorded every piece of information, which was disseminated to further index cards and cross-referenced. Therefore, if a witness had seen an unknown man get out of a car near the scene of a crime carrying a newspaper and an umbrella, a detailed description of the man would be entered on one card, as much detail as possible about the car on another, and the fact that he was carrying a newspaper and an umbrella on other cards, all of them cross-referenced with each other, together with the statement from the witness which would have been allocated a number. On the office manager's copy of statements, each factor – man, car, newspaper, umbrella – would be underlined in red. With each new statement, the content – man, car, whatever – would be checked against the existing cards; if not identical, then fresh cards would be made out. It was laborious, but it was 'the system' – and what's more, it worked.

But if these were the days before computers, mobile phones and pagers, the police were also deficient in just about every other kind of technological support. One year before this incident, personal radios had just been introduced to the Met – they were not altogether reliable – and ballpoint pens had just replaced pencils to inscribe details in officers' pocket books. Given that a ransom demand had been unexpectedly made, with the caller's promise that further communications would be made, it would have been sensible to install sophisticated recording equipment in St Mary House, and eventually it was. But initially there was none to be found, so one of the detectives brought in his own tape recorder from home and attached it with a rubber suction pad to the McKay's telephone. He had to explain to his colleagues and to the McKay family how it worked.

Meanwhile, let's take a look at the top brass. First, there was Commander Herbert Guiver, head of the Met's No. 4 District, who was a detective to his fingertips and highly experienced; he was in overall charge.

The day-to-day running of the enquiry was in the hands of Detective Chief Superintendent Wilfred 'Bill' Smith, who had joined the force on 3 March 1947, following wartime service with the RAF. A native of Burnley, Lancashire, Smith had walked the beat as Police Constable 410 'F' and had been commended for arresting shop- and house-breakers. Rod Bellis, a detective at Tooting police station at the time, recalled him as being 'a lovely guy, with a great sense of humour; always of a happy disposition'.

Smith's deputy was the elaborately named Detective Inspector John Henry Ecclestone Minors, who like Smith had served with the RAF during the war. Joining the Met five months before Smith, he had also served a tough apprenticeship, starting on 'M' Division's streets of Southwark.

Other detectives filled the desks to cope with the 2,000 incoming telephone calls and 1,150 letters, some helpful, others misleading, some malicious and some from cranks – but each one had to be followed up. A man telephoned the police with a car's registration number which he believed had been involved with Mrs McKay's disappearance; it turned out to be a black Morris Oxford registered to an Ayrshire farmer who could fully account for his (and his car's) movements on 29 December.

There were 'sightings' of Mrs McKay, one by Albert Tietjen, a company director who was certain he had seen her on a bus travelling from Felixstowe to Ipswich; but following an investigation, Suffolk police were obliged to report, 'We have drawn a complete blank.'

The Spanish newspaper *Diario de Barcelona* reported another sighting by someone who stated quite unequivocally that 'either Mrs McKay or her double' had been seen boarding a ship at Las Palmas in the Canary Islands which then docked at Barcelona; but it must have been her double.

Rather more promising was the report from the General Secretary of the Bank of England's sports ground, Priory Lane, Roehampton; two men had been seen leading a blindfolded woman from the sports ground into a car, which then drove off. Since this was about 1½ miles from Arthur Road, police dogs were brought in to track the ground, but the description of the persons and their car, seen in the dark, was so imprecise that the lead, which could have been encouraging, petered out.

Somewhat less promising was the anonymous call to say that Mrs McKay was in an underground passageway of a church. An inspection of the passageway revealed that it led from a parish church to an old rectory – and what's more, it had been blocked up for decades.

Quite suddenly, attention was focused on the seaside town of Bournemouth; it was thought that Mrs McKay could be in one of the hundred care homes there; then enquiries spread to Thanet, and there were two reports of Mrs McKay having been seen in Ramsgate; but she hadn't been.

A woman was identified as the missing person at a Bloomsbury hotel – but she wasn't. Nor was she on board the London to Glasgow express; detectives carried out a thorough but fruitless search of the train when it was stopped at Huntingdon. Letters arrived at St Mary House three times a day addressed to Alick McKay; each one was carefully opened by a detective before passing the letter to him. Thousands of posters were printed at Scotland Yard showing a photograph of Mrs McKay with the caption 'HAVE YOU SEEN THIS WOMAN?' Photographs of the billhook were published and enquiries were made at pawnbrokers and jewellers to try to trace Mrs McKay's jewellery, without success. A photograph of the telephone box from where the 'M3' call had been made was published in a newspaper, to see if anyone had seen anything suspicious at 1.15 on the morning of 30 December – but travellers at Bell Common, Essex were few and far between on the road at that time. The telephone kiosk was dusted for fingerprints – there were a lot – and the pay-box was emptied and similarly tested for fingerprints.

Wimbledon Park, then the Common, were searched by sixty members of No.1 Unit, Special Patrol Group (SPG); police frogmen started work at the lake at Wimbledon golf course but found nothing. The area of Epping and Waltham Forest was searched by 150 police officers with thirty-four police dogs, and mounted police combed rough ground in the area of Chessington – all without success.

Sheds, derelict buildings, anywhere that might house a body: all were searched. That included the attic and the garden at St Mary House – just in case.

House-to-house enquiries were carried out, using pro formas: 'Where were you between 5.50 and 7.30 pm on 29 December and who can verify it?' 'Did you see or hear anything at all which you thought was suspicious?' Police Constable Martin Reeves was one of the SPG officers used in that capacity – without success. The same applied to the Revd Clifford Smith, who lived at Wimbledon Vicarage next door to St Mary House and said, 'We heard no noise at all.'

But others did. June Maxwell-Robinson lived opposite to St Mary House; between 3.00 and 4.20 pm she saw someone whom she described as 'a young coloured man' standing by a grit-bin in Arthur Road. He was carrying a broom, or perhaps a shovel, but she thought he was too smartly dressed to be a manual worker.

There was more. At about 5.45 pm – and this was thought to be the approximate time that Mrs McKay would have arrived home – Janszen Zarzycki, who lived nearby, saw two men whom he believed to be Indian walking along Arthur Road, opposite the McKays' residence. Fifteen minutes later, Mona Lydiatt saw a dark saloon parked on the driveway of St Mary House.

Meanwhile, roadblocks were set up in Wimbledon. 'Were you in the area on 29 December? If so, did you see anything suspicious – something that excited your attention? If not, were you in the area prior to that date – did you see anything odd, then?' There was something. Alfred Anderson, a local motorist, had been driving at 4.40 pm on Wimbledon Parkside, which runs alongside the common. He overtook a very slow-moving Volvo in which were two men whom he described as 'a tanned, Arab colour'; he recalled the incident because ten minutes later, he saw the same car turn into Church Road, which leads into Arthur Road. It meant nothing at the time, but the details were inserted into the appropriate index cards and filed away.

Members of the press flooded the area, filling the pubs and hotels, speaking to everybody, police and public alike, getting confused and contradictory information but publishing it anyway. Reporters and photographers from France arrived and decided that St Mary House did not look grand enough to house a Fleet Street mogul; to satisfy their readers they published photographs of a far more upmarket home.

Although the police were properly treating this matter as a major enquiry, they were still groping in the dark – Britain had never experienced a kidnap coupled with a ransom demand before. They consulted the Federal Bureau of Investigation, who had – could this be the work of the Mafia? Yes, they knew that the Mafia had featured during the recent Kray investigation, but that was to do with stolen bearer bonds and gambling junkets. Was there a British branch of the Mafia? Did 'M3' mean anything? The answer was 'no', to both questions.

There was a telephone call which had been picked up by David Dyer; a woman's voice had whispered, 'Grey Hillman' before being cut off. He thought the caller might have been his mother-in-law but couldn't be sure. Diane Dyer had been told by her mother of silent, heavy-breathing-type telephone calls which had been made, usually on Thursday afternoons, over a period of several weeks. But although this might have provided a lead, it did not. No one knew this at the time, but the kidnappers had previously been unaware of the McKays' home telephone number. They only acquired it after it had been ripped from the telephone's disc at the time of the abduction.

CHAPTER 8

Mystery and Mediums

Back, now, to the afternoon of 30 December, when Smith and Minors were at St Mary House talking to the family. The press appeared to be everywhere, and the family seemed split; some favoured liaising with the police, others put their faith in the press, while there was a third line of thought that it was best to act independently and deal with the kidnappers alone.

In this highly charged atmosphere, Smith convinced the family that it was imperative to let the police handle the case. They must under no circumstances go it alone, but should play along with the kidnappers. It was then at 4.59 pm that the telephone rang; it was picked up by David Dyer.

'Wimbledon 2656 – hello?'

'Hello.'

'Hello.'

'This is M3 speaking again.'

'Yes?'

'Do cooperate.'

'I see.'

'For heaven's sake, for her sake, don't call the police. You have been everywhere, you have been gone, you have been followed.'

'I'm sorry, I didn't catch that last part.'

'You have been followed, did you, did you get the message?'

'Yes.'

'And the money?'

'I'm sorry.'

'Did you get the money?'

'Just a minute . . . '

At that, the caller hung up.

This time, the speaker had not used a telephone box; the call had been made on the automatic STD system and so was untraceable. The tape was taken back to Wimbledon to be transcribed and listened to; Wally Whyte felt sure that it was the same voice he had heard earlier in the day.

Meanwhile, on 30 December at 8.50 pm, Diane Dyer made an emotional appeal on BBC television news for information regarding her mother. It was understandable for the family, who wanted to try anything to get Muriel McKay back; but infuriating for the police, who were submerged in a flood of fresh telephone calls and letters, largely useless, while trying to deal with and evaluate the existing pile of paperwork.

On the morning of 31 December a letter arrived at St Mary House. Addressed to Alick McKay, it was postmarked '6.45 pm, 30.12.69, Tottenham, N.17'. Inside the envelope was a letter written on a piece of blue, lined writing paper. Despite the almost illegible hand, Alick McKay nevertheless immediately recognised the writing as Muriel's:

> Alick DARLING
>
> Please do something to get me home. I am blindfolded and cold. Only blankets. Please cooperate for I cannot keep going.
>
> Love, Muriel
>
> I think of you constantly and the family and friends. Have been calm so far, darling. What have I done to deserve this treatment? Can you do something soon.

It appeared from this that Muriel McKay had still been alive the previous day; although it was odd that when the caller had spoken to David Dyer the previous afternoon and asked, 'Did you get the message?' the letter had only just been posted. However, that was symptomatic of the gibberish that would be conveyed by the kidnappers.

Nevertheless, Smith felt – quite properly – that the contents of the letter must be kept from the press. This was paramount; there were items in there – references to 'blindfolded' and 'blankets' – which would be crucial in any future interview with a suspect. Only a genuine suspect would know of those words, so Smith swore his men to silence. At the evening press conference, the McKay family made an emotional appeal in which David Dyer mentioned that they had received a letter from Mrs McKay; he also read from a statement by Alick McKay (who was too ill to attend) informing the kidnappers that he was willing to do 'anything within reason' to get his wife back.

Smith was furious, just as furious as he had been when he was approached earlier by a journalist from the *Sun* who told him that he knew about the letter and that the newspaper intended to publish it in full the following day.

The *Sun*'s editor, Larry Lamb, stated that the contents of the letter had been released by the police; Commander Guiver in return insisted that the letter had been released to the press by the McKay family 'and their associates'.

Who was responsible? It was the police who had given the letter to the *Sun* to publish in full; not the McKay family.

It had been released to the *Sun* by a very stupid, self-important senior police officer who had had too much to drink; and not for any pecuniary advantage, either. It was purely an ego trip, to show how clever and well-informed he was. It was obvious that Smith knew the culprit; he therefore telephoned the Press Association and gave all the newspapers the contents of the letter, so as not to show partiality to the *Sun*. The officer concerned should have been sacked; but to have done so would have caused immense damage to the already floundering enquiry. If Mrs McKay was still alive, the most important thing was to get her back, not to give the press information about a stupid police officer who was not fit for traffic warden duties.

* * *

The next day was 1 January 1970, a new year, a new decade – and the beginning of new problems.

The previous day, David Dyer had received a telephone call from an anonymous nurse who told him that she had been praying for all of the McKay family and that she could put them in touch with a spiritualist. On New Year's Day, Dyer telephoned the number given and spoke to a medium named Mrs Nora Blackwood, who stated that whilst she was unable to meet the family 'to meditate' with them, because she was fully booked for a month, she did happen to mention that by an incredible coincidence she had already received 'a message' from Mrs McKay.

According to Mrs Blackwood, there were three people involved in the kidnap, the Seven Sisters Road featured strongly in the message and Mrs McKay was now being kept in 'a very scruffy place', the motive for the abduction being 'spite or malice'.

Frantic for any hint of assistance, the family pounced on these crumbs; the letter from Mrs McKay was postmarked Tottenham – and the Seven Sisters Road ran into that area. Three people in the kidnap? M3 had said they were part of a gang, and it was clear from the messages that they were both spiteful and malicious. Kept in 'a very scruffy place'? Just what Muriel had written: 'cold' and 'blankets' – this must be right!

Of course, these details had been already mentioned in the *Sun*, but David McKay announced to the press at 11.10 that morning that he had consulted one spiritualist and was now about to contact another.

So whilst the family's anxiety was understandable, so was the reaction of the police, who experienced an 'Oh, fuck!' moment – and the reasons were these. They knew that now Dyer had broadcast this news, every medium would come crawling out of the woodwork to offer their information – and they were right. They also knew that every so-called piece of 'evidence' unearthed by the mediums would have to be followed up and checked out by the investigating team. And finally, whilst they were aware that in Dennis Wheatley's 'black magic' books, the intrepid Jean Armand Duplessis, aka the tenth Duc de Richelieu, and his chums might go dashing about all over the astral plane seeking evil-doers and bringing them to justice, it was all bollocks.

The second medium was contacted by Eric Cutler, a friend of Alick McKay's; his name was Gerard Croiset (born Gerard Boekbinder), an alleged parapsychologist, psychometrist and psychic, who lived in Holland. Cutler flew there and upon arriving at Croiset's home at 21 Willem de Zwijgerstraat, Utrecht showed the psychic a photograph of Muriel McKay.

A trance or two later, Croiset provided the following information: Muriel McKay had been taken away from her home on a route heading north-north-east out of London. He could 'see' a white barn surrounded by trees, and a green barn. There was a deserted airstrip, a concrete building and an old motorcycle half-submerged in a pond. She had definitely been taken against her will, and if she was not found within fourteen days she would be dead.

Cutler returned to London, and a *Daily Mail* team – reporter, photographer and driver – slavishly followed the clues supplied by Croiset. Whenever a landmark in any way resembled one of Croiset's 'sightings', the crew went into transports of delight. But most of them simply didn't materialize.

Although Croiset had drummed up terrific publicity for his powers (the police apparently relied on him to reveal the whereabouts of every missing person and every murder victim), the truth was rather different.

The sceptic, James Lett, wrote:

> The truth is that the overwhelming majority of Croiset's predictions were either vague and non-falsifiable, or simply wrong. Given the fact that Croiset made thousands of predictions during his lifetime, it is hardly surprising that he enjoyed one or two chance 'hits'.

Croiset claimed that he had helped to solve the case of an assault of a girl in Wierden, Holland, but the chief of police of that area stated that the information provided by Croiset was inaccurate and his input was not used in the case. The matter was investigated under controlled conditions by the Belgian Committee for the Scientific Investigation of Phenomena Reputed to be Paranormal; they found no evidence that Croiset possessed psychic ability.

Croiset's mentor, Professor Wilhelm Heinrich Carl Tenhaeff, had stated that Croiset had genuine psychic powers which had materially assisted the police. However, Piet Hein Hoebens, an investigative journalist with the Dutch newspaper *De Telegraaf*, discovered that Tenhaeff had manipulated reports and was utterly unreliable and fraudulent.

In fact, where Croiset's predictions had proved to be accurate, the police claimed that they would have solved the case in any event, without his help.

So Croiset, who claimed he could only work in complete silence, sipping milk and whipped-up raw eggs in between trances, and who said, 'I don't want anything out of this; I am helping for humane reasons', stated that 'Mrs McKay will be found within two weeks, probably by someone confessing', then bowed out of the case clutching a fee of £2,000.

Next was 73-year-old Mrs Clara Palmer of Romford, Essex. Mrs McKay's spirit had visited her twice asking for help and it guided her to a grave at St Peter's Church, Woodmancote, Sussex, which appeared to have been recently dug. She said:

> When I was in a trance I was shown a grave which, I believe, is the one in the church cemetery. I was also shown a narrow road, bordered by trees, and a large old-fashioned house. I'm sure this road is the one that runs along the front of the church. As I passed the church I had a strange feeling and when I saw the grave, I came over cold. I believe that Mrs McKay is no longer alive and that she is buried in that grave.

Not so. The wife of the vicar, Mr S. P. Terry (who had been ill and confined to bed for the previous five weeks), was able to state quite categorically that there had been no burials for at least six weeks.

And still they kept on coming: 1,400 messages from soothsayers, I Ching experts, palmists, fortune-tellers, people possessing Tarot cards and Ouija boards, and tea-leaf readers. Spiritualists invited police officers to attend séances, and mediums were not the only ones to go into trances – the eyes of the investigating team glazed over as their investigations got slower and slower and the costs of the operation spiralled, while they wasted time investigating trash such as this.

One incredible move which absolutely beggared belief came when a detective sergeant from the Essex Constabulary actually constructed identikit pictures of two men believed to be responsible for Muriel McKay's kidnap based on images provided by a member of the public who had seen them in a dream. If that particular officer went on to attain high rank, it may explain many of the ills that the police service is suffering from today.

The net result was that while the frantic McKay family became ever more frustrated and disappointed, the newspapers got splendid copy for their readers, the mediums and other cranks grew richer and the investigators more and more thoroughly pissed-off.

A senior Scotland Yard detective visited Arthur Road and told Smith that he was wasting his time, since Mrs McKay had obviously gone missing of her own volition. It was advice that nobody on the investigating team found particularly helpful.

Chapter 9

Copy-Cat Demands

During that evening of 1 January there was another telephone call from M3 which was answered by Diane Dyer. It was the usual blend of stupidity and gibberish, the caller asking, 'Where's your Mummy; can I speak to her?' followed by 'It has gone too far now.'

The call was then abruptly terminated; perhaps the caller was seeking advice on what to say next, because four minutes later, he rang again, and again the telephone was picked up by Diane Dyer.

'They've got to get a million, a million pounds. I'll contact them tomorrow and they have got to get it in fivers and tenners.'

'Where do you get a million pounds from? I wouldn't know.'

'Well, I don't know. That's not my business.'

'Well, if you want it, it is your business, isn't it?'

That night, an illiterate, ungrammatical and misspelt letter written in block capitals was put through the letterbox of the *Hornsey Journal*, a local weekly newspaper paper covering North London:

> I am writing to your newspaper corse it don't try to corrupt young people like the News of the World does. Why should that rotten organisation worry that I might murder Mrs McKay? They don't worry very much about all the kids' souls they murder with their evil pens. They pay out hundreds of thousands of pounds to no good girls to write their rotten stories so why shouldn't they pay me for not murdering Mrs McKay?
>
> I lost my 12 year old daughter corse she was influenced by all the money those dirty girls got paid for telling everyone about it. And now my girl is missing and the last I heard about her was that she was living with niggers like that Christine Keeler was and she went with married men to. She got VD three times and the last I heard of her was three months ago. She may be lying dead somewhere for all I know so if Mr McKay chose to aid and abet in the corruption of my child and lots of other children then he should complain or expect me to care what happens to his wife who lives off his filthy earned money.
>
> A million pounds won't really compensate me for the loss of my darling little girl but it wasn't me who asked for it.

> Fuck the permissive society and fuck all the newspaper that encourage it.
>
> P.S. I will let Mrs McKay go if the News of the World and the Sun publikly announce that they will not corrupt our kids any more by printing all that filth

Although the letter received a wide circulation, no one really believed that it came from the kidnappers; rather that the writer was a near-deranged father letting off steam and mourning the loss of his daughter's youth and innocence to undesirables. He was later identified and questioned; in the belief that he should be pitied rather than scorned, no prosecution followed.

But while there were plenty of letters and cranks telephoning to demand money, no one had contacted the family to arrange a meeting. On 2 January, someone did.

* * *

The caller told Alick McKay that if he wanted his wife returned to him he would have to pay £500. That sum was quite at variance with the million pounds previously demanded, nor did the caller sound anything like 'M3'; but then again, M3 himself did not sound particularly professional.

However, this particular caller had insisted that the £500 should be brought in a suitcase to Wimbledon railway station to meet the 5.20 pm train from Waterloo arriving at platform five.

Alick McKay, his hopes raised, was more than willing to go, but Smith put his foot down firmly. This was a job for the police and the police alone.

Smith and Minors were provided with hats and topcoats from Alick McKay's wardrobe, and one would have thought that a little subterfuge might have been called for; for example, taking the clothing and the money – 'tops & bottoms'[1] – in the suitcase and driving to the police station; then from there, dressed in the borrowed clothing, being taken in an unmarked observation van to the railway station to keep the rendezvous.

They did nothing of the kind. Wearing the loaned-out finery and carrying the suitcase, they walked out of St Mary House through the throng of reporters, inevitably attracting the attention of a local journalist, who followed them to the railway station.

---

1 Genuine currency interspersed with paper cut to the size of the notes

There he saw Smith wearing an unaccustomed fur hat and waiting on the platform, suitcase in hand, as the train from Waterloo pulled in. The crowds who alighted from the train drifted away, leaving one expectant-looking young man who was swiftly collared.

He was an 18-year-old waiter named William Alexander Peat, who lived in a fantasy world at a bedsit in Gilling Court, Belsize Grove. Lucky to be charged only with attempting to obtain £500 from Alick McKay by means of criminal deception, he appeared at Wimbledon Magistrates' Court, and when he was committed for trial to the South-West London Quarter Sessions in custody, his solicitor was quick to ask for reporting restrictions to be lifted so that his client might apologise for 'adding to Alick McKay's distress'. On 17 March 1970, Judge F. H. Cassels fined him £100, to be paid immediately or suffer the consequences of three months in a detention centre, telling him, 'I propose to make you pay for all the time you have wasted and the trouble you have caused.'

This episode would be followed by a letter addressed to Alick McKay which contained the words:

> You have suffered enough. I want £2,000 in used notes. You will send someone to the toilets outside Maryland Point station.
>
> If the police are anywhere near or even told about this, it will do you no good.
>
> If the money is delivered with no trouble, your wife will be set free within a few hours.

The brown paper parcel of 'money' was delivered to the railway station's toilets as requested; the officers who were keeping observation saw Roy Edward Roper, aged twenty-six and unemployed of Jason Road, Leytonstone, enter the toilets, and when he emerged having claimed the parcel he himself was claimed. Shown the letter, Roper said, 'I will tell you the truth. It was me. I don't know why I did it.'

The reason why he did it was simple: to be £2,000 the richer; and of Mrs McKay's whereabouts he had not the faintest idea.

He appeared at the South-West Quarter Sessions and pleaded guilty to both attempting to obtain £2,000 by deception and blackmail. The same Judge who would sentence William Peat more leniently told him, 'This was a very wicked and cruel thing you did', and packed him off to prison for three years.

These were just two examples of greedy men aching to line their pockets which the police could do nothing to control – the same applied to another anonymous caller who wanted £25,000, telling the family, 'A woman's life is worth more than money.' Nevertheless, police investigations were proceeding, albeit slowly.

The copy of the *People* which Alick McKay had dismissively screwed up and thrown away upon his arrival at his house on 29 December had been retrieved and submitted to the Forensic Science Laboratory for ninhydrin tests; these revealed a palm print. There was also a fingerprint on Mrs McKay's first letter which did not emanate from her – that had been confirmed by prints taken from her bedroom and other parts of the house. Both the finger and the palm print were compared with the millions contained in Scotland Yard's C3 Fingerprint Department. There was no match. Had one of the kidnappers left his palm print on the newspaper? He might have done, but so might anybody discarding a newspaper. Was it his fingerprint on the letter? Since it was not Mrs McKay's, then yes, almost certainly.

Who had written the letters purporting to have been written by Mrs McKay? Alick McKay had no hesitation in saying that it was his wife's handwriting, but Smith needed confirmation. Identifying handwriting was not a precise science; experts at Forensic Science Laboratories up and down the country varied immeasurably. They could be brilliant, bringing charts to court to impress upon a jury their expertise in detecting similarities between known and questioned handwriting; conversely, they could be little better than halfwits, stuttering through their evidence and on one splendid occasion stating that it was a strong possibility that the officer in the case (me) had written the lines in question.

The owners of hardware shops in and around the Wimbledon area were questioned about the billhook, without success. It was later established, by casting the net further afield, that the manufacturers stated these tools were often sold in the area of Bishop's Stortford, Hertfordshire. It was a clue, albeit not a very promising one. It appeared every farmer in the region possessed such an item.

The ball of twine and the elastoplast were non-starters – they could have been purchased anywhere in the country. Then there was Mrs McKay's jewellery; fortunately, photographs were available and they were circulated in the confidential publication *Police Gazette* and enquiries made of jewellers and pawnbrokers – but without success. None of the jewellery has ever been recovered.

By now, thirty detectives had been brought in to work full-time on the case. The best clue was the fingerprint on Mrs McKay's letter – that, and the hope that the kidnappers would break cover, with the fingerprint belonging to one of them. The officers could carry on with their enquiries because neither M3 nor anybody else was contacting them. The burning question was: is Mrs McKay still alive? Among the cynical detectives, the belief was, no, most probably not. The McKay family clung on to every vestige of hope, Alick McKay appearing on television on the evening of 9 January 1970 and pleading to meet anybody who might assist in disclosing his wife's whereabouts.

The next day, Saturday, the editor of the *News of the World*, Stafford Somerfield, received a letter marked 'Personal and Urgent'. Posted in the E1 area of London, it was written on blue-lined white writing paper in a backward-sloping hand:

> I am writing these lines to you because I can't get through to Aleck McKay by phone, for it is bugged by the police. If you are his friend, you will contact him discretely, telling him his wife is safe and well. She is being treated by a doctor from abroad. How long this will continue depends on how much co-operation Aleck McKay will give us when he authorise the police out of his home and he is free to talk, I will telephone him giving him instructions and proof of his wife existence for a ransom of one million pounds to be collected on two occasion of half a million each. If he co-operate, he shall see his wife. If he don't co-operate, I shall not be contacting him anymore and his wife will be disposed of. If he had obeyed me on the Monday, when I telephone by not calling the police, the matter would have been solved already.
>
> 1. A clue for him to know she is alive, Muriel said that Rupert Murdoch left for Australia on Christmas Eve for six weeks. Secondly, he has not paid off for St Mary House. She said he hasn't the money but he can borrow it from firms he know. Immediate attention is important and he is in no position to bargain. I shall telephone in a few days to confirm, give a code number when telephoning.

A few days later, on 14 January and by the strangest of coincidences, Somerfield did receive a telephone call from the inaccurate and ungrammatical letter-writer. Somerfield was on first-name terms with Sir John Rennie KCMG, the head of MI6, the Secret Intelligence Service. Since its inception, the head of 'The Firm' had always been known as 'C', after the surname of its founder, Captain Sir Mansfield George Smith-Cumming. But due to the popularity of the James Bond books and films, when Somerfield's secretary received a telephone call from a person who introduced himself as 'M', she believed this to be a reference to the factual head of MI6 (as opposed to the fictional one, at that time portrayed by Bernard Lee), and thinking the caller was Sir John, she put him through immediately to Somerfield.

He was surprised to hear someone whom he later described as being 'a coloured man, possibly with a West Indian accent' instead of the urbane, measured tones of his friend Sir John and was told, 'This is M speaking' and later, 'It is M3.'

Somerfield demanded the caller's name and address, only to be told, 'Tell McKay to get a million. I have proof of Mrs McKay's existence.'

Somerfield later listened to a number of recorded telephone calls to the McKay house; he identified the speaker on a call from 'M3' as being the caller to his office.

At 4.13 pm that day, Ian Burgess, Alick McKay's son-in-law, picked up the ringing telephone, before passing it to Alick; it was the usual, rambling, imbecile message:

'This is concerning your madam, your mistress . . . did you hear from your editor? . . . We'll send you a letter from your wife, giving you enough proof and we'll tell you where you've got to give us the money. All right? . . . You got to cooperate and you'll get your madam back.'

McKay then said, 'Well, now, look, can you, can you tell me one thing, has she had any . . . any . . . any of the drugs she needs, or medicines?'

'Yes.'

'She has had treatment?'

'Yes.'

'And she is quite well?'

'Oh, yes.'

'You're, you're quite sure about this, are you?'

'Yes, honestly, honestly, I promise you that, she's costing me a lot, now.'

But the promised letter did not immediately arrive, and nothing more would be heard from the kidnappers for a further five days. During the interim period an incident occurred which involved some mind-blowing stupidity.

* * *

On 12 January, a caller demanded £250,000 for the return of Muriel McKay. He stipulated that Diane Dyer travel on a No.47 bus from Catford garage and bring the money in a suitcase.

Three murderers and a victim

Right: Michial Onufrejczyk.

Below left: Paul Russell Corrigan.

Below right: Peter Reyn-Bardt and (victim) Malika Maria de Fernandez.

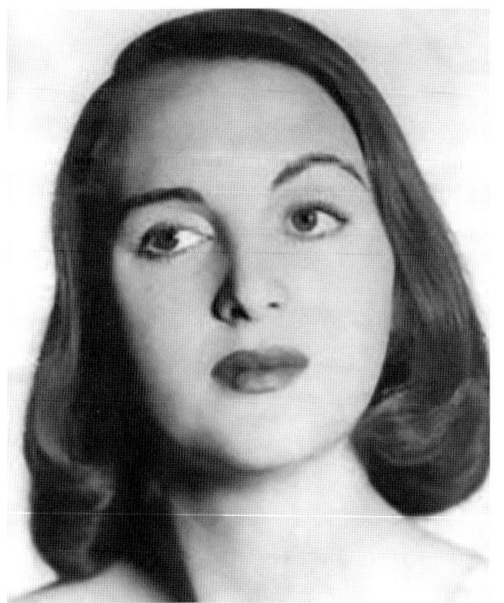

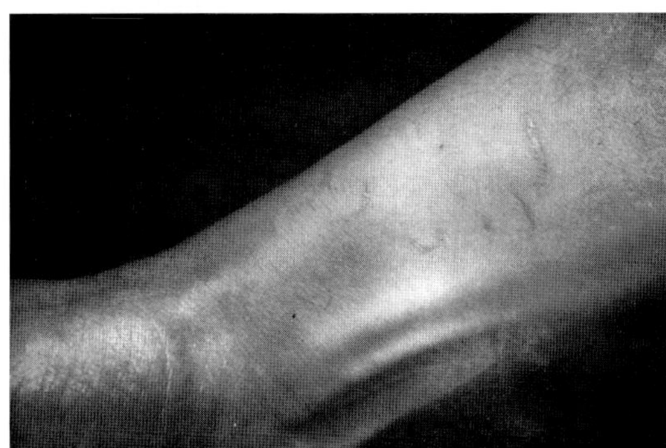

Above left: Gay Gibson.

Above right: James Camb.

Left: Scratch marks on the wrist of James Camb.

Cabin 126, showing the bell pushes in close proximity to the bunk.

Above left: Divisional Detective Inspector Shelley Symes.

Above right: Woman Police Sergeant Maudie Lambourne.

Haigh leaving court.

Above left: Haigh leaving court.

Above right: Professor Keith Simpson and his secretary Jean Scott-Dunn searching the factory at Crawley.

Below: Police search the factory site at Crawley.

Some of Haigh's victims

Above left: Mrs Durand-Deacon.

Above right: Donald McSwan.

Dr and Mrs Henderson.

Darling Alick — I am deteriorating in health & spirit please cooperate
excuse writing I'm blind folded & cold —

Please keep the Police out of this and cooperate
with the Gang giving Code No M3 when telephoning
you. The earlier you get money
the quicker I may come home or
you will not see me again. Darling can you
act quickly Please
please keep Police out of this if
you want to see me. Muriel

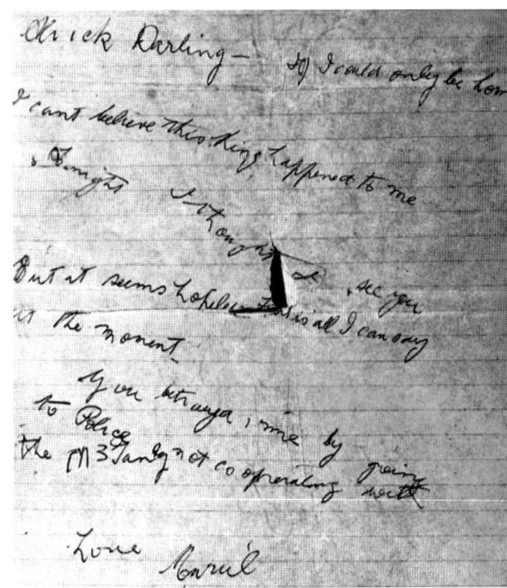

Alick Darling — If I could only be home
I cant believe this thing happened to me
tonight
But it seems hopeless see you
at the moment. this is all I can say
You betray me by going
to Police
the M3 Gang not cooperating with
Love Muriel

Above left: Letter written by Mrs McKay.

Above right: Second letter written by Mrs McKay.

Mrs Muriel McKay.

Above left: Arthur Hosein.

Above right: Nizamodeen Hosein.

Below: (L) Detective Chief Superintendent Wilfred Smith (R) Detective Inspector John Minors.

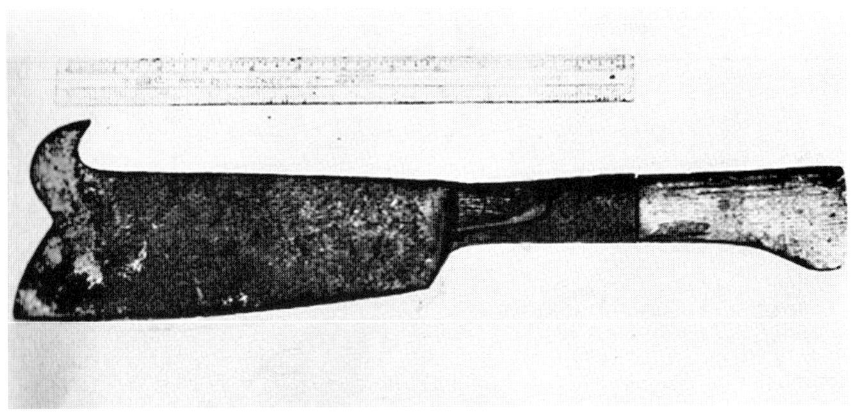

The billhook found at the McKay house.

An aerial view of Rooks Farm.

She should then alight at the last stop before Stamford Hill, when a car would draw up behind her, flash its lights, and the transfer – money in exchange for abductee – would be carried out. The call did not sound as though it emanated from M3, but nevertheless, the matter had to be properly covered. Prior to the commencement of the journey, armed officers were secreted in and around the area of the proposed handover. There was, of course, no possibility of the police permitting Mrs Dyer to participate in this venture, and a substitute wearing clothing provided by her had to be found. This should not really have presented a problem; there were scores of plucky policewomen ready for such an opportunity – in fact, just a few years earlier, two of their number from nearby 'Z' Division had been awarded George Medals for volunteering for dangerous decoy work.[2]

Despite this, a bizarre decision was taken by Smith to get a male officer to dress in female clothing and take Mrs Dyer's place. That officer was Wally Whyte, who now describes what happened:

> So far as I can recall, there were no female officers actually involved on the enquiry at that stage. Some of the guys more familiar (so to speak) with the female officers available at 'VW' discounted those for various reasons, and time constraints left us with the unlikely situation of employing a male officer. Of those then present in the house some were (if you'll forgive me) of the wrong age and/or wrong shape. Of those still remaining, only Johnny Hodgson and I had any chance of getting our feet into the pair of ladies' boots offered by the family, along with the other necessary bits of apparel and wig. Given that Johnny later fathered a scrum-half who wore the England shirt a few times, you may understand, I hope, that he had a naturally slightly lower centre of gravity than my then more willowy frame. In answer to your rather pointed question, Bill Smith was the final arbiter, and no, I didn't have to audition via the casting couch for the part!

Ian Burgess, Alick McKay's son-in-law, volunteered to drive the substitute 'Diane Dyer' to Catford in his Bentley; on the first bus out of Catford garage at 5.45 am, Whyte and two other officers disguised as early-morning workmen to act as minders and picked up en route were the only three passengers. The suitcase contained just £5,000, all that could be scraped together in time, but that – and the person conveying it – was never in any danger.

---

2 For further details of these courageous women, see *The Brave Blue Line: 100 Years of Metropolitan Police Gallantry*, Pen & Sword Books, 2011

The two minders saw to that, and there was substantial back-up, not only from the waiting, armed detectives at the rendezvous point, but also in the shape of two unmarked police cars who were following the bus so closely that the driver reported them as suspicious to Stamford Hill. The conductor, too, saw through the disguise of the passenger with the suitcase immediately. There were, of course, no flashing headlights, no reception committee, no nothing – except a great deal of embarrassment. Whyte, who suffered a considerable number of jibes from his fellow officers, told me, 'After two or three hours on my delicate little "dancers", neither the boots nor the dancers, I think, were ever quite the same again!'

Never again was Whyte required to 'drag up', and now, retired and in his eighties, he still exhibits the same fierce heterosexuality that would have put a Viking raider on East Anglia's coastline, a millennium earlier, to shame.

The police quickly came to the conclusion that once more this had been a hoax, after the caller telephoned the following day, apologising for failing to keep the rendezvous but explaining that he had been unable to deliver Mrs McKay to Stamford Hill because of his lack of funds to purchase a car. Therefore, Mrs Dyer should board a train to Catford and when she saw a bonfire by the railway line should throw out a parcel containing £200 to buy a car. This time, it was decided at the highest level that no one – not Mrs Dyer, a male officer impersonating Mrs Dyer or anybody else – should board that train to Catford. The way things were going, had a bonfire actually been seen, the £200 tossed from the train's window would probably have landed slap-bang in the middle of the flames and been consumed by them.

Chapter 10

A Revealing Conversation

The long-awaited telephone call from M3 was finally made, five days after the last one. Quoting it here in full demonstrates the idiotic, taunting, cosy familiarity of the kidnapper, but more than anything else, the anguish of Alick McKay. It commenced at 2.25 pm on Monday 19 January when the caller asked to speak to 'Alex'.

'Yes?'

'Who's speaking, please?'

'Oh, it's McKay, here.'

'Hello, Alex, this is the M3. We contacted you last week concerning Muriel.'

'Yes.'

'Now she's very worried, you see, why we did not send a letter and we contacted you, because we got a tip from CID that she contacted them, you see.'

'Well, you see, this is ridiculous, you know. I cannot understand someone having the mentality that this is going on, you know.'

'Now, we have got many in the CID as far as you know, that's why they will never be able to solve this case. Now, you shall hear from us, I've, I've told you already. Muriel is very nice.'

'I know she is.'

'She is very cooperative. She is all right, well taken care of.'

'Well, she must at least have told you the truth, that in fact, that I haven't got the money you are talking about.'

'Well, she told us you haven't got it, but could get it from firms. That's what she said.'

'Get it from firms?'

'She said you could borrow it, she said, she's very worried and all our problems . . .'

'Oh, you know, you know the situation that . . .'

'Nervous, she's terribly worried now.'

'How do you think I am?'

'Eh?'

'How do you think I behave, do you think I'm worried about it?'

'You're worried as well?'

'Of course I'm worried. I want to get her back again.'

'I know, she's, she's . . .'

'Do you, you must, you must, you must make a reasonable demand so that I can meet the situation.'

'You see, we have got to have a price, I am now, now in a few days' time, if you want some proof about it.'

'Why in a few days?'

'She is, she is with us, ah well now, she, she is wearing a low-heeled cream shoe with chains on the front, with a piece of chain to the front of it. She's wearing a green skirt and bodice, with buttoned down bodice, and a double-way coat, black and brown, light brown. She hasn't got her glasses, her eyes are going a bit bad now, she can't read, we gave her books to read.'

'Is . . . can't you get her to write to me, you ask her to write in the full names of her children?'

'The full names of her children?'

'Yes, and give their full Christian names.'

'Yes, she told us the children, she told us what the son-in-law do for a living, she told us everything, now all you've got to do, we will send you a letter, we'll send you instructions what you've got to do if you want her back.'

'Well, look, you ask her to get . . .'

'We'll give you time, enough time to do it. Now . . .'

'Ask her what she got for Christmas presents.'

'Now, you'll get a letter from her as well as instructions from us.'

'Well, you ask her what she did . . .'

'Police . . .'

'You ask her what she . . .'

'You are to be blamed for if the police, now let me tell you, we're running this in such a way that, er, whatever we're doing, I mean, forever now, we'll contact you, for we're looking for a place where you should meet us to bring the money.'

'I want to do that.'

'You want to do that?'

'Now, the police are looking for her, as you know and I know, but I want to get her back.'

'Yes, well, we will tell you the place where you got to bring the money, all right?'

'Yes, of course it is, but it, you know, has got to be the amount of money that I can get.'

'Right.'

'I can't get an unlimited sum of money, I can't get it.'

'Now, on the first delivery, you will have to bring half a million.'

'Oh.'

'You will speak to her, and two days after that . . .'

'Look, bring a gun here and shoot me rather than ask unreasonable situations.'

'We, we . . .'

'It's ridiculous.'

'Now, we want a million, we want a million in two different stages.'

'Nobody's got a million pounds, and I mean, quite frankly, it's ridiculous to talk about it.'

'Now, if we send you this letter, we give you a few days, and . . .'

'You might as well give me ten years. You might as well kill me now.'

'If you don't cooperate . . .'

'I am cooperating, but I can't cooperate with impossible sums that . . .'

'Now, if you don't cooperate within the time we give you in the letter we will be sending – you're to be blamed for not seeing your wife again.'

'Well, look . . .'

'Yes?'

'I'll never be blamed for that, my boy, because I can't meet impossible situations, but what you've got to do, is this ...'

'Yes?'

'What you've got to do is ask her what she got for Christmas presents and then put that in the letter to me, so I know she's alive.'

'She is alive. You'll be able to speak to her.'

'She is well?'

'Yes, she is.'

'When can I speak to her?'

'As soon as, after the first delivery, you'll be able to speak to her.'

'Look, the first, er, make this a reasonable sum of money, man, you know I haven't got this money. If you had been with her, you would know I can't get it.'

'But now, Mr McKay, this is not one person this group, this is in a world-wide international.'

'Look, it may be a world-wide international, but if the world-wide international's as big as you say it is, at least they know I haven't got that money.'

'Yeah.'

'And they know I haven't got any hope of getting it.'

'I run this branch in England, you see, and I'm repeating the code again for you. Don't take any telephone calls from anyone else, unless they say it's M3.'

'Well, give me something, oh you've given me something now.'

'M3.'

'M3, yes, that's all right, we've had other people saying 'M' and all sorts of things, you know.'

'Now this is our code – M3.'

'Right.'

'The Mafia 3.'

'I believe you.'

'You believe me, and if you believe me, you shall hear from your wife.'

'Look, can you make it quickly, make it quickly, because quite frankly, I mean, and mention a reasonable sum of a first delivery, because I haven't got that money and I can't get that money?'

'This is the first delivery.'

'I haven't got that sort of money and you know it.'

'What, what will you do for the first delivery, how much will you give on the first delivery?'

'I mean, hell, I mean, I'll give you everything I've got.'

'Yeah, well, the first delivery, we want to be sure, you see, that you are honest, that you've decided to cooperate.'

'What are you trying to do?'

'To give half a million.'

'What have I done to deserve this?'

'Well, I don't know.'

'My God, I wish . . .'

'But I'm very sorry we had to do this because your wife is such a nice person.'

'She's the most . . . she's the quietest and most charitable person you've ever met.'

'She's very nice and very cooperate, it wasn't intended for her, but I gave the instructions to the boys what they got to do, they traced down the car ULO 18F and they went there and they got her instead, you see. Now on the delivery . . . you, the letter you got, you got to use ULO 18F.'

'If you ask, if you ask for all that money, I tell you it's impossible for me to get, and I know impossible, how impossible it is and it's no good and you must have been in my house. It's an ordinary house. It's got a mortgage on it, I cannot get that money.'

'You know people. I am not concerned about . . .'

'Look, if I knew you, would you lend it to me?'

'It's costing me out of my pocket, now.'

'Would you, I'll pay what you are out of pocket, I'll pay even more on top of that, but I can't pay impossible amounts. It's ridiculous for you to suggest it.'

'How much would you pay at the first delivery?'

'Pardon?'

'How much would you pay at the first delivery?'

'Well, I will give you, er, you make a reasonable sum, say twenty thousand pounds.'

'Twenty thousand! Over here. No use. Twenty thousand pounds only cost of cars.'

'But you see, you can't handle cash. My money is tied up in pensions. I have got to raise money from the banks. You can't get money from companies.'

'That's not my concern. It's my order and it's an order.'

'Would you lend me the money?'

'It's your own, or to reject, accept or reject half a million.'

'I can't find half a million pounds, I'm sorry.'

'Well, we'll give you a letter. You got to do something about it.'

'I know I got to do something. I can kill myself!'

'There is no reason to shout.'

'I can kill myself. That will solve a problem!'

'I've got to leave tonight for Malta. I got another job in Malta, you see. I got to go around to Malta to see about this job and then back to America tomorrow.'

'Yes, okay, well, I don't know you, see? I mean you're making impossible demands on me that I can't . . .'

'It's not up to me, you see, I got to contact Head Office and that's, that's what I say.'

'You got to contact who?'

'The Head Office, and that's what I say, you see.'

'Well, the head of that organization, whatever you say it is, must know exactly because he must know what I'm worth. He must know what I can raise. He must know how silly the question is that you are asking.'

'We got private detectives, we got CID men within this business.'

'You might have everybody in the world, but the situation is, the point about it is, you must also know, you might even have a bank manager, you might even have my bank manager, but I'll tell you what, anybody that says I can raise half a million pounds must be, must be out of their minds, because I can't do it and I'm nearly out of my mind.'

'Well, I don't have much time, because my taxi is waiting and I've got to go a long way.'

'You have to go. I don't know where you've got to go, but I'll tell you what . . .'

'I've got to go to the airport.'

'I haven't got that money and I mean, it's no good of you putting pressures on me to ask more of a sum.'

'I thought that before I go down to the airport, I should ring you and let you know because I've got to go to the airport to receive one of the boys coming down today.'

'Well, I can't help where you go. I don't know.'

'Well, it's left to you, now. I told you, you got to get half a million, we will tell you the place, give you the route number, you got to leave there at such a time. It will be you alone and the chauffeur of ULO 18F, the Rolls-Royce.'

'The Rolls-Royce is smashed and in the garage and that car doesn't belong to me and you know that.'

'If you don't use that, you use the Capri, all right? Your wife's Capri, she says she's got a Capri, a green Capri.'

'Yes, did she tell you I've not got my own car?'

'Pardon?'

'What is my own car?'

'The Capri is her car.'

'Her car, yes.'

'Yes.'

'Well, okay then, expect to hear from us again.'

'Well, look, make it soon.'

'We'll be giving you the instructions of what you got to do.'

'But it's no good asking for half a million, because I'll tell you what . . .'

'Your wife is safe, don't . . .'

'Have me instead, take me instead.'

'Take you instead?'

'Yes, have me instead.'

'This is my order and that is final. I've got nothing more to say.'

'Well, I can . . . I can't give you . . . what you can't give . . .'

And with that, the kidnapper hung up, leaving Alick McKay at his wits' end. The kidnapper had been on the telephone for 35 minutes, quite the longest call so far, and as he had told Alick McKay, he had nothing more to say.

In fact, it transpired that he had said too much; far too much.

Chapter 11

Ian McKay Takes Charge

But before the kidnapper's mistake was revealed, much more had been going on. No letters appeared, but two days after the call to Alick McKay, at 12.17 pm there was a further telephone call from M3; this time Ian McKay, who had flown in from Australia, took the call, explaining that his father was too ill to speak to the caller. Although M3 tried to insist, Ian was adamant and, what was more, M3 agreed to negotiate with him, which was precisely what he and the police wanted. In fact, Ian scored a major point when M3 mentioned the police, because he was able to say, 'Well, we would, our problem is, you see, we don't know how to get rid of them. If we'd had a note right from the start, we would have known not to call them, but we can't get rid of them.'

It was a good start, but things became even better when Ian told M3 that the police suspected Alick. It surprised the caller, who asked, 'Suspect who – your Dad?'

'But, you know, they even suspect him', replied Ian, 'and you know, well, you know, he's very upset because, well, he hasn't done anything and, er, you know, but if only we'd . . . if only you could have left a note, he would never have panicked, you see, in the start.'

It was a clever move, because it appeared that Ian was willing to negotiate and also that he and the police had become alienated. 'Yes, yes, that's it', replied M3 eagerly. 'You see, we had the note delayed but it so happened that your Mum, you know, she was a bit upset.'

The illogical talk from the caller rambled on: 'Well, I control the M3, well, you know, at the moment . . . And, er, that is the Mafia Gang Three . . . And the instructions were given to go to this room and get this chap, but it so happens we got your Mum. You see? . . . Well, we had, we had conferences about it, but it so happened that, er, they, we, want a million pounds.'

It was during this call that M3 stated that they had called a doctor in from abroad to take care of Mrs McKay. And then the caller made this disgusting claim: 'She has even been trying to give herself to the doctor . . . she has been offering herself to the doctor to get away . . .'

The caller rang off but a few moments later called back saying that Alick and Diane would be receiving letters from Muriel McKay and also instructions about what the family had to do. A date, 1 February 1970, was stipulated and Ian was told, 'We want a million but the first delivery gotta be half a million . . . Now, we've got where you gotta go and what you gotta do. Okay? And that's all. Bye.'

The following day, 22 January, letters arrived at St Mary House postmarked Wood Green, N22 at 2.15 pm the previous day. Both were written on the same cheap notepaper and the one addressed to Diane read:

> Dearest Diane I heard you on TV . . . Thank you for looking after Daddy . . . Would you please persuade Daddy to co-operate with M3 Gang . . . they will telephone you giving you that code M3 . . . M3 . . . You will then be sure you are speaking to the right party . . . Act quickly for my sake dear . . . Please keep Police out of it if you want to see me alive . . . Negotiate with Gang as quickly as possible and discretely for the gang is too large to fool . . . All my love to you . . . Mumm.

The letter addressed to Alick read:

> Darling Alick I am deteriorating in health and spirit . . . please co-operate . . . excuse writing I'm blindfolded and cold . . . Please keep the Police out of this and co-operate with the gang giving Code No M3 when telephoning to you . . .the earlier you get the money the quicker I may come home or you will not see me again. Darling can you act quickly . . . please, please keep Police out of this if you want to see me. Muriel.

Additionally, there was a ransom note; it read:

> This is your instructions. Please obey. No error must happen. The police must not be informed. If you disobey, you will be blamed for the consequences. On the first occasion you must place half a million pounds in a black suitcase in £5 and £10 notes. Drive your wife's Ford Capri from your home and get on the North Circular Road and then take the A10 Cambridge Road on your own. At the first set of lights at Church Street, London, N9 there is a telephone box (01-360-3578). Enter the telephone box and wait for us to telephone you with further instructions at 10pm on first

> February. We shall use our code number for identification, M3. Your wife Muriel has pleaded with us that you cannot obtain one million pounds. If you send the first half million the gang will hold a conference whether to accept the half a million. Your wife will be returned to you two days after business is finished. Make sure the suitcase with the money is locked. We are sending a totally strange person who will be paid to do a job. His job will be to collect a black suitcase. If he is caught he will not be able to assist you or the police. My men will be watching your house. Any error on your part will only take two minutes and you will never see your wife. You will see her dead and delivered to your door.

It was as a result of these communications that police came to the following conclusions: that they were not dealing with the Mafia, or even criminals who could half-way purport to be professional. Whoever was responsible for the kidnapping, they were little better than cretins.

Half a million pounds in £5 and £10 notes represented a sizeable volume of currency. The total weight would be approximately 80kg, and if the kidnapper was later to stipulate used notes, the dirt and grease adhering to them would make the weight considerably more; pristine or grubby, it would be quite heavy enough to pull off the handles of the three very large suitcases – not one – which would be needed to contain the money.

Next, it seemed that these letters written by Muriel McKay were out of sequence; they were letters which had obviously been written far earlier and could (or rather should) have been sent far sooner. And although the police were keeping this to themselves, they were under no illusion that Muriel McKay was still alive. But on the plus side, the writer's left palm print was found on the ransom demand.

On 23 January, there were three telephone calls from M3 to 20 Arthur Road in fairly quick succession, all of which were answered by Ian McKay and the first of which came at 11.56 am.

Ian stated that they had received the letters but added that they could have been written weeks before (as they certainly had).

'I told you what she is wearing', replied M3. 'What do you want me to do? Take her clothes off and send them to you? We are in business and want to cooperate to sell good stuff. If you do not cooperate you will get her dead on your doorstep. I'm asking you for the last time, I'm asking you, and that's if you intend to cooperate, yes or no?'

Ian wanted proof that his mother was alive; M3 refused to supply it. Tempers – particularly Ian's – were becoming raised. Ian wanted M3 to get Muriel to write something that he directed, such as wishing all her family and friends a Happy New Year, but that quite obviously was an impossibility. Ian told M3 – on several occasions – that he had got the money, but this was completely ignored, with M3 saying inexplicably, 'If you don't cooperate, well then, we shall not contact you again and you shall be blaming your own self.'

Even more inexplicable was when M3 said, 'Well, it's a pity, if our phone was not bugged, our phone is bugged, you see, she could have used a telephone now. We don't want to take her out, you see.'

On and on it went, with more threats from M3 about Muriel McKay being delivered dead to Ian's door, and Ian demanding that his mother be allowed to write today's date in full. That resulted in M3's reply: 'I've told you, we won't be letting her write again any more.'

Losing his patience, Ian shouted, 'Because you haven't got her.'

M3 hung up but telephoned again at 1.55 pm saying that he had spoken to head office; then he uttered the following gibberish:

> They said this is final, what I've got to say now, it's either you cooperate, it is what is, what is on the paper, or if you, if you, intend to cooperate we shall proceed and if you don't intend to cooperate, well we shall drop the matter there, and, um, we won't be needing the money and you won't be seeing your Mum.

Ian now explained that through friends and relations they had raised a quarter of a million. This was a seriously good strategy; it was a long way from Alick truthfully saying he hadn't a million pounds and was unable to raise that sum, to now, weeks later, Ian stating (untruthfully) that at least they had been able to raise a substantial sum. It should have been a turning point, but M3 was so blinkered about getting a million pounds in two instalments – either that, or he was so stupid – that he ignored it. Instead, he babbled on about how the family had been under observation by the gang and, quite apart from having an agent in the CID (as he had previously mentioned), he now added that they had agents in the Post Office as well to monitor the progress of the letters. There was the matter of the quarter of a million pounds, said Ian; M3 wanted to know if he would cooperate. Of course, he wanted to cooperate, replied Ian – all he wanted was proof that his mother was alive.

'Well, look, you are not going to get any further more . . .' replied M3, before he was interrupted by Ian furiously shouting, 'Because you haven't got it! You got a corpse, you got a corpse, you got a corpse! . . . You've got a dead person, you haven't got her at all, you know she's not alive, so you are just trying to trick us, you're trying to trick us, you're trying to trick us!'

M3 went on to say that they had never murdered anybody yet but there would always be a first time. He was told by Ian, 'Don't be silly, quarter of a million pounds, a lot of money to get. You can't pass this up', only to reply, 'Yes, well, look, we don't deal with the quarters, we deal with the wholes.'

After fifteen minutes' conversation M3 hung up but at 2.11 pm he telephoned again, this time wanting to speak to Alick McKay. Ian refused, saying that his father was in bed and had had drugs administered to him, and that he, Ian, was the family's spokesman. M3 stated he wanted the deal to go through on the Sunday night but as he said, 'We don't have to cooperate with you . . .' Ian, however, wanting definite proof that his mother was still alive, had the final word: 'The headlines on tonight's paper . . . and the date in full, and I'm going to hang up on you – goodbye.'

And that concluded business for Friday, 23 January. The family would hear nothing more until the following Monday.

Chapter 12

Enter C11 Department

On Monday, 26 January, three letters arrived in a single envelope posted in Wood Green, N22. Two were from Muriel McKay, the first of which read:

> Alick Darling – If I could only be home. I cant believe this thing happened to me . . . tonight . . . I thought I see you . . . But it seems hopeless . . . this is all I can say at the moment . . . You betrayed me by going to Police and not cooperating with the M3 Gang . . . Love Muriel

The second letter read:

> Darling Alick – You don't seem to be helping me. Again I beg of you to cooperate with the M3 gang. You do understand that when the . . .

The writing tailed off; something had been cut from the letter. In addition, there were two pieces of material cut from the clothing Mrs McKay had been wearing when she was kidnapped, a green suit and a black coat, also a piece of cream patent leather cut from one of her shoes.

The third letter was a ransom note. It was written in a backward-sloping hand, full of spelling and grammatical mistakes, and it read:

> I am sending you final letter for your wife reprieve. She will be executed on the 2nd February 1970 unless you keep our business date on the 1st February without any error. We demand the full million pound in two occasions, when you deliver the first half million you wife life will be saved and I personally shall allow her to speak to you on telephone. We will not allow you to tell us how to run our organisation. We are telling you what to do you cannot eat the cake and have it this is our 4th blackmail we have absorbed 3½ million pound we did not murdered anyone, because they were wise to pay up and their family were returned to them. You do the same and she will return safely. My next blackmail will be in

> Australia some time this year. Looking forward in settling our business on the 1st February at 10pm as stated on the last letter in a very discreet and honest way, and you and your children will be very happy to join Muriel McKay and our organisation also will be happy to continue our job elsewhere in Australia we shall look forward to see you son Ian when we visit Australia. You see we don't make our customer happy we like to keep them in suspense in that way it is a gamble that is why we don't accept you Ian telling us what to do we give the order and you must obey
>
> M3

On the letter commencing 'Alick Darling' there was a thumb and fingerprint; on the envelope's 4d stamp, a left thumb print. None of them belonged to Mrs McKay.

* * *

Following the end of each recorded telephone conversation, the tapes were re-run, listened to and carefully typed up, then scrupulously checked and re-checked for mistakes. When the investigating officers were satisfied that the transcripts were entirely accurate, they sat down to study them, to see if the caller had slipped up in any way, if he had left any kind of clue, no matter how tenuous. And they discovered that when M3 telephoned Ian McKay on 19 January he had done just that.

What was it he had said? 'I gave the instructions to the boys what they got to do, they traced down the car ULO 18F and they went there and they got her instead, you see.'

'They traced down the car.' What did that mean? That they had gone to the *News of the World* offices, seen the car and followed it to Arthur Road? It could do (and of course, they had), but then surely the expression used would have been 'followed' or 'tailed'?

No, 'traced down' were the words M3 had used. The officers went to the Greater London Council offices, just as M3 had done, to check on the ownership of registration number ULO 18F. There they found the form upon which M3 had requested the details of Murdoch's Rolls-Royce. The name of the enquirer? That was shown as Sharif Mustapha of 175 Norbury Crescent, Norbury. In fact, it would later transpire that the address given was one of M3's cousins, Shuffi Ali; the name on the form was that of a school-friend.

The reason for M3's enquiry? It was because the enquirer's car had been involved in a slight accident with the Rolls. His vehicle's details? A blue Volvo, registration number XGO 994G. That could be false, as well – except that it wasn't. The registered owner was shown as Mrs Elsa Hosein of Rooks Farm, Stocking Pelham, Hertfordshire. Who else lived there? A check on the electoral roll revealed the details of an Arthur Hosein. The investigators dug a little deeper . . .

But before we go any further, I need to introduce an allegorical story to lead into the next and very important part of this tale.

* * *

Fast-forward by about six years. I am walking towards the departure lounge at London Heathrow Airport, smartly attired as one should be when travelling with other business class passengers and carrying an expensive-looking briefcase. I had no boarding pass, but a discreet nod from the resident Special Branch officer to the official on the gate let me through to mingle with the other passengers.

Suddenly, there was a shout: 'Dick! Over here!' Damn – I'd been spotted!

I turned to see a press photographer hurrying towards me. 'Let's have one of you with the briefcase, Dick!' he called. Sporting a rueful, rather embarrassed grin, I held the briefcase up to shoulder height, rather like a reluctant Chancellor of the Exchequer.

'A bit higher – one more – and another – great!' The photographer enthusiastically clicked away, and the other passengers all looked in my direction. Who could this celebrity be, they thought, someone well-known who's travelling on the same flight as us?

And then the flight was called and the passengers filed out towards the waiting aircraft; I stood back courteously to let them pass me and smiled, as celebrities do. As the last passenger left, so did I – in the opposite direction, back to the headquarters of the Yard's Serious Crime Squad.

A few weeks later, three members of an international gang responsible for the forgery of everything from driving licences to diplomatic passports, cheques, letters of credit and banknotes of every denomination and currency, sat glumly in the police cells wondering how on earth the police had been able to form an association between them. Those men, just three of dozens of members of what was known as 'The Hungarian Circle', had been in the departure lounge with me. Not one photograph of me holding that briefcase aloft existed; several of the three gang members, staring at some unknown celebrity off camera, did.

Because the photographer was not a member of the Press Association at all; he was a covert photographer employed by Criminal Intelligence – or C11 Department at the Yard.

C11 had been formed in 1960. Its members seldom if ever gave evidence in court. They gathered information about the most dangerous criminals in the country, the 'Main Index Men', using their informants, telephone intercepts and listening devices. Their surveillance operatives blended in seamlessly with their surroundings, using whatever transport was necessary or available – cars, vans, trains, buses or just plain shoe leather – and passed their often whispered intelligence to each other by means of covert radios, using an unbreakable frequency. Their expertise was much admired and their services eagerly sought by the proactive squads at the Yard: the Serious Crime Squad, Flying Squad and Regional Crime Squad. And when their work was done, the followers drifted away, back into the shadows from whence they'd come.

One of the C11 photographers who was much in demand was Detective Constable Jim Smith. Previously a member of the Special Patrol Group, Smith had been awarded a well-deserved British Empire Medal for gallantry in tackling three armed men.

On Wednesday, 28 January 1970, Smith was called into the office of Detective Chief Superintendent David Clarence Dilley, the second-in-command of C11. Dilley had joined C11 Department as a detective inspector in 1964; he would remain there until his retirement as commander in 1976. He would last in that post three years longer than Smith, who posed a threat to him; equally, Smith believed that Dilley was as straight as a corkscrew.

But on this particular day, Dilley told him to shut the door, then gave him his assignment. The next day, he was to go to Old Street Magistrates' Court, where a man named Arthur Hosein would be appearing to answer a traffic summons. When he appeared, Smith was to photograph him, then report back to Dilley. That was all.

So on the Thursday Smith set out for the Magistrates' Court. He was accompanied by Police Constable Eric Turner, one of the '42s', C11's covert motorcyclists. Smith got into the back of his nondescript van parked opposite the court entrance. Dressed in his motorcycle leathers, Turner looked no different from many others in the court awaiting condemnation for breaches of the Road Traffic Act. He positioned himself inside the court building; in that way, he would be able to identify Hosein when he arrived and, when his case was dealt with, follow him outside and surreptitiously identify him to Smith. Following that, Smith would be in possession of the photographs and Turner could clandestinely follow Hosein wherever he went.

Unfortunately, although both officers remained *in situ* until the court closed for the day, Hosein – for whatever reason – did not appear, and Smith returned to the Yard and informed Dilley of the non-appearance.

Precisely why Smith had been tasked to photograph the man who was supposed to answer a summons at a Magistrates' Court he had no idea, and Dilley did not enlighten him. Smith had never heard of Arthur Hosein, and few other people in the world of law enforcement had, either. He was certainly not a C11 'Main Index Man'.

In fact, Arthur Hosein did not possess a criminal record at all; that was why his fingerprints were not on file.

Chapter 13

A Drop is Arranged

Back at Wimbledon, it certainly appeared that Sunday, 1 February was going to be the date when the ransom was dropped, and arrangements were being made to deal with that eventuality.

Of course, Ian McKay would not be allowed to attend the meet; a police officer posing as him would be substituted. It had been stipulated that Muriel McKay's Ford Capri should be used, but it was necessary that whoever made the drop should be accompanied by at least one other officer, and a Capri would have insufficient room for the officers and the load of ransom money. But the Rolls would prove ideal. Minors would act as the chauffeur, and Detective Sergeant Roger Street would pose as Ian McKay, since he was of approximately the same height and build as the younger man.

Next, the money. They acquired £7,500 in genuine £5 notes with their serial numbers recorded. But for the rest of the cash it would be too risky to attempt the usual 'tops and bottoms' trick to give the appearance of £500,000; nor could such an amount of money be procured. Therefore, the investigating officers took a decision that though necessary was probably unlawful. They approached Bradbury Wilkinson & Co., the firm responsible for the printing and engraving of postage stamps, share certificates and banknotes, which had moved to New Malden, Surrey in 1917. In conditions of great secrecy, what purported to be 242,500 £5 notes were printed – except that there was a thick white band running through the middle of them. Contained in their wrappers, with genuine notes top and bottom, anyone riffling through them would be convinced of their authenticity. The secrecy extended to every police officer in the know; if word that half a million pounds was going to be transported leaked out, it could lead to rival gangs trying to hi-jack it. Its authenticity would make little difference to a gang – if the money was genuine, all well and good; if not, it could still be used in its counterfeit form as a bargaining chip for their nefarious activities. And therefore, bearing in mind the leaking to the press of Mrs McKay's letter in the investigation's early stages, the lid had to be kept well and truly tight on this matter. The printing company's managing director had been profoundly shocked when the matter of manufacturing the fake fivers was put to him; he was only assuaged by the compelling reason for the request and the solemn assurances of the police that as soon as the investigation was completed, the notes would be returned for destruction, as indeed they were.

It was also decided to fit the suitcase with a tracking device, or 'lump' as it was colloquially known. It was held that when such a device was being monitored by specialist operators, its whereabouts could be established at any distance from 50 miles down to a few feet. Unfortunately, this assertion was bollocks.

These devices (and those monitoring them) could be gloriously imprecise. In fact, some fifteen years later, when such a device was fitted to a stolen car used by bank robbers, careful monitoring of it revealed to the occupants of the Flying Squad vehicles, who were acutely interested in the robbers' activities and movements, that for some considerable time they had been following a marked police area car. 'Lumps' have greatly improved since then.

But this enquiry was chock-full of ifs, ands and buts. The kidnappers had first demanded that the Roll-Royce be used for the drop, then the Capri – but would they accept the Rolls once more? The Assistant Commissioner (Crime) Peter Brodie OBE, QPM, was eager to offer any assistance needed to the enquiry – firearms, vehicles, surveillance and electronic techniques, manpower – because it was utterly essential to bring it to a successful conclusion.

With the best of intentions, Brodie supplemented the enquiry team with personnel from the Flying Squad, the Regional Crime Squad and C11, and contacted the Assistant Commissioner 'A' Department to authorize assistance from the Special Patrol Group. This was felt necessary because with a crime such as this, unprecedented in the annals of Metropolitan Police, the officers were pretty well searching in the dark.

Unfortunately, with the assignment of 180 police officers and 56 unmarked vehicles, the operation planned for Sunday, 1 February was doomed to suffer from overkill.

* * *

The next call from M3 came on Friday, 30 January at 11.30 am and as usual was taken by Ian McKay. Immediately, Ian said, 'We know you're the right people and we want to cooperate', to which M3 replied, 'All right, er, just remember any error will be fatal, remember that.'

The details of the drop and the place were mentioned, and then Ian suggested taking the Rolls to the meet because Mrs McKay's Capri was in the garage; if it were suddenly driven off, the press would notice and take photographs of it. Additionally, Ian stated that as well as not knowing North London very well he had injured his hand, and therefore he wanted the chauffeur to drive. M3 concurred, and Ian also got him to agree to let him see his mother at the drop-off.

Saturday saw a flurry of activity in police circles, with the telephone box and the surrounding area being plotted up for surveillance; in the McKay household there were no further telephone calls, and tension was rising.

Sunday, 1 February: during the afternoon, Minors and Street (with his hair touched up) arrived at St Mary House; Minors changed into the chauffeur's uniform and Street into one of Ian McKay's suits. His arm was in a sling, to support Ian's assertion that he had injured his hand, and concealed in the sling was a two-way radio. At 7.50 pm there was a call from M3, who wanted Ian's assurance that when his mother was returned to him she would not be interviewed by the police or the press. It was an odd demand, but of course Ian readily gave his guarantee that no such interrogation would take place. M3 also wanted to know if the Rolls contained what he described as a 'telecommunications set', which Ian denied.

'Now, any calls going to the police and coming from the police, we got a tracking radar, will tell us, and we will know', stated M3, and Ian was quick to assure him that he would not take that kind of a risk.

An hour later, with Minors at the wheel and Street in the back, the Rolls-Royce swept down the driveway and headed towards the capital.

Since 6 o'clock that morning, Jim Smith had been in the manager's office at Edmonton cemetery, from where he was able to view the telephone box in Church Street. He had seen no connection between this assignment and his observation at Old Street Magistrates' Court three days previously; there was no reason why he should have.

'By today's standards of equipment, ours was very low', he told me. 'It was a 35mm film camera, Sony reel to reel video equipment with a 12-minute battery life. I managed to connect the equipment to the mains electricity. Throughout the day, I photographed and videoed every person entering the phone box throughout the daylight hours. Whilst I was doing this, I was dialling TIM [the speaking clock] on the office phone and recording it on to the video tape.'

Roy Medcalf, then a uniformed officer in plain clothes from Tottenham police station, was also keeping observation of the telephone box; he was one of many.

Just after 10.00 pm, the Rolls arrived at the Church Street telephone box, which Street entered. Immediately, the telephone rang and a voice said, 'Who's that?'

Mimicking Ian McKay's Australian accent, Street replied, 'Ian McKay – who's that?'

'This is M3', said the caller. 'These are your instructions. Proceed along the Cambridge Road away from London. At the second set of traffic lights on the left is Southbury Road with a telephone box on the corner. The number is 01-363-1553X. Go there and wait for another call from me. Any error will be fatal.'

Street asked, 'How's my mother?' and was told, 'She is all right. Soon you will see her.'

Returning to the car, Street told Minors what had transpired, and while they drove off, Street passed the news by means of the concealed radio.

From his vantage point in the cemetery manager's office, Jim Smith had seen the Rolls draw up and a man with a plaster cast on his right arm get out and go to the telephone kiosk. But when the car drove off, as he told me, 'with a convoy of Squad cars following, as it drove off to the A10, they were joined by some C11 motorcycles. When Dilley and Lovejoy [Detective Superintendent Frank 'Little Legs' Lovejoy, Dilley's second-in-command] were working on a job, it became known in C11 as the RAC club.'

It appeared the C11 motorcyclists had disguised themselves as Hell's Angels but they were riding in an upright, almost military position. As the late Detective Sergeant Terry Brown GM told me, 'They might just as well have worn fucking uniforms.'

One of the Flying Squad cars was manned by officers from 10 Squad. The vehicle was one of the few Squad cars fitted with a multi-channel Pye radio which could pick up the more secure Regional Crime Squad (RCS) transmissions, and all three officers were armed. The officer in charge was Detective Inspector Bill O'Hara, who had been awarded a well-deserved Military BEM whilst serving with the Royal Ulster Rifles in Korea. Equally tough was Detective Constable John Corner, who had previously appeared as a leading light in the 'N' Division boxing team. Detective Sergeant Tony Stevens was a highly successful Squad officer who was known throughout the Yard as 'Gary Glitter'.

When a very senior officer demanded to know why, he was told by the head of the Squad, ''Cos he's a fucking star, Guv.'[1]

The Rolls arrived at the Southbury Road telephone box about three-quarters of an hour later. M3 duly telephoned and told Street to look on the floor, where there was a cigarette packet with further instructions written on the inside flap. 'Go down the A10 through Hoddesdon and Ware', said M3. 'You'll see a place called High Cross. You'll know it because you'll see an Esso gas station. You'll come to a road with a sign pointing down it called Dane End. On the corner there, over by the side of the road, you'll see two paper flowers. Leave the money there and go back to the first kiosk at Church Street, where you'll get a phone call saying where your mother is.'

An anxious Street (who was busily scribbling down the directions), having been assured that 'his mother' was all right – 'Just leave the money and you'll see her again' – got back into the Rolls, and as Minors headed back towards Edmonton, he relayed the latest information on the radio.

It was almost midnight as the car approached Dane End and slowly came to a halt, since driver and passenger had seen the paper flowers, pink and yellow, planted on a grass bank. Both men went round to the boot of the car and with difficulty lifted out the weighty suitcase and deposited it between the two flowers.

The tale is now taken up by Tony Stevens:

> We are only a couple of minutes behind and when we arrive, it's chaos. There are C11 bikes behind the Rolls-Royce and behind them is a long line of RCS cars, it seemed like twenty cars. Remember, this is midnight on a Sunday, there's no other traffic on the road. We pull to the other side of the road and overtake cars and motorbikes. As we pass the Rolls-Royce we can see the case being unloaded on to the verge.

Bill O'Hara went to the scene and saw movement behind a tree. Drawing his service revolver, he hissed, 'Don't move or I'll blow your fucking head off!'

'It's me – John Minors!' replied the 'suspect'.

'Oh Christ, sorry – thought it was them!' came the response.

---

1 The originator of the nickname, the singer Paul Gadd, was later sentenced to sixteen years' imprisonment for a variety of disgusting offences, and the sobriquet was immediately discarded by Stevens, who made it quite clear that in future he preferred to be known as 'Tony'.

Half a mile further on was a transport café, where the Squad car parked up and turned its lights off – and there they waited.

Not long after their arrival, a car pulled round close to them and stopped. Tony Stevens in the front passenger seat saw that it was a Volvo containing two men. One of its rear lights was out. Stevens particularly noted it since he wanted to buy one because of the manufacturer's safety record; he remarked on this to the other occupants of the Squad car. He was not the only one to make a remark concerning vehicles in that vicinity; at home, his wife had been listening to a programme on the radio which included a report that there was a traffic jam on the A10 north of Ware.

The Volvo drove off, after more cars from the Regional Crime Squad arrived at the café. 'Bill O'Hara was not pleased', commented Tony Stevens.

Other police vehicles secreted themselves, but Hertfordshire Police Constable John Weeks discovered some when he drove into the very small yard at Ware police station to find four men sitting in a car. 'They identified themselves as Met officers', he told me, 'but would not say what they were doing there. I don't know if anyone else at the station was aware of their job, but I suspect not.'

During the three hours that the police waited at Dane End, details of about a dozen passing vehicles were logged and passed to the operations room at Scotland Yard. Included was the Volvo, although no registration number had been recorded.

Back to Church Street went the Rolls, and the officers waited for an hour by the telephone kiosk for a call that never came. The occupants of the Volvo had high-tailed it for home.

At 2.35 am Minors and Street returned to Dane End. There was the suitcase, undisturbed. They retrieved it, and Minors raced back to Arthur Road, in case M3 wished to make further contact. But he didn't, and according to one eye-witness, the Rolls was left steaming on the driveway.

Naturally, there were recriminations amongst the police officers. But some good had come out of the operation: the Piccadilly cigarette packet containing the kidnappers' instructions was adorned by a left-hand thumb print. And it matched the thumb print found on the 4d stamp on the envelope containing the letters from Mrs McKay and the ransom note from the kidnapper.

The following day, nothing was heard from M3. But at the debriefing it was felt, from the recordings of the telephone calls, that the caller might be Asian – or perhaps West Indian. Bill O'Hara's team was sent to the vicinity of Dane End to make further enquiries. The owners of small shops and garages were spoken to, and the officers struck gold. Yes, they were told, there was a remote pig farm run by two Indians at a place called Stocking Pelham. Equipped with binoculars, Bill O'Hara scanned the farm. It did appear to be run by two Indians. And there was a Volvo parked there, together with a Morris Minor. Further enquiries were made. Yes, the brothers were known and no, they were not liked. The local police sergeant was engaged in casual conversation; yes, he knew the brothers. They had come to notice after committing various traffic offences. However, he thought they were Pakistanis.

All of this information was sent back to the incident room, where it was logged and indexed – as was the location of the two brothers. It was known as Rooks Farm.

Chapter 14

The Second Drop

M3 made contact on Tuesday, 3 February. He told Ian that there had been a meeting between the component parts of his group, the 'intellectuals', the 'semi-intellectuals' and the 'ruffians'. They were aware that police had been present during the intended handover, and one of the police motorcyclists, who was in their pay, had reported to 'the head boy'. M3 went on to say that the 'intellectuals' were laughing at him and indeed, he had broken down in tears; what was more, his life was now in danger. But one matter he was adamant about: he demanded that when he next called he should speak to Alick McKay.

Two days later, the call came. Alick McKay was far from well; he had spent much of the recent time in bed, heavily sedated, but with tremendous willpower he rallied and took the call at 10.25 am. In fact, he went on the offensive and told M3 that Ian had had an hour's start on the police and, had the kidnappers not led Ian on what he described as 'a Cook's tour', the changeover could have been accomplished in half an hour. But now M3 stipulated that at the next ransom drop it should be Alick who brought the money (which, said Alick, was currently being held in the bank) together with his daughter Diane – and M3 would phone back with the details of the drop.

At 11.17 am, he did. He stated that Alick and Diane should make the journey at 4.00 pm the following afternoon, to the same telephone kiosk at Church Street that Ian had gone to. With mind-boggling inanity, M3 demanded that the money should be in 'two small briefcases'. When Alick protested that the money would never fit into luggage that small, M3 relented and told him, 'Two suitcases'.

There was a great deal of work to be done by the police in just over 24 hours. There would be no repetition of the fiasco that had been 'Operation Cargo'. That had been run from Wimbledon, but although Smith and Minors were experienced detectives and murder investigators, neither had served on the proactive squads at the Yard dealing with tailing, watching and finally ambushing criminals. A special operations room was set up, next door to the Information Room at Scotland Yard. The man in overall charge was Commander Guiver, and the other commander present was Norman Hoggins MBE, the head of C11. Also from C11 was Hoggins' deputy, Dave Dilley, and from Wimbledon, Bill Smith. Dave Bowen, a temporary detective constable from Mitcham police station who had been seconded on to the enquiry, was there, and the radio operator was Detective Constable Dave Kerney, who had been one of the 42s the previous Sunday.

Except in emergencies, radio transmissions had to be kept to a minimum. Communication was to be made via telephone kiosks to the operations room – it was all very much like Flying Squad operations of the 1930s. Although there would be covert surveillance, there would be none of the saturation following of the previous Sunday. Detective Chief Superintendent Ron Harvey of Hertfordshire Constabulary – he had once been a Yard officer – coordinated Flying Squad and Regional Crime Squad teams outside the A1, A11 and A10 trunk roads, working on the assumption that if the kidnappers followed the same route as before, the teams would be able, if necessary, to home in on them in a pincer movement.

So secrecy was paramount. That extended to the press as well. Thanks to the Sunday night debacle, there had inevitably been speculation about police activities in Ware, Hertfordshire. The Commissioner of Police authorized a directive to be sent to the Press Association requesting editors to refrain from any mention of police activity in the area, since to do so might well jeopardize the safety of Muriel McKay; he assured them that as soon as it was safe to do so, any pertinent information would be made available to them.

Naturally, neither Alick McKay nor his daughter would be permitted to keep the meet. McKay would be impersonated by a disguised John Minors – his moustache had to be sacrificed – and Diane's part would be taken by Woman Detective Constable Joyce Armitage of the Flying Squad, a plucky 31-year-old who had taken part in several other undercover operations. Both were dressed in clothing from the McKay and Dyer wardrobes.

The two suitcases would be put into the boot of the Rolls-Royce, and they would be accompanied by Detective Inspector John Bland, who was halfway through his second tour with the Flying Squad. At a quarter of an inch over five feet eight, and a former Petty Officer with the Royal Navy, Bland had boxed in all divisions from flyweight to light-middle. All of his seven commendations by the commissioner were for arresting violent individuals, mainly for armed robbery. It was considered that Bland was probably the best man for a rather tricky job.

The 'lumps', the usual tracking devices, were inserted into the suitcases.

At the same time as inserting the 'lumps', someone at the Home Office thought it a good idea to use white phosphorous paint on the roof of the Rolls, so that if the 'lumps' failed to provide adequate tracking, then the police helicopter could be used to monitor the Rolls-Royce's progress. It would have been prudent for the academic in question to have ascertained if the Metropolitan Police actually possessed a helicopter. They didn't – it would take several more years before 'India 99' was launched on its maiden flight – so one was loaned by the *News of the World*. Just when it looked as though 'Operation Capture' would go the same way as its predecessor, common sense intervened; the helicopter, no doubt full of eager press photographers all keen to snap a scoop as they exhorted the pilot to swoop down lower and lower and make a dog's breakfast of everything, was quietly shelved and the roof of the Rolls was scrubbed down.

On Friday, 6 February, Ian McKay received a telephone call from M3 at 2.34 pm. Ian told the caller that his father and sister had left, as indeed they had; they had gone to Wimbledon police station. Ian stressed that there was no chauffeur, just the two family members, confirmed that they were going to the same telephone kiosk that he had gone to and assured M3 that there would be 'no tricks'.

Uttering his usual, near-incomprehensible gibberish, M3 said, 'I hope it is not well souped-up or well covered as the last time, because the last time, it was well covered up, you know. It was all sealed or closed up, that booth there.'

'Look, all we want to do is get my mother back, well, look, it is, I can assure you that there's nothing like that, at all', replied Ian.

'I see, because this will be the last and final chance', said M3 and on that chilling note ended his eighteenth and final telephone call to St Mary House.

* * *

The Rolls arrived at Church Street punctually at 4.00 pm, but it was another 45 minutes before the telephone rang in the kiosk. Giving a very creditable impersonation of Alick McKay, Minors was told by M3 to go to another call box, this one in Bethnal Green Road. This was not only unexpected but also deprived the occupants of the Rolls of the protection they were expecting from the other officers in their close vicinity. Relaying this unforeseen change of plan to the operations room, Minors was told to drive back to Bethnal Green but not to hurry; other officers would have to get there first. The Rolls arrived at 6.00 pm; had M3 queried the amount of time it had taken to arrive, Minors would have put the blame on the Friday night traffic; but no such query came. Now Minors was told to leave the Rolls at Bethnal Green Underground Station and take the Central Line tube – together with the suitcases – to Epping where, at a kiosk in the booking hall, he would receive a further message. M3 then wished to speak to 'Diane' – and with great presence of mind, Joyce Armitage sobbed, 'I'm upset – please talk to Daddy.' And so the receiver was passed back to Minors, who was told, 'No error must be made. If the police are around this time, we will execute Muriel and no one will ever see her again.'

A decision was made to drive the Rolls to Theydon Bois, one stop from Epping, and get on the train there. The reasoning was this: the promised telephone call at Epping might well be a blind. If the police trio had got on a train at Bethnal Green, it was twelve stops to Epping, and if the gang were to board the same train, filled with Friday night commuters, and matters were to go badly wrong, there might well be a bloodbath. Although Bland was armed with a revolver, it would be impossible to have any further police back-up accompany the train; and if the gang were to grab the money, they could get out at any of the twelve stops into a waiting car. Far better to pin hopes on the promised phone call at Epping, and for the support team to go to the Epping area and await further instructions.

The Rolls drove into Theydon Bois station car park, Bland got out of the boot with the suitcases and, as the next tube train for Epping arrived, Minors and Joyce Armitage boarded it, with Bland in the next carriage. The six-minute journey was uneventful; Minors, struggling with the suitcases, got off and waited by the telephone kiosk. At 7.30 pm, Epping 3077 rang. These were M3's instructions:

> Get a cab and go to the Stortford Road, just past the junction with the A11 London to Newmarket Road. Go to Gates Garage, London Road, Bishop's Stortford and leave the money by a used Mini car for sale, for £450 on the forecourt, UMH 587F. Any error will be fatal to Muriel and Diana. We deal with hi-powered telescopic rifles and shotguns. Anyone who attempts to interfere, we will let them have it.

Once they had placed the suitcases by the van, 'Alick' and 'Diane' were told to return to Epping; there they would be given directions on how to retrieve Muriel McKay.

Minors telephoned for a cab, and immediately afterwards called the operations room for the latest instructions; once more, Minors was advised not to rush the 13-mile journey to Bishop's Stortford, to give time for an armed team of Flying Squad detectives to get into position. One of them was Detective Sergeant Colin Kinnaird, a member of 1 Squad and a marksman; another was Detective Sergeant Jack Quarrie BEM, an immensely tough character who had been a wartime member of No.9 Army Commando, which had seen fierce action at Lake Comacchio.

The cab duly arrived and the suitcases were lifted into the boot. Bland, meanwhile, had slipped out of the station and stood by a bus stop. The cab moved off, but the driver, Robert Kelly, was surprised when Minors told him to stop, the rear door opened and a dishevelled, disreputable character got in and lay down on the floor. Mr Kelly, understandably disturbed, wanted to know what was going on, only to be told, 'We're playing a joke on a friend.' Mr Kelly, who later said, 'I didn't sleep properly for about three days', drove in stunned silence to Bishop's Stortford. The suitcases were transferred from the boot to the back of the car, then, as they reached Gates Garage, the cab was directed to swing around and stop beside a nearby hedge, opposite the garage's forecourt. There, the rear door opened, Bland slid out and disappeared into the hedge. Minors got out, retrieved the cases and, spotting the beige Mini, took them across the road and placed them alongside it. The time was now 9.00 pm. 'They'll get pinched there, Guv'nor', said Mr Kelly, but Minors simply told him to take him and his female passenger back to Epping. He did so, and after they had spent a considerable time waiting for a telephone call that never came, he took them to Theydon Bois, where they picked up the Rolls.

Meanwhile, back at Gates Garage, just five minutes after the cab's departure, Bland saw a blue Volvo driving very slowly towards him. The car's registration number was XGO 994G. There was just one occupant, who stopped the car, wound down the window and looked at the suitcases, before driving off again.

Bland was not the only person to have seen the Volvo. Earlier, it had gone to Gates Garage, where the driver had asked for his tyres to be inflated. Michael Byers, the forecourt attendant, had seen the Volvo several times after that, before the garage closed at 10.00 pm. When it had stopped, Byers asked the driver, who was looking at a sheet of paper with writing on it, to move on.

Half an hour later, the Volvo returned, this time from the opposite direction. There was still just one man in it who looked once more at the suitcases before turning the car around and driving off. And then, at 10.57 pm, the Volvo returned. This time there were two men in it. It appeared that they were about to get out of the car, and the armed detectives were tensed and ready; but not for what happened.

A local married couple, Peter and Joan Abbott, had also spotted the suitcases and stopped their car. They were seen by C11 motorcyclist Brian Norris, as well as the watching detectives. The Volvo moved off, the couple then called the police, a Hertfordshire Land Rover arrived, and the cases were taken into Bishop's Stortford police station, where they were quickly retrieved by the Metropolitan officers.

But now everything about that muddy blue Volvo had slotted into place. Brian Norris lived quite close to C11's Commander Norman Hoggins and he received a very late telephone call from his chief. 'Pick me up at 5.00 am', he was told, and they drove to Bishop's Stortford, where they liaised with quite a number of other officers, both Metropolitan and from Hertfordshire. On that morning of 7 February they set off in a convoy; their destination was Rooks Farm, Stocking Pelham.

Chapter 15

Rooks Farm, Arrests and Searches

Hoggins was just one of about twenty officers who arrived at the farm at 8 o'clock that morning; others included Detective Chief Superintendents Ron Harvey from Hertfordshire and Bill Smith from the Met. The door was opened by Mrs Elsa Hosein, and Smith produced a search warrant, saying that he was looking for stolen jewellery. Elsa was joined by her husband Arthur, who invited the police into the house, telling them, 'I know nothing. I earn over £150 a week. I do not deal in stolen property. You can look where you like.'

And the police did. Detective Inspector John Bland went upstairs to assist the searchers; there he saw a young man whom he recognized. Telling him to come downstairs, Bland informed Smith that this was the man he had seen driving the Volvo. His name was Nizamodeen – also known as Nizam – Hosein, and he was Arthur's brother.

Just then, Jack Quarrie also informed Smith that he recognized Arthur as the passenger in the Volvo the previous evening.

There was no sign of Mrs McKay or her jewellery, but other items were discovered. In one of the children's bedrooms, some blue and yellow paper flowers were found; they were identical to the flowers found at the first drop at Danes End. Another flower was found between the driving seat and the door of the Volvo. On top of a radiogram there was a tin of elastoplast, as well as some baling twine, both similar to those found at Arthur Road, and an empty packet of Piccadilly cigarettes similar to the one containing the ransom instructions found in the telephone kiosk. In Nizam's bedroom a blue-lined exercise book was found, and in due course a forensic examination would show indentations on the pages which corresponded with the letters written by Mrs McKay. In the pocket of Nizam's trousers was found a piece of paper; written on it was the registration number UMH 587F, which belonged to the beige Mini at Gate's Garage.

Two pairs of tailor's shears were found, as was a billhook similar to the one found at St Mary House. It had been used, said Arthur, to chop up a calf which Nizam said had been fed to the two snarling German Shepherd dogs chained up in the yard.

The head and bones? 'Last time we saw it, it was out with the rubbish', said Nizam. A hacksaw blade had been borrowed from a farmer before Christmas; when it was returned on 1 January, the owner stated that the sharpened blade was quite blunt. A shotgun was found; Arthur accepted ownership but declined to say where he had acquired it. Nizam admitted that he had sawn off the barrels. A ballistic examination would reveal that although the gun had been fired, the sawn-off ends were clean.

And while Tony Stevens had been unable to record the registration number of the Volvo during the first ransom drop, the faulty rear light he had noticed corresponded with a defective one on the Volvo currently at Rook's Farm.

A search of the farm now commenced; it would continue for weeks. Uniformed officers from the Met, Hertfordshire and Essex took part, including Robert Needham, an Essex dog handler. 'A bleak, foggy morning with a sharp frost, everywhere', he recalled. 'Still very much in my mind was the presence of a media helicopter which almost came to grief with the overhead power lines on site, such was the density of the fog. Being so cold, I could not help but feel sorry for the Underwater Search Unit that I saw breaking up the surface ice on ponds as they entered them for their part of the search.'

One of the members of the Underwater Search and Recovery Team was former Royal Marine Ken Wright; the unit covered Essex, Suffolk, Norfolk and Hertfordshire and were equipped, as Wright told me, 'with basic diving suits and equipment, even our sole vehicle was an old police van, which had seen better days.' Abortive searches were carried out in freezing water, including a dive into a water tower near the farm. Ken German of the Met's Underwater Team tried unsuccessfully to do the same in the lake at Wimbledon Park, but the ice was too thick to permit an underwater search.

Dog handlers from Hertfordshire also attended, one of whom was John 'Jock' McNeil, whose photograph, complete with dog, was displayed in the *Sun* newspaper. Later, photographers – having been warned away from Rooks Farm – were seen snapping another farmhouse. When McNeil pointed out it was the wrong one, the photographer replied, 'I know that, you know that, these are for Australia – they won't know that!'

McNeil and Woman Police Constable Janice Parry (later Stephens) worked together at the farm, where one of their tasks was to answer the telephone first, to deflect calls from the press away from the family. In addition, Miss Parry's job was to amuse the children, then aged seven and eight. When Elsa Hosein made phone calls, they were usually in German. One day, the boy started to count in German and McNeil joined in: '*Eins, zwei, drei, vier, fünf . . .*' after which, Mrs Hosein made all her telephone calls in another room; she was not to know that counting to ten represented McNeil's total grasp of the German language.

Miss Parry's claim to fame (as she told me) was the following:

> One shift, Elsa was upset because the Aga cooker had burnt out so the house was cold and she had no idea how to light it. My parents had always had an Aga, so I offered to light it. Her delight soon turned to anger when the kitchen began to fill with smoke until I could damp it down again, and she stormed off. When I opened the cover at the base of the flue, we were faced with white pieces of what looked like bones, not black soot. I scooped the pieces into a tissue whilst 'Jock' looked on.
>
> Back at Hertford station, neither DCS Ron Harvey nor the two DIs Cyril Thomas and Lew Kirby were there, so I took my find back to my lodgings. The next day, I explained and showed Ron Harvey. Straight away, they organised for the Aga to be inspected by experts. It was dismantled, my find was tested and not found to be bone but what it was remained a puzzle and was never identified.

Police Constables Gary Purser and 527 Peter Ryan were members of Hertfordshire's Tactical Patrol Group who spent days searching the farm's pigpens. Ryan now recalls, 'wet days, mud and the isolated farm . . .', and Police Constable Tony Craighill from No. 2 Unit of the Met's Special Patrol Group was there slightly longer, 'issued with overalls, welly boots and with rakes and sticks' but had the same lack of success. 'It was cold and grotty work; pleased when we were withdrawn', he told me, adding, 'Anguilla was better!'[1] Those sentiments were echoed by fellow SPG officer Police Constable Trevor Wilson; the Anguillan temperature of 90° plus was a stark contrast to the freezing weather at Rooks Farm, and after three or four days hard work (wearing wellington boots 'that fitted if you were lucky') all that was found was some women's clothing which had obviously been discarded years before. But the SPG were nothing if not inventive; they found an unoccupied house for sale, in which the heating had been left on. A bottle of malt whisky was exchanged for keys with the estate agent, and food

---

1 This was a reference to 'Operation Sheepskin', when in March 1969, British troops and a contingent of the SPG were sent to the Caribbean island of Anguilla as a peace-keeping force, following civil insurrection.

procured from the local butchers and bakers was consumed in comfort.

But although the searches continued for weeks, then months as fresh information arrived, no trace of Mrs McKay was found – not in the house, the Volvo, the eleven acres of ground or anywhere else.

The Hosein brothers were first taken to Wimbledon, then to Kingston-upon-Thames police station for further interviews; but before we see what was said and what evidence accrued, the background of the murderous brothers who ludicrously purported to be members of the British branch of the Cosa Nostra should be examined.

Chapter 16

Background to Two Murderers

The community of Dow village, within the borders of Couva-Tabaquite-Talparo on the Caribbean island of Trinidad, is populated mainly by people of Indian origin who annually celebrate a religious play entitled 'Ram-Leela'. Until recently, Caroni (1975) Ltd's Brechin Castle sugar factory provided employment to many of the local inhabitants.

But not all. Shaffie Hosein was a successful tailor, as well as being an elder at the local mosque, and he and his wife Siffiran, living in a four-bedroom timber-framed house in Railway Road, raised a family of seven children strictly according to the teachings of the Koran.

Arthur Hosein was born on 18 August 1936 and grew into an extremely boastful, attention-seeking character but also a very hard worker. He attended the local commercial college before turning to his father's trade of tailoring, displaying quite a talent for the work.

In 1955 he decided to move to England, where he had one or two fairly lacklustre, poorly paid jobs before returning to his original trade of tailoring. Renting a room in Mare Street, Hackney, he rapidly achieved success working as a cutter for some of the district's tradesmen. Soon he was earning £100 per week and was ostentatiously buying drinks for often complete strangers in the area's pubs, usually with £10 notes. That, coupled with his boastfulness, earned him the soubriquet 'Nutty Arthur'.

Called up for National Service, his army career in the Royal Pioneer Corps was nowhere near as successful as that in the tailoring trade, and after continually being rude, insubordinate and absent without leave, Private 23623918 Hosein was charged with desertion and sentenced to six months' imprisonment in the glasshouse – the military prison at Aldershot – an institution which was nowhere near as comfortable as its civilian counterparts. 'He was immeasurably the worst soldier it has been my misfortune to have under me . . . that is, when he wasn't absent or in detention', commented his commanding officer, and Arthur was dragged off to the cells shouting, 'Watch how you go with me – I'll be worth a million one day!'

Before his dishonourable discharge Arthur, then aged twenty-three, had met Elsa Fischer, a German woman some ten years older. She had been married to a British serviceman, but once her divorce came through, she and Arthur married. He returned to the tailoring trade and moved into an upstairs shop in Kingsland High Street in London's East End. The couple settled in Marden Ash, Ongar, Essex in a semi-detached house called 'Longfields' which was purchased for £3,750 in 1965 and had two children, a daughter Fareed and a son Rudeen.

Two years later, the house was sold at a profit of £625 and, putting down £5,500, Arthur obtained a mortgage of £9,000 from the Halifax Building Society and purchased for £14,500 what he described as 'his country estate'. The seventeenth century Rooks Farm stood in eleven acres of grounds in a village of 170 residents at Stocking Pelham, Hertfordshire.

One of the farm's outhouses was converted into a tailor's workshop and now, with dreams of opening a shop in trendy Carnaby Street, Arthur was on a high; his mortgage of £75 per month and hire-purchase payments of £38 per month on the Volvo could easily be managed on his weekly income of £150 – good earnings in those days. By way of comparison, a police constable's weekly wage at that time was £17 12s 8d.

Meanwhile, back in Dow village, the youngest of Shaffie's family, Nizamodeen, had been born on 1 July 1948. He appeared the complete opposite of his elder brother Arthur, whom he looked up to; slack-jawed, with an almost oriental slant to his eyes, Nizam appeared depressed and shiftless. He also had a propensity for violence; in December 1967 he attacked his brother Charles with a knife, inflicting serious stomach wounds, and on 3 January 1968 he was placed on probation in the care of his parents. Some fifteen months later, he was charged with assault and battery on his father; on 14 May 1969, the case was not proceeded with, but his mother entered into a recognizance of 150 Trinidadian dollars as a surety for her son's good behaviour for three years, and his probation was renewed.

In May 1969, Nizam arrived in England to study accountancy and initially lived with his brother Adam, in Thornton Heath, Surrey. Three months later, he went to live at Rooks Farm.

Arthur's grandiose plans were expanding; he would employ twenty girls from Bishop's Stortford, bussing them in to the farm every day to work on the fine raiment which would soon launch him into millionaire status, just as he had predicted to an incredulous Court Martial several years previously. In addition, he would use the three piggeries to raise pigs, ten at first but then twenty and thirty more; he also purchased calves and chickens.

There were two pubs in the village, The Cock and The Raven; Arthur frequented both, buying drinks for all and sundry, but the denizens of Stocking Pelham, unlike their counterparts in Hackney, were less tolerant of the brazen boasting of a man of colour. Telling them he wanted to be 'a snob – the greatest snob ever', he revealed his lack of comprehension of English colloquialisms. What he actually aspired to was to be regarded as a 'nob' – the diminutive of 'nobility'. Diminutive or not, 'a (k)nob' was precisely how Arthur was regarded by many of the inhabitants of Stocking Pelham.

Known locally as 'King Hosein', some of his drinks were refused and others were spat into; and his plans to turn Stocking Pelham into a rural economic miracle were seriously frowned on by those who lived in the area and wanted to keep its rustic charm exactly as it was. And so, when he applied to have the outbuilding at Rooks Farm turned into a factory, the planning officers at Bishop's Stortford turned him down flat; it would, they said, ruin the amenities of the village.

What was more, the pig experiment was floundering; the brothers had no idea of how to care for the livestock, and the pigs became undernourished and ill. Arthur's income dropped to £100 per week.

His behaviour became more and more irrational; he still bought drinks but he also started getting into violent arguments with residents of the village, reporting them to the police and threatening lawsuits, before making fawning apologies.

Nizam's six-month visitor's permit would soon be running out. He applied to join the RAF at Norbury, Middlesex but decided to turn up for the interview with lank hair and dressed in dirty jeans and an equally grubby T-shirt and plimsolls. Having given insolent answers to the board, he was unsurprisingly rejected, whereupon he accused them of being racially prejudiced. It was an early example of playing the race card; one that Arthur wholeheartedly endorsed, too.

The two brothers still visited the local pubs; Arthur, cocky, ebullient, saying that he had £750,000 in the bank and that the Indian Prime Minister had been coming to stay at Rooks Farm for the weekend but had been forced to cancel at the last moment, and Nizam silent, sulky, usually sitting in the corner, saying little. Nizam was often seen in the village wearing a blue steel helmet together with a long, leather coat, sometimes with the snarling Alsatians, Rex and Reggie, and he told one bemused resident that he worked for a Trinidad security company.

And then on the evening of 3 October 1969, the brothers sat down to watch *The David Frost Show* on television; on it they saw the very wealthy Rupert Murdoch and his beautiful wife, and the germ of a get-rich-quick scheme was hatched . . .

Ideas were dreamed up, improved upon, then discarded and reassessed, until their plans took an immense step forward. On 13 December 1969, Elsa Hosein, the two children and the Hoseins' sister Haffiza, who was staying at the farm, decided to go to Germany to spend Christmas with Elsa's parents and to return on 3 January 1970.

The next step for the brothers was to find Murdoch's home address; nothing was found in the telephone directory, from directory enquiries or in Kelly's Street Directory, so the *News of the World*'s offices were visited and the Rolls-Royce was spotted; that was followed by the enquiry at the Greater London Council's offices to discover the car's owner. Then it was a matter of following the Rolls to Wimbledon, where the brothers believed that the Murdochs lived.

Shortly after arriving in England, Nizam had met pretty, 27-year-old Mrs Liley Mohammed, a divorced Trinidadian nurse. In fact, she was already known to Arthur, since back in Trinidad, her sister was the mother of Arthur's illegitimate son. On Christmas night, Nizam telephoned her, inviting her to spend Boxing Day at Rooks Farm, an invitation she accepted. She brought with her the six paper flowers made from tissues and paperclips which would later be found at Danes End, at Rooks Farm and inside the Volvo. Shortly afterwards, the two brothers came to blows over her, and Nizam was so badly beaten up that he telephoned the police. Liley, terrified, left the following morning.

At about the same time, Alick and Muriel McKay returned to St Mary House, having spent the Christmas with their daughters and grandchildren; now Mrs McKay could focus on the planned trip to Australia in the New Year to visit their son.

On the morning of 28 December, the farm received two visits from the police. One was from Detective Sergeant Gerald Sommerville and Detective Constable Graham in respect of an allegation of assault on Sunday, 21 December, when two men, one white, one black, had attacked an elderly white farmer. It was on that date that M3 had made two telephone calls to Ian McKay. The officers left saying they might have to return, and they did, on 5 January.

The other visitor was Police Constable Dick Felton, in response to Nizam's allegation of assault by Arthur, but this case appears to have petered out.

That evening, apparently reconciled, the brothers were drinking in the Plough public house at Great Munden, Hertfordshire. Arthur was in his most expansive, bragging mood, telling a fellow customer that the Ghanaian ambassador and the Trinidadian High Commissioner had been due to attend a Boxing Day party at Rooks Farm; regrettably, it had had to be cancelled due to his wife going to Germany. He had also been invited to a dinner party at the house of Rupert Murdoch but had been compelled to refuse.

Precisely what happened at St Mary House on 29 December 1969 will probably never be made known; suffice it to say that a terrified, middle-aged woman, 5 feet 9 inches tall, with dark brown hair, was abducted, having been mistaken for a blonde woman some thirty years her junior by two out-of-control, obsessional, egotistic and greedy brothers.

Liley Mohammed telephoned Rooks Farm that evening to make a date with Nizam. There was no answer at 8.00 pm or 9.00 pm. At 10.30 pm Arthur answered. Nizam, he said, was out.

With the search for Mrs McKay well underway, Elsa Hosein returned from Germany and Arthur met her at Liverpool Street station. It appeared that his behaviour was becoming more erratic. When his car was stopped by police during a routine search, he flew into a rage and demanded action from his solicitor. He demanded that Elsa leave the farm (she did not); the brothers would often go out in the evenings and when they were at the farm they would engage in whispering sessions.

Chapter 17

Interviews

And now both brothers were under arrest. Their fingerprints were taken, and Arthur's matched prints found on the ransom notes, envelopes, the cigarette packet and the discarded *People* newspaper. Let me make it quite clear; fingerprinting is a precise science that leaves no room for manoeuvre. In circumstances such as these, it is never a case of someone at the Fingerprint Branch giving the prints a cursory glance, then dismissively saying, 'Yeah, that's him.' In my experience, when a suspect is in custody, prints are checked and checked again, not by one expert but by several, with the officer in the case taking periodic telephone calls from the Yard: 'Have you still got him? Good – keep him there!'

The interviews were now underway. Arthur was shown the paper flowers and said, 'I've never seen the flowers before.' Next, the lined paper from Nizam's bedroom: 'I've never seen paper like that before; I never do my own correspondence. As it was in Nizam's bedroom, you'd better ask him.'

Arthur refused to sign his interview notes; then it was Nizam's turn, who was asked by Jim Parker where he was on 29 December, whereupon he started to tremble and shake his head.

'Where did Arthur say I was? I was with my brother Arthur.'

'Did you go to Wimbledon?'

No reply.

'What's the matter?'

'I want to die – let me die!'

'What's troubling you?'

'My brother Arthur will kill me. He beats me.'

'Why should he kill you?'

'I can't speak – I mustn't speak – let me see Arthur!'

With that, Nizam began to bang his head on the edge of the table and was restrained by Parker. 'Why don't you kill me?' sobbed Nizam.

Minors, probably less tolerant than the avuncular Parker, snapped, 'Don't be ridiculous!'

The following day, there were more questions, with Smith asking Nizam about his movements on 1 February when the first ransom drop was made and getting the response, 'When can I speak to Arthur? What has he said? Has he blamed me for something?'

'Wimbledon?'

'I don't know the names of places.'

'Were you there with Arthur?'

'No. Not Wimbledon.'

'If you don't know the names of places, how do you know you weren't there?'

It appeared there had been a row between the brothers, that night. Arthur had told Nizam to go into a pub to get some cigarettes; instead, Nizam stayed for a drink and Arthur subsequently hit him.

Shown the flowers from Danes End, Nizam started shaking once more: 'Let me die! I want to die!'

In contrast to the previous snivelling heap of humanity, Arthur was quite self-possessed in the interview room with Chief Superintendent Smith, saying, 'I want to help you all I can. I realise you have a very difficult case.'

Arthur agreed to provide a sample of his handwriting, as did Nizam. Shown the billhook from St Mary House, Arthur stated, 'It's like the one I borrowed from George to chop up the calf.' Asked if he wrote letters to Alick McKay, Arthur replied, 'No. I don't write letters to anyone.'

Nizam was asked once more about his movements on the night of 6 February, the second ransom drop. He provided a list of names and addresses that he and Arthur visited in London, finishing at about 7 o'clock, after which he had a date with a girl named Susan – a girl who it was later proved did not exist. After that, he drove to a pub named The Raven, where he saw Arthur. Arthur said he wanted to drive to Bishop's Stortford, which they did in the Volvo; they did nothing there, and went home.

But shown the billhook, the sticking plaster and the baler twine from St Mary House, there came the almost expected trembling and head-shaking, and the wailing, 'Let me die!'

Arthur was once more at his most urbane: 'That's all right, Mr Smith. You have a very difficult case and I am genuinely sorry for you', but then his and Nizam's stories began to diverge; Arthur said that after they had finished delivering clothes to tailors in London at 4.30 pm, they went to Bishop's Stortford, where he let Nizam have the Volvo while he took a taxi to The Raven. This was pointed out to him by Smith, who said, 'Nizam has told me he met you in the Raven and you asked him to take you to Bishop's Stortford.'

This produced an immediate change to Arthur's smooth, faux-helpful line of patter: 'Nizam's a fool to have told you that – we did not go!'

Now Smith told Arthur that his fingerprints had been found on those incriminating pieces of evidence: 'That's impossible!' he retorted. 'You're just trying to trick me, Mr Smith.'

Smith also suggested not only that Arthur had written the ransom notes to Alick McKay but that when he provided his handwriting samples he had deliberately attempted to disguise them – all of which was denied.

Arthur had already spoken on a telephone to the McKay household, where the calls were tape recorded so that a comparison might be made between his voice and that of M3 – he did so willingly, since he had not made any of those eighteen calls to St Mary House. But Nizamodeen reacted differently: 'It's a trick! Has Arthur done it? I don't believe it – I don't want to do it!'

He had already been shown the cut pieces of material from Mrs McKay's clothing and cried, 'Let me die! Let me die! Why don't I die?' When asked why he was behaving in such a fashion and more importantly, whether Mrs McKay was dead, he refused to answer. The same applied when David Coote, a solicitor acting for the brothers – who could obviously see which way the wind was blowing – told him, 'If there is a possibility that Mrs McKay is alive and if you have any knowledge of where she is, then you must tell the officers.' The solicitor met with the same lack of success as the police.

While the brothers were in custody, Minors instructed junior officers to spend the night in the cells with the prisoners. This was normal procedure, and its purpose was twofold: (a) to prevent the detainees from harming themselves, and (b) to record any incriminating statement they might make.

Steve Williams was a temporary detective constable at Wimbledon tasked with such a duty; he told me:

> Switching between cells throughout their stay and engaged in playing cards and conversation, at the end of each shift I was to record as much detail about the conversation, then hand my record to DI Minors. Arthur was very engaging but his brother was quiet and reserved. Arthur continually protested his innocence and was convinced he would be acquitted. He talked openly about his pig farm and the oven . . . his last words to me before he was remanded in custody were, 'My pigs are very tasty.'

Still the search of the countryside around Rooks Farm continued; the area expanded to cover 25 acres, with 200 officers employed. At one time the Hoseins had kept seven Wessex Saddleback pigs; by the time the police went to the farm, four of the animals had been sold, leaving a boar and two sows. By now, speculation was growing that Mrs McKay had been killed and fed to the pigs; and if that were so, there might well be traces of cortisone (which Mrs McKay had been taking as medication) in their bones. But although the sold-off animals were traced, they had since been slaughtered.

The brothers had now been in custody for four days, and the press speculation was becoming ever more insistent, and more worrying. There were now stories appearing in the press regarding the forged currency on the drops, as well as the paper flowers (it appeared that once again someone had been inappropriately blabbing), and if there was much more of this it could prejudice any trial the brothers might face.

On 10 February, Arthur and Nizam Hosein were taken back to Wimbledon police station, where both of them were charged with firstly, murdering Muriel McKay between 29 December 1969 and 7 February 1970, and secondly, making an unwarranted demand from Alick McKay of £1,000,000 for the safe return of his wife.

Dave Bowen took the antecedents of both brothers and told me, 'Without doubt, Arthur Hosein appeared to be the brains behind the kidnapping and murder, but Nizamodeen, who was about eleven years younger, appeared to me to be the more "criminal, evil-minded" type . . . Arthur Hosein at the time was quite relaxed and calm when I was speaking to him, whereas Nizamodeen was "up-tight" and "nasty".'

The next step, the following day, was Wimbledon Magistrates' Court, where the brothers were remanded in custody to Brixton prison. This was the first in a series of seventeen remand hearings at the Magistrates' Court.

There was no let-up in the police investigations. Obviously, they wanted to discover the whereabouts of Mrs McKay's body, but they also wanted to trace her missing jewellery and hopefully connect the brothers with it. Whilst they would be unsuccessful in both quests they were nevertheless cobbling together a strong case for the prosecution, and no details seemed to be too small. For instance, they found that each Sunday the brothers took the *People* newspaper, a discarded copy of which (containing Arthur's palm print) had been found at St Mary House. Had it been brought to conceal the billhook? Quite possibly. Then there was the sighting of the Volvo by the motorist prior to the abduction in Wimbledon. Even though he might not be able to identify the occupants, it was still a useful piece of circumstantial evidence.

More convincing was the existence of the Hoseins' brother Adam, who lived in Thornton Heath, approximately five miles from Wimbledon. Was it possible that Mrs McKay had been taken there on the night of the kidnapping? It was known that Nizam had gone there that night, and what was more, he paid off a debt of £3 10s 0d. What was unusual was that the money was peeled off a roll of notes, for Nizam seldom had any money of his own; Arthur paid him pocket money to look after the pigs. Did that money come from Mrs McKay's handbag, which had contained approximately £25? It was also known that on the same night Nizam had called upon his cousin Shuffi Ali, whose address he had used when making enquiries regarding the Rolls-Royce – and he lived in Norbury, a stone's throw from Wimbledon. Both properties were searched, but whatever suspicions the investigators might have had, the fact remained that neither Adam Hosein nor Shuffi Ali could be connected with the crime.

But when Adam visited Nizam at Brixton prison on 13 March, a prison officer saw Nizam hold up a piece of paper against the window which separates prisoner from visitor. It was seized, and the note read:

> Do not say anything to no-one, not even solicitor, that I was by you on Monday night. Two farmers are saying that Arthur was down there by them that day and at 6.30 pm I was home.

'Monday night' referred to the day of the kidnap, 29 December. It certainly appeared to put Nizam in the Wimbledon area at the time of the offence.

Still the remand appearances dragged on; the brothers were separated at Brixton after Arthur beat Nizam up during an exercise period, but it did not stop Arthur getting messages through to his brother telling him what, and more specifically, what *not* to say.

On the evening before their committal to the Old Bailey, Nizam asked to see Smith and Minors at Wimbledon police station. Was he going to impart pertinent information that would perhaps alleviate the pressure the McKay family were under, or assist the police and ultimately himself? But no; there was the usual blubbering, to such an extent that a doctor was called, and when he was interviewed a week later, again in the presence of his lawyers, and shown items cut from Mrs McKay's clothing and the billhook, the result was the same. 'Let me die, let me die', he wailed, and by now, in all probability, the detectives and his lawyers were wishing he would.

Charged the following day with the offences for which they would stand trial, Arthur replied, 'I am innocent of all these charges. All those charges are false.' Nizam's answer was, 'I know nothing about these charges.'

With the brothers back in Brixton, still the enquiries continued. Rooks Farm was searched again. As well as the Aga, the fire grates were examined. And although reports were coming into the police, many of them bizarre, there was one piece of information which was quite chilling.

It came from a woman who lived in the Stocking Pelham district, about a mile and a half from Rooks Farm, and what she told the police was this. Around 1 January her dog had started to howl as it sat on her lawn. The dog was an unusual breed, a Catahoula Leopard Dog, an alert watchdog used mainly in Louisiana for hog and cattle minding, and it had an acute sense of smell. Going outside to discover the cause of the dog's howling, she detected an odour coming from the direction of Rooks Farm; she said it was reminiscent of the smell one associates with a crematorium. It was also about that time that another witness had stated there had been the sound of a gunshot from the direction of the farm.

Just as interesting was information from Police Constable John Wright, who was then attached to Stoke Newington police station. He frequented a barber at Glading Terrace, N16 who stated that he was a refugee from Tito's Yugoslavia. This address was in the vicinity of both Mare Street, Hackney and Kingsland High Street, where Arthur Hosein had had tailoring shops. Wright takes up the tale:

> Round about the time when Mrs McKay's disappearance was top of the news, I went for my monthly cut. The barber told me that some time before the disappearance, two men he described as of Indian appearance had approached him in the shop and asked if he knew of anywhere they could rent where they could store something on the QT. It was obvious that the barber was concerned about this and on my return to Stoke Newington, I informed the incident room.

It was sufficient for Detective Chief Superintendent Ron Harvey to pay a visit and, accompanied by a local officer, make a tour of the area to see of any likely boltholes might be found; again, without success.

CHAPTER 18

The Trial – the Case for the Prosecution

The trial commenced in No.1 Court at the Old Bailey on 14 September 1970.

The prosecution was led by the Attorney General, Sir Peter Rawlinson QC, MP. Born in 1919, Sir Peter had served with the Irish Guards in 1940, had been wounded and Mentioned in Dispatches in 1943. Demobilized in 1946 with the rank of major, he resumed his legal studies and was called to the bar. He was one of the junior counsel prosecuting in the case of Ruth Ellis, who in 1955 was the last woman in Britain to hang for murder. He was appointed Solicitor General in 1962 and Attorney General in 1970.

He was assisted by Mr E. J. P. Cussen, who as Major Cussen had served with MI5 during the Second World War and was now Senior Treasury Counsel. Brian Leary, who had been called to the bar in 1953, appeared as Junior Treasury Counsel.

Mr W. M. F. 'Barry' Hudson QC, who had defended in the trial of the three men accused of shooting the three murdered members of the Q-Car 'Foxtrot One-One' and also in the Kray brothers' trial, appeared for Arthur Hosein, assisted by Mr Hubert Dunn.

Nizamodeen Hosein was defended by Mr Douglas P. Draycott QC, assisted by Mr Leonard Woodley.

The Judge was the charismatic 63-year-old Sir Sebag Shaw, who had been a superb advocate as a prosecutor and of whom it was said, 'There is no one today at the Bar who could match his command of simple descriptive language or his flow of eloquence and charm.' He had been appointed Queen's Counsel in 1967 and a High Court Judge a year later. Like the Attorney General, he had been a junior counsel in the case of Ruth Ellis.

The brothers were brought up to the dock to hear the Clerk of the Assize read the seven charges against them: that between 29 December 1969 and 7 February 1970 they murdered Mrs Muriel McKay; that on 29 December 1969 they stole and unlawfully carried away Mrs McKay against her will; that between

29 December 1969 and 7 February 1970 they assaulted and imprisoned Mrs Muriel McKay against her will in some secret place; that on 21 and 26 January 1970 they sent unwarranted demands for £1,000,000 with menaces; that on 21 and 26 January 1970 they sent letters to Mr McKay threatening to murder Mrs McKay.

To all these charges, the jury of nine men and three women heard both brothers plead not guilty.

The Attorney General, the country's leading lawyer, briefed by the Director of Public Prosecutions (who was also in court), outlined the case for the prosecution to the jury. He was compelling. He took his time – 5½ hours – over it and he finished with one inescapable fact in respect of St Mary House: 'Altogether, there were eighteen telephone calls and five letters. Since the day before the police came to Rooks Farm, there has been complete and utter silence from M3.'

With that, the witnesses would be called to give their evidence for the prosecution; but before this could happen, something astonishing occurred.

* * *

It does not happen very often. Seldom during a criminal trial does the defendant make an admission, for his defence will have been carefully cooked up weeks before. In fact, it happened only once in one of my trials, when an armed robber got caught out during some scintillating cross-examination by Michael Stuart Moore QC and was obliged to admit perjury in his testimony.

But it was different in the trial of the Hosein brothers. Nizamodeen Hosein made not one admission but seven – and that was right at the commencement of the trial, before any of the evidence had been heard.

Telling the Judge 'that the admissions do not involve any knowledge of, or intention to commit the offences in the indictment', Douglas Draycott outlined the admissions from Nizamodeen as follows:

1. That he made the application on 19 December 1969 to the Greater London Council.
2. That on 1 February 1970, he placed two paper flowers where they were subsequently found by police near the junction of Dane End and the Cambridge Road.

3. On 6 February 1970 at about 8.00 pm he drove the Volvo, XGO 994G, to Gates Used Cars; that he did so in order to look for two suitcases, that he drove around and waited for about an hour, that he saw the two white suitcases on the pavement, opposite the Minivan.
4. On 6 February 1970 he drove the Volvo to The Raven public house, arriving at about 10.00 pm.
5. At 10.47 pm on 6 February 1970 he returned in the Volvo to Gates Used Cars.
6. That the note (Exhibit 83), the small note referring to the Minivan, is in his handwriting.
7. That the note found by the prison officer when he was searched is in his handwriting.

Mr Hudson for Arthur Hosein immediately objected, saying there was one item in respect of his client that he was not prepared to admit; but as the Judge pointed out, one accused cannot prevent another from making admissions.

Well! Until now, one would have thought the brothers would offer a joint defence – basically, that they knew nothing about anything – but not any longer. It appeared that there was going to be what is colloquially known as 'a cut-throat defence', with each accused blaming the other.

When Alick McKay gave his evidence of returning to the empty house at 20 Arthur Road on 29 December, it appeared that both the Judge and Mr Draycott wished to spare him unnecessary distress, although Mr Hudson was keen to establish that there had been a number of false leads, misleading information and people attempting to extort money from him.

Other members of the McKay family gave their distressing evidence, as did detectives on the ransom drops.

Mr Rosenthal was a witness in the tailoring business who had arrived at the farm following Elsa Hosein's return from Germany but prior to the arrests. He had left a packet of Piccadilly cigarettes there, and the imputation was that it was that packet which had been found in the telephone box giving Sergeant Street instructions and which bore Arthur Hosein's left-hand thumb-print. Mr Hudson challenged Mr Rosenthal on his evidence, saying that he had gone to deliver goods, not receive them; it turned quite acrimonious, with Hudson suggesting that Rosenthal was a liar and Rosenthal retorting, 'I was there and you weren't.' An invoice dated 9 February was produced by the defence, with Hudson suggesting that Rosenthal had been telephoning Mrs Hosein for payment; but the matter appeared to be resolved after the Judge noticed the word 'verbal' written on the invoice which suggested that an order had been given over the telephone. In fact, the case did not turn one way or another on whether the items were delivered or collected.

Detective Chief Inspector Brine gave evidence about comparing Arthur Hosein's fingerprints with marks found on the various incriminating documents, saying that eight similar characteristics were 'satisfactory', ten were 'good' and eighteen 'beyond doubt'. He had found sixteen characteristics to compare with Arthur's fingerprints; Mr Hudson suggested that there were only six.

Re-examined by the Attorney General, Brine, who had twenty-two years' experience in the Yard's Fingerprint Department, stated that he assessed thousands of fingerprints in a month, and the Attorney General asked if the chief inspector ever speculated in his judgement?

'No.'

'Are you satisfied?'

'Yes.'

'By what standards?' asked the Judge.

'I'm sure of it', replied Brine.

Asked if there were any points that could be challenged, the chief inspector answered decisively, 'No.'

The detectives who had seen two men in the Volvo on the final night of the observations were questioned, with some hostility in the case of Jack Quarrie who had unhesitatingly identified Arthur; but Quarrie was quite sure his identification was 100 per cent accurate.

There was evidence from the licensee of The Raven public house and his wife who said that Arthur had entered the pub at about 7.00 pm, that at 10.00 pm, Nizam had arrived, and that they stayed until approximately 10.30 pm. Arthur had gone to the pub's toilet twice, at about 7.30 and 9.30 pm, and after Nizam's appearance, had asked for six pennies in his change. The inference was that he wanted to use the telephone kiosk which was about 100 yards away from the pub and was of the old-fashioned kind which required pennies. This was denied, although the question was academic; no other telephone calls were made by M3 that night, although the suggestion mooted was that Arthur required the pennies in case a further call had to be made.

Mrs McKay's GP was called to say that she was in good health; this was to obviate any suggestion that she might have died not at the hands of her kidnappers but as the result of shock or exposure.

DI Minors was called to say that when he received the telephone call at Church Street, Tottenham in his guise as Alick McKay, the voice on the telephone sounded 'very similar' to the voice he had heard on the tape recordings at St Mary House.

He was led through the interviews at Kingston police station, and then there was the odd interview on the eve of the committal proceedings on 12 June which Nizam had requested with the detectives, without the presence of his solicitors.

'Is anyone stopping Liley from seeing me?' he had asked. 'Has my brother Adam told her not to? Could I speak to her? . . . I could get out of 90 per cent of this trouble if I put my cards on the table.'

'What do you want to tell us?' DCS Smith had asked.

There had been a silence. Then – 'I want to think . . . I'll leave it to another day.'

This led Mr Draycott smoothly into cross-examining Minors about that impromptu interview: 'He was on the brink of telling you something? He wanted to, but something held him back?'

'We felt it did.'

'Many times during the interview, he showed marked signs of feeling afraid, did he not?'

'Yes.'

'He was certainly afraid?'

'Yes.'

'Very distressed?'

'Yes. We called for a doctor.'

'What seemed to be hold him back was fear?'

'Fear, sir.'

'Would you agree with me that, having seen these two brothers over a long period, it is abundantly clear, abundantly plain, that Nizam's relationship with his brother is unusual, in that it is not based on brotherly affection, but fear?'

'That would appear to be the case.'

And having established that no trace of Nizam's fingerprints was found at St Mary House, Mr Draycott sat down.

Now Mr Hudson stood up. He suggested that at the farm the police did not mention Mrs McKay to Arthur; Minors replied that they did. Concerning the matter of Minors giving evidence of having shown Arthur the sheets of paper from Nizam's bedroom to which Arthur had replied, 'I've never seen the paper before. You must ask Nizam', Hudson suggested that Arthur had told Minors that he had used the paper to write to Ipswich County Court.

'Absolutely incorrect', replied Minors.

When Wimbledon had been mentioned to Arthur, he had replied, according to the police, 'Where is Wimbledon?' This was denied by Hudson, who suggested that Arthur had said he had been dog-racing there.

'I think he made a reference to dog-racing', admitted Minors, adding, 'I have a feeling he mentioned Clapton.'

One last question before Hudson sat down; did DCS Smith slap Arthur across the face? 'That's news to me, sir', replied Minors.

Draycott had no questions for DCS Smith, and although Hudson questioned him about the various searches of Rooks Farm and the surrounding countryside, he saved his big one up to last: 'I now put this to you personally. I suggest that during some parts of the investigation at Kingston police station you punched Arthur Hosein and slapped him across the face.'

'That', replied Smith, 'is not true.'

An important witness was farmer Leonard Smith; prior to the kidnap, he had conveyed purchases in his truck to the brothers at the farm; he left behind his spare wheel and the billhook (Farmer Smith insisted it should be called a 'bill'), which he positively identified as his, saying, 'It's nothing near as sharp as it was when I lost it.' The brothers later returned the spare wheel but not the billhook (or 'bill'), which was the one found at 20 Arthur Road.

Liley Mohammed told of how she stayed at Rooks Farm on the night of 26 December, that there had been a fight between the two brothers and that Nizam had called the police. She telephoned Rooks Farm several times on the evening of 29 December, finally speaking to Arthur at 10.30 pm. She did speak to Nizam the following day, and then on 31 December she saw both brothers in the Volvo in London and they persuaded her to go to the farm, where she stayed until 2 January, preparing meals for them. Liley mentioned that Nizam left the farm on the afternoon of 1 January, apparently to get something for a stomach-ache. However, it was during the early evening that two calls were made to Diane Dyer, by M3. In re-examination, all Liley could say was that the nearest time for Nizam's absence she could give was between 2.00 and 6.00 pm. There was the matter of the paper flowers given by her to Nizam and the chopped-up calf; she also felt free to go wherever she liked on the farm and did not get the impression that the brothers had anything to hide.

A Principal Scientific Officer from the Metropolitan Police Forensic Science Laboratory, Mr Fryd, was called as a handwriting expert. He had already correctly identified Nizam as having written the application at the Greater London Council, as well as the note at Brixton; following the seven admissions, these were matters which were not now in dispute.

Asked if Nizam might have written the ransom notes, Mr Fryd dismissed this as 'bordering on the ludicrous'. But as for Arthur having written them, Mr Fryd's opinion was that 'there was a considerable probability that he did'.

'I'm not likely to get you to change your opinion', commented Mr Hudson, and this was skilfully countered by Mr Fryd when he replied, 'I'd change it if I saw cause to.'

That was the case for the prosecution; and in the absence of the jury, both defence counsel submitted that the murder charge should go no further and should not be put before the jury; the Judge disagreed.

Chapter 19

Arthur Hosein's Defence

Opening the case for the defence, Mr Hudson told the jury, 'Arthur Hosein's defence is that he had nothing to do with this dreadful crime at all.'

Called into the witness box, Arthur appeared to be wearing a dinner suit with a waistcoat, an evening-dress-style shirt and a black bow tie. What he had to say was that on 29 December he was at the farm when Nizam told him there was a telephone call from his solicitor, David Coote; the same Mr Coote who later exhorted the brothers, at the police station, to tell the police if they had any knowledge of Mrs McKay's whereabouts. The call came in, said Arthur, at between 5.15 and 5.30 pm. If that was the case, it was a perfect alibi. There was no way that the brothers could have driven to Wimbledon in that time to kidnap Mrs McKay.

When Arthur gave that evidence, Mr Coote was present in No.1 Court – but the fact remains, he never gave evidence in the case. Why? If the claim was true, it was the perfect defence; it would have led to the case being stopped and the brothers undoubtedly freed. If it was true . . .

This was the first time Arthur had mentioned the alleged telephone call from Mr Coote. Had he mentioned it during his interview at the police station, there is no doubt a statement would have been obtained from Mr Coote by the police to verify the claim. Furthermore, no notice of alibi was served on the prosecution by the defence naming him as a witness – not before, during, or after the seventeen weeks of remands at the Magistrates' Court. That, of course, was when Mr Coote was representing Arthur. His name could hardly have slipped Arthur's mind. When an air-rifle and pellets were found during the search at Rook's Farm, Arthur explained that they belonged to his friend, Mr Coote – over the previous six months, he and his girlfriend had visited him at the farm. And as the brothers were leaving the farm under arrest, en route to Wimbledon police station, Arthur asked, 'Can I inform my friend and solicitor, Mr David Coote? He and his girlfriend come here for the weekend.' Mr Coote was informed; but the telephone call was never mentioned by or to him.

Arthur did mention four mysterious men – one British, one American and two French – who arrived at the farm on several occasions at between half-past one and two o'clock in the morning before and after Christmas and were there to help Nizam stay permanently in the United Kingdom. He would have told DCS Smith about this, said Arthur, had not Smith treated him so badly.

Dealing with the events of 1 February, Arthur said that during Rosenthal's visit he accepted a Piccadilly cigarette from him, leaving the packet on the bar in the lounge; and then he and Nizam left to go to the finishers.

Now there was the call to Ian McKay at St Mary House at 7.55 pm. After that there were the calls to the telephone kiosks at 9.55 pm and 10.45 pm (these were received by the detective purporting to be Ian), and that was followed by the sighting at midnight of the Volvo (although not of its registration number) containing two men.

According to Arthur, he and Nizam had left Hackney Wick at about 7.50 pm, and that was followed by a row between the brothers after Arthur had sent Nizam into a pub to buy some cigarettes. He had left to find his own way home; he, Arthur, had returned to Rooks Farm at 9.15, and his wife had told him that Rosenthal had left a quarter of an hour earlier. Nizam returned at midnight, soaking wet through, having apparently hitchhiked home. Arthur did not want to question his younger brother 'for fear of provoking him'. So the important point was that – according to Arthur – the Volvo was at Rooks Farm from 9.15 pm onwards; and if that were true, whichever Volvo Tony Stevens and Bill O'Hara saw at midnight, it could not have been the Hoseins'. If it was true . . .

On the night of the second ransom drop, when M3 made telephone calls to the kiosks in Church Street at 4.45 pm, Bethnal Green at 6.00 pm and Epping at 7.30 pm, Arthur stated that he and Nizam were at a tailor's in Bethnal Green at 4.30 pm and left half an hour later. On the way back, Arthur said that Nizam wanted to see a girlfriend in Bishop's Stortford; he had therefore let him have the Volvo and caught a taxi to The Raven public house, arriving there – 'I shall remember it to my dying day!' – between 7.00 and 7.05 pm. Nizam arrived at the pub at approximately 10.00 pm, and twenty minutes later, drove Arthur home. Although he had consumed, by his own reckoning, ten or eleven double scotches, Arthur remembered the time quite explicitly: 'I have to! I believe it is essential – my life depends on it!'

Matters were beginning to hot up in the witness box. Did a police officer identify him at the farm as being in the Volvo the previous night? 'No!' Or at the police station? 'No, no!' The matter of the box of elastoplast found at the farm was brought up.

'This was planted, after my arrest!'

'Chief Superintendent Smith asked, "Have you ever been in Wimbledon?"' said Mr Hudson. 'And you said, "Where is Wimbledon?"'

'I'm an NGR member! I own greyhounds! I've taken greyhounds to Wimbledon!'

'Mr Smith asked you about reading the newspapers and watching TV. You said, "I never watch TV and never read newspapers".'

'Those are the police's own words! It is an example of the vindictiveness of the police, indicative of the cruel way they work!' He then addressed the Judge: 'I hope my Lord is aware of these things!'

Back to Mr Hudson, who before being interrupted said, 'Did you say to the police, "I want to help you all I can? I realise that you have . . . "'

'I have cooperated in every way with the police and I've been very badly treated by them! Tortured mentally and physically! Smith beat the hell out of me while under the influence of drink! He had a bottle of scotch in front of him. He hit me in the belly and slapped my face. Commander Guiver was not so bad; he held my head when I was about to faint. I had sleepless nights for two nights – I was wakened by the police every ten minutes! That is the truth, the whole truth!'

Right.

A little more examination in chief – he denied writing the ransom letters and making notes on the cigarette packet – and then it was the turn of Mr Draycott for Nizam to cross-examine.

He wanted to know about the relationship between the two brothers. 'And you treat him gently and kindly all the while?'

'I don't treat him gently and kindly all the while. I try to make him realise his position as a stranger. I try to be lenient and semi-lenient.'

An odd expression, reminiscent of M3's talking of 'the intellectuals and the semi-intellectuals'.

'What do you mean by lenient and semi-lenient – does it mean chastising him?'

'Good heavens, no!'

'There's no reason to say he's afraid of you?'

'No reason at all.'

Arthur had said that on 29 December, feeling unwell, he had gone to bed at 8.30 to 9.00 pm, leaving Nizam to visit his relatives; something he hadn't known then but did now.

Turning to the four mysterious men who had visited Nizam in the early hours of the morning, Mr Draycott asked if he could identify one of them. 'I'm not vindictive and I don't wish to say – I haven't enough proof . . . I believe it was Robert Maxwell, Member of Parliament.'

So the inference was that Nizam was associating with Maxwell, who had tried to buy the *Sun* newspaper but had been outbid by Rupert Murdoch, the man whose wife had been the intended target of the kidnapping all along.

And that was the reason for Arthur attacking his brother whilst they were on remand at Brixton prison; he wanted to find out who these sinister people were. It was a contrived defence, and a supremely silly one.

It was at variance with what Nizam would use as a defence, said Mr Draycott: that on Sunday, 1 February, it was Arthur who told him to plant the paper flowers at Danes End – that there was a quarrel, because Arthur wanted Nizam to pick up the suitcase and Nizam refused, wanting to know why. And that on 6 February, Arthur had told Nizam to pick up the two suitcases at Gates Garage – 'I'm not concerned with what he'll say!' – and after Nizam arrived at The Raven, they both went to Gates Garage: 'I was not implicated in any crime!'

Now it was the turn of the Attorney General, who mentioned the police turning up on two occasions at Rooks Farm on 28 December: the police constable in respect of Nizam's allegation of assault by Arthur, and also the two detectives investigating an assault on a white man by two men, 'one white and one coloured'.

Regarding the matter of Mr Coote's alleged telephone call to Arthur on 29 December, the Attorney General almost casually asked, 'Is Mr Coote going to give evidence?'

'No.'

There was a pause. Then, from the Judge: 'What did he ring about?'

'He wanted to bring his girlfriend for the weekend of the fourth.'

'When did you remember that call?'

'When I was in my cell I remembered.'

The four men – one of whom, according to Arthur, was Robert Maxwell – received a mention. 'I have reason to believe these four persons knew what was going on and have used my brother', said Arthur. 'He thinks they were going to assist him to stay here permanently.'

It appeared they might have assisted Arthur's case as well, after it was alleged that the palm-print on the copy of the *People* was his. 'So I've been told', replied Arthur. 'It's not proven, not yet', and then, with a flash of genius, 'These people early in the morning of 29th. It is possible *they* may have taken my paper.'

'Assume it is your palm-print', said the Judge. 'Can you imagine how it could have got to St Mary House?'

'That paper could have been taken from my place', exclaimed Arthur. 'My brother has said there were four people at my farm at 2.00 am on 29 December.'

'Assume the billhook was the billhook Mr Smith lost at your farm', said the Attorney General.

'Another person will say it is another billhook!'

More outbursts: 'In captivity, I lose my sanity – what little I have, I'm trying to control it!'

The matters of the letters and the fingerprints were raised, especially Arthur's fingerprint found over the stamp on the envelope. 'If this is factual, not an assumption, and this is my fingerprint or thumb-print, then there is no other way of explaining it than someone has used my home behind my back!'

'Would you say your brother has been used?' asked the Attorney General.

'People helping him to remain in this country were telling him to do things, take my car . . .'

It sounded like desperate blustering, even more so after the Judge asked, 'Has your brother any reason to say you told him to do it?' because Arthur burst out with 'If my brother says I told him to do that . . . if you believe I told my brother to do these things, then you can find me guilty of all the charges, not just one!'

All the matters which Nizam would suggest were put to him: being with Nizam at Danes End on 1 February, told to take the paper flowers, pick up the suitcases on two occasions, being together at Gates Garage – false, all false.

Asked why he had not told the police about the existence of the four men, Arthur assumed wounded innocence: 'If I'd been treated humanely by the police, you'd have found most likely I wouldn't be facing you here, today . . . I'm not vindictive, my Lord. If I have some ideas, I want backing, I want grounds . . . Crime was not on my mind.'

On Arthur being handed an album of photographs, the question arose as to how one got into the shed where the dogs were kept, and the Judge instructed Arthur to show the jury. He did so and with a dazzling smile told them, 'It's all right – I'm not dangerous!' But the jury didn't find the remark funny, none of the nine men and none of the three women.

The ransom letters, together with the various spelling mistakes, plus Arthur's handwriting samples which also revealed spelling mistakes as well as inverted 'V's on the letters which corresponded with indentations on writing paper found in Nizam's bedroom became the subject of spirited discourse.

'I will be honest', he said. 'I wouldn't put anything past the police to get a conviction. Anyone can make alterations. I have never corresponded with unknown persons. There are doubts. If the handwriting is mine, then I have no excuse. Mr Hudson says there is a slight probability . . . Smith showed me the ransom note and said, "Spell it like that" . . . I know it is not good English but it is what I was told to write . . . I have written fifty pages of ransom letters. After I was beaten, I was told, "I want you to write it this way" . . . I wanted to avoid a beating.'

Back now to the matter of fingerprints, especially the one on the Piccadilly cigarette packet: 'Persons who were using my brother absorbed it from my brother. Why didn't you find Mr Rosenthal's fingerprints on it? Only mine! I am the scapegoat of this affair! As Attorney General, Sir Peter, you should have taken more care!'

So should Arthur – 'absorbed' was one of the curious phrases used on the telephone by M3.

Suggesting that when Arthur saw the solicitor, Mr Coote, he did not complain about being ill-treated by police, the Attorney General stated that it was because the allegation was an invention. 'I'm not vindictive; I'm not a person to invent', replied Arthur, adding, 'A policeman has never yet been found who admits to having beaten up a person!'

But after the examination and cross-examination was complete, Arthur was compelled to make a dramatic announcement to the jury before leaving the witness box:

> Believe me, I have great sympathy for the McKay family. I have a mother myself. I am no murderer, even if I am found guilty. These hands are artistic, not destructive. I believe in the preservation of man. That is what I am living for.

After that outburst, various witnesses were called who had visited the farm; they could say there was nothing suspicious about the brothers' behaviour but could not provide alibis for them at the pertinent times when the M3 telephone calls were made. Then Elsa Hosein was called.

She mentioned Nizam coming to live with them after he was 'thrown out by Adam' and said that Nizam and Arthur's relationship was 'brotherly – quite good'.

She mentioned the night that Nizam returned to the farm soaking wet but then appeared to be unsure of which Friday that had been: 'I'm getting confused.'

'My wife wants a glass of water!' bellowed Arthur from the dock and then repeated this shout, which earned him a rebuke from the Judge. Elsa then referred to the day of the arrests, saying, 'The police were not very nice.'

'Well, it was hardly a social visit . . .' commented the Judge before he was interrupted by a furious cry from Arthur: 'I refuse to sit here before that Judge! I would like him changed – he is partial!' As he leapt to his feet, he was grabbed by the warders and cried, 'Take me down!'

It was an exercise in control, that was all. First, demanding water for his wife who hadn't asked for any, then trying to put the Judge in his place, then demanding to be taken to the cells – which he would have been, in any event. 'King Hosein' was in his court, dictating to his subjects who was who and what was what.

Back to Elsa, who suffered losses of memory about some matters and suggested that the police might have taken some items and left others. She denied suggesting that on the night when Nizam came home soaking wet, it was because Arthur had been out with another woman; nor did she believe that Nizam feared her husband.

The elastoplast tin was produced; she thought her son used a tin like that as a money-box, which rather kicked into touch the allegation that police had planted it. Otherwise she was quite antagonistic in her replies: 'The police told me to shut up . . . I couldn't watch everywhere . . . why were they looking at papers?'

But one thing she was sure about; on the night of the second ransom drop, when the police alleged that Arthur and Nizam were seen at Gates Garage at 10.47 pm, Arthur had definitely been at Rooks Farm between 10.15 and 10.30 pm. And when the Attorney General suggested that the time he returned home was 11.00 pm, her adamant reply was, 'No. Earlier.'

The brother, Adam Hosein, gave evidence for the defence that Nizam had arrived at his house in Thornton Heath on the night of the kidnap at about 11.30 pm to deliver some trousers. His testimony was negative, even sanitized. People were helping to get Nizam a visa; he did not know who. On the night of the kidnap, Arthur was in bed, ill. Nizam didn't get excited when he was stressed. Nizam was his ordinary self that night, nor was he, Adam, surprised to see Nizam. He had no idea how long it took to drive from Thornton Heath to Epping.

The note from Brixton was produced: 'Did you read it?'

'Not really.'

'Did you realize he was asking you not to tell anyone that he had been to your home on Monday evening?'

'At the time I didn't understand.'

Former intelligence officer Dr Julius Grant, just approaching his sixty-ninth birthday, was called by the defence as an expert witness on fingerprints, handwriting and the weight of paper. With regard to Arthur's handwriting samples and the ransom notes, this was Dr Grant's judgement:

> I find a number of similarities in the writing and I reached the conclusion that there is a reasonable doubt that Arthur Hosein wrote the letters. But I cannot exclude the possibility that he did . . . I cannot exclude the possibility that they were written by Nizam.

Such wrigglings would continue throughout examination and cross-examination, and when it came to his expertise in comparing fingerprints, Dr Grant admitted that he had no experience in a fingerprint bureau but said, 'I have attended lectures, read widely.'

He was obliged to agree that the five separate marks – a total of 62 points by the prosecution – came from the same man but was unable (or unwilling) to agree the same number of points that Chief Inspector Brine had found.

'You're not suggesting your evidence is always acceptable?' asked the Attorney General.

'No', asserted the defence's star witness pompously, adding, 'I'm not saying it's always rejected, either.'

CHAPTER 20

Nizamodeen Hosein's Defence

Now it was the turn of Nizamodeen to enter the witness box. It was his voice on the M3 recordings, said the prosecution, but although it had already been decided that those recordings would not be played in court, his speech was so quiet that it would be suggested by both Judge and barristers that he was trying to be inaudible. His own barrister appeared the most brassed-off: 'Speak up – or you'll find me getting annoyed!'

First, Nizam painted a picture of being dominated by his brother: 'I was afraid of him . . . whenever I don't do something he tells me, he has a go at me . . . he punches me in the chest . . . he beat me on several occasions.'

He described Arthur driving him to County Hall on 19 December to get the name of the owner of the Rolls-Royce and admitted he had given a false name: 'I didn't want any more trouble . . . I gave my cousin's name in Norbury Crescent, because it was the only one I knew . . . I just put the incident out of my mind.'

On the night of Boxing Day, when Liley Mohammed wanted to go home and Arthur wanted her to stay, Nizam described phoning for a taxi, only to have Arthur jump on him and punch him.

His account of his movements on the day of the kidnapping was that he and Arthur were at the farm until 3.00 pm, when Arthur left in the Volvo to go to the finishers. He returned at 8.15 pm, complained of the 'flu and went to bed. Nizam then decided to visit his relatives in Norbury and Thornton Heath and drove to those addresses in the Volvo; and whilst he could have made the first of the M3 calls at Epping at 1.15 am, of course he did not.

Could Mrs McKay have been at the farm without his knowledge? She could not have.

On Sunday, 1 February – the day of the first ransom drop – having gone to London to deliver trousers, he had been told by Arthur to go to Dane End and put the paper flowers in the ground which he did, ('I do as I'm told'); he was then told to pick up a black suitcase, which would be found where he had deposited the flowers. Nizam refused, there was a row and he walked home in the rain; Elsa Hosein thought they had been out with other women, and Arthur told her to shut her mouth.

On to 6 February. The brothers had been to London, and at Bishop's Stortford Arthur told him to go back to Gates Used Car Lot, where he would see two black briefcases by a Mini – Arthur dictated the Mini's registration number to him which he wrote down on a piece of paper – and to pick them up, not to open them, but to bring them to him at The Raven public house.

So off to Gates Garage went the obedient and cowed Nizam; only to discover two white suitcases by the Mini. Thinking they might contain stolen property, and seeing they were the wrong colour, he drove to The Raven and informed Arthur that the suitcases were white, not black. Arthur then said, 'Drive me back, and we'll go and have a look.'

That's what they did, and that was how the police saw the Volvo and recognized them. Of course, this completely contradicted Arthur's account, but that was by the by – and when the police arrived the following day, Nizam was told by Arthur, 'Keep your mouth shut.' And Nizam did. But when he was shown the paper flowers and the billhook from St Mary House, he then realized that he was in a precarious position: 'I was frightened, scared . . . I was scared . . . I didn't know what would happen. I was scared . . . I was scared of Arthur . . . I thought he is my brother – and it was very hard for me to say.'

The Judge now intervened. 'What did you think Arthur had done?'

'I thought he had some part in . . .'

'In what?'

'In the affair.'

'What affair?'

'The Mrs McKay affair.'

Oh, dear. Bad news for Arthur, certainly, and it was about to get worse. The note shown to Adam at Brixton? 'Arthur told me to say it.' In fact, things were about to get a *lot* worse. The four men who were at the farm during the early hours of 29 December? There was no truth in it, the men did not exist, said Nizam – 'That's the story he was telling me to tell.'

He was furiously cross-examined by his brother's barrister, Mr Hudson, who asked him: 'Are you anxious to disguise your voice?'

'No, sir.'

'Do you swear it?'

'Yes, sir.'

'Why didn't you agree to speak on the telephone at the police station, as your brother did?'

'I didn't know what was happening. I was frightened . . .'

'Why were you frightened?'

'I thought it was a trick . . .'

But what Mr Hudson wanted to do was to show that far from being a shrinking violet, Nizam could be aggressive, and he cross-examined him regarding his violent behaviour in Trinidad, stabbing his brother Charles and beating his father. Nizam now fared very badly; the stabbing incident was an accident, he said, and he had never assaulted and beaten his father. This left Mr Hudson suggesting, 'You're perfectly capable of defending yourself!'

The Attorney General was no kinder, with Nizam responding to practically every question about his dealings with the police, 'I was scared stiff . . . I was trembling . . . I was saying, "Let me die!"'

'You didn't tremble and say "Let me die!" when you were asked to speak on the telephone', snapped the Attorney-General. 'You said "No"!'

Although Nizam had admitted going to County Hall he denied following the Rolls-Royce and when he was asked, 'Were you involved in the fact that Mrs McKay was missing?' he replied, 'I was involved with the paper flowers.'

'Then why should you say, "Let me die!"?'

'Mr Smith said I'd murdered her. Mr Smith said it was not a calf I'd chopped up, it was a woman . . .'

And on it went: 'I was scared . . . I was scared stiff . . . I didn't know what I was doing, what to say . . .'

Some interesting points arose. The first was when the Judge said, 'So far as the evidence goes, there was only one enquiry about the user of ULO 18F. Only one. That was you. M3 says, "I told the boys to trace the car." How would you describe what you did at the GLC office?'

'I was finding out the car owner.'

The second occasion was after Nizam admitted being in Bethnal Green after M3 had directed Inspector Minors (in his role as Alick McKay) to go to a telephone kiosk at that location. The Judge asked, 'Are you accepting that you were in Bethnal Green, near to the telephone box?' to which Nizam replied, 'I could see the box.'

There was one of those stunned silences in court, after which the Attorney General asked, 'Were you watching the call box to see if Mr Alick McKay went into it?' and when Nizam replied, 'No, sir', it did not, given his previous answer, sound convincing in the slightest.

The third occasion arose after the Judge asked, 'If you passed Gates Garage and saw the Minivan, why should you have to write it down?' It was a good point; the only reason to write it down in his guise as M3 was to pass it on to 'Alick McKay'.

The Attorney General pushed on relentlessly, to more wailings from Nizam: 'I was scared . . . Arthur told me to keep my mouth shut . . . I never knew why I was involved . . . I never knew what trouble I was in . . . I'd rather die than be charged with murder!'

Chapter 21

Summings-Up, Verdicts and Sentences

There was some re-examination of Arthur being a wife- (as well as a brother-) beater, before the closing speeches of both prosecution and defence.

The Judge in his summing-up asked the jurors to consider count two – the kidnapping – first, and then, if they were satisfied that one or both of the brothers were guilty, they could discuss the murder charge. If, on the other hand, they were satisfied that neither of the brothers was involved with the kidnapping plot, then the charge of murder must fail.

The evidence was carefully dealt with (as it had been by both the defence and the prosecution), and then the Judge discussed the matter of the alleged telephone call which Arthur had stated had come from his solicitor, 26-year-old David Coote, who was now in the well of the court looking studiously at his shoes. 'You may ask yourselves "why",' said the Judge. 'Mr Coote may have forgotten about it. You might expect Mr Coote to come into the witness box and say, "I may well have telephoned Arthur in the afternoon." But Mr Coote didn't come to say that. Is the reason, you may ask yourselves, because he'd have to say he never made the call?'

On 6 October 1970, the Judge finished his summing-up with the words, 'You must not convict except on evidence that makes you sure of guilt. Where the evidence falls short, you may say "not guilty", not as a matter of charity but as a matter of law; you must be unanimous.'

And with that, at 12.35 pm, the jury filed out to consider their verdict, to ruminate upon what the seventy-nine witnesses had told them.

At 4.10 pm they returned to deliver guilty verdicts on all of the counts in respect of both brothers, with a recommendation of mercy in respect of Nizamodeen.

Arthur reacted with a predictable outburst, first to the court in general: 'I claim this privilege to say that justice has not only been done, it has also been seen and heard by the public gallery, to be done through the provocation of your Lordship! You have shown immense partiality. To his Lordship I would say that from the moment I mentioned Robert Maxwell, I knew you were a Jew, not that I am anti-Jewish myself. You have shown throughout this case that you have directed the jury only on one side, to the Crown. I have produced thirty witnesses and not once have you mentioned anything on my behalf; you have denied me justice!'

Then, Mr Hudson got to his feet: 'Your Lordship, may I have a word . . .' only to be told, 'He doesn't need your help, Mr Hudson.'

'Thank you, members of the jury!' bellowed Arthur. 'It is a grave injustice!'

In passing sentence, the Judge said:

> The kidnapping and confinement of Mrs McKay was cold-blooded and abominable. She was snatched from the security and comfort of her home and so long as she was alive, she was reduced to despondent despair. The punishment must be salutary.
>
> You, Nizamodeen, are many years younger than your brother but I am not sure you are any the less culpable. There cannot be a worse case of blackmail. You held her family on the rack for weeks and months.

Both brothers were sentenced to life imprisonment for Mrs McKay's murder. For the kidnapping, it was twenty-five years' imprisonment for Arthur and fifteen for Nizamodeen, to run concurrently, plus concurrent sentences for both of fourteen years for blackmail and ten years for sending threats to murder.

With Arthur still raving and Nizam smiling, they were led off to the cells, and the Judge gave the jury 'the thanks of the City of London and indeed the whole of society for the service you have rendered to the administration of justice'; he also thanked DCS Smith: 'The community owes a debt of gratitude to you and your colleagues. It was brilliantly done. There is no other way to describe it and it has enabled justice to be done in this court.'

Jim Parker's commissioner's commendation was published in *Police Orders* but others were not. Tony Stevens told me, 'After the trial, John, Bill and I were told we'd been commended but that it would not be published to avoid publicity', and he was right; amongst others, John Bland's commendation was entered on his Central Record of Service, dated 10.11.70, with the words, 'Commissioner's: for valuable assistance in a difficult case of murder – not in *Police Orders*'.

All very odd; it was the sort of thing that happened during wartime, when women police officers (whose identities were never revealed in court) performed daring undercover work.

Of course, there was an appeal. It was heard at the High Court on 29 March 1971 before Edmund Davies, the Lord Justice of Appeal, accompanied by Lord Justice Karminski and Mr Justice Melford Stevenson. It was dealt with in a day; they did not need to hear the case for the Crown, having read the court transcript of the case beforehand.

Delivering judgement, Lord Justice Edmund Davies said:

> In the combined experience of the three members of this Court of Appeal, both at the Bar and then at the Bench, this is, in some ways the most terrible case with which we have ever had to deal, whether as counsel or Judges. No more a terrible crime could, in our judgement, be conjured up.

The appeal was dismissed, the sentences stood and the notoriety of the brothers earned them a place at Madame Tussaud's waxwork museum.

Chapter 22

The Aftermath

Following the arrest of the Hosein brothers, Alick McKay put St Mary House up for sale; it went for just over £30,000.

On 18 November 1970, Rooks Farm was auctioned after a cautionary note was put up by the auctioneers:

> It is essential that appointments be made to view as there are two Alsatian Guard Dogs at the property and applicants are strongly advised not to view without a prior appointment having been made through the auctioneers, so the guard dogs can be shut up. The auctioneers and the vendor wish to make it quite clear that they can accept no responsibility should applicants fail to observe the above viewing arrangements.

It was a prudent move. The dogs had already killed a nanny goat and a kid, pets belonging to the licensee of The Cock public house, as well as a sheepdog. However, the warning proved unnecessary. The day before the auction commenced, the dogs, who were due to be destroyed on the day of the auction, were reprieved after they were taken to a dog-training establishment at RAF Debden. It is unlikely that they were taken there for re-homing purposes.

Bidding for the farm commenced at £5,000, and it was sold to Mrs Arthur Lilley for £18,500.

Also present was Elsa Hosein. Arthur had wanted the proceeds of the sale to go to his parents in Trinidad; the very next day, Elsa presented herself at the Divorce Court Registrar at Somerset House, where she obtained an emergency injunction restraining Arthur from disposing of half the proceeds of the sale. A week later, she filed for divorce on the grounds of cruelty, and on 2 December 1970 Arthur appeared at the Divorce Court, where he agreed to the Judge making an order freezing the proceeds of £10,000 from the sale until the hearing of the divorce action.

However, Mrs Lilley was unable to raise the capital to buy the farm. The following year, it was re-sold to an East End publican, Anthony Wyatt, for £17,500, with Sworders the auctioneers demanding the difference of £1,000 from Mrs Lilley. With her share of the proceeds, Elsa stated, it was her intention to return to Germany and set up a business there.

But before that happened, she received a letter from Nizam saying he had been beaten up at Winson Green Prison, Birmingham. This was denied by the Home Office, although he was transferred to Wormwood Scrubs and it was there that she saw him and said that he told her, 'Sis, they beat me up – but I can't tell you who did it.'

Arthur had also been moved; he had commenced his sentence at Wandsworth but had been moved to Leicester where, when Else saw him, he was sporting a black eye. 'But he looked in a terrible state', said Elsa. 'He had obviously had a rough time.'

Arthur had not wanted to speak about his experiences which, given the circumstances, was understandable. The explanation was provided by a senior prison officer, who described what had happened: 'One of our inmates was sitting opposite the Hosein inmate; they were having breakfast. The inmate said to Hosein, "Now it's all over, what did you do with Mrs McKay?" Hosein reached over, pointed to the bacon on the inmate's plate and said, "You may be eating her now!" A serious fight broke out between the inmates, and Hosein was injured and was then transferred to another prison.'

Elsa Hosein had run sobbing from the court when the verdict was announced, saying, 'I still believe in my husband's innocence. I am shocked at the verdict. It is terrible, terrible.' This was understandable and typical of many wives' reactions to the sentencing of their husbands in bitterly contested trials.

However, what was not said by Elsa at the trial but revealed later in an exclusive interview with a tabloid newspaper, was that Arthur appeared fixated on Rupert Murdoch, saying that he would be worth a lot of money if he could be held captive. With all the publicity about Murdoch's purchase of the *News of the World* and the *Sun*, Arthur thought that he ought to be more careful: 'You can never tell what might happen to him.'

There was more. Included in her revelations, after she returned from Germany on 3 January, Elsa said she had seen that the curtains had been ripped off the railings in her bedroom, and that in the spare bedroom occupied by her sister-in-law (who had accompanied her to Germany), someone had been using the bed. In the bed was a woman's blue-green vest which was too big to fit her daughter; believing that the brothers had held a party with women in her absence, and obviously annoyed, Elsa threw the vest on the fire in the sitting room.

She was furious with Arthur but when she tasked him with what might have happened in her absence, in her words 'he went berserk' and ordered her and the children out of the house. According to Elsa, Nizamodeen begged her not to go and, shaking and trembling, he held out his hands to her, saying, 'You see these hands, sis? They can kill. Please, for goodness sake, don't leave me here. These hands are able to kill.'

Elsa was in no doubt in her own mind that Nizam had murdered Mrs McKay. This view appeared to be confirmed when she accompanied a reporter to see him at Winson Green Prison. She wanted him to provide details of what had happened to Mrs McKay's body, in order to pass the information to the McKay family.

Nizam told her that early in the evening of 29 December, he and Arthur had gone to the Victoria Sporting Club in the Edgware Road, where Arthur had become quite drunk; and then he told Elsa, 'Yes, sis. We had her.'

He denied killing Mrs McKay with the sawn-off shotgun which had been found by the police, but when Elsa persisted, asking how she had died, he replied, 'Do you remember that night you were going to leave us? Do you remember that night, sis?'

He refused to tell Elsa what had happened to the body, in the same way that he refused Alick McKay's written pleas to both brothers for them to reveal the whereabouts of his wife's remains.

So the jury never heard about the state of Elsa's bedroom, the spare bed having been slept in or the blue-green vest which might have belonged to Mrs McKay but had been consumed in the sitting room fire.

That was not all. Whilst the brothers had been on remand in Brixton, a fraudster serving a six-month sentence told the police that one or perhaps both of the brothers had admitted murdering Mrs McKay and disposing of the body in the Thames at Windsor. It was all rather confusing, and although he gave evidence at Wimbledon Magistrates' Court, his testimony was not used at the Old Bailey trial. With the confusion about who said what, it is perhaps understandable that the prosecution did not call him.

But it was very odd that another piece of evidence was not called. That was the testimony of Shuffi Ali, the brothers' cousin who lived at 175 Norbury Crescent. It was that address that Nizam had written on the GLC form when tracing the owner of the Rolls-Royce; the same address which he had visited on the night of the kidnap to repay his cousin's loan. A spent cartridge had fallen out of his pocket and Ali had asked what it was. Nizam pulled out several other spent cartridges and said he had been shooting at the farm. That was coupled with the sound of a gunshot being heard in that vicinity a day or so later.

And yet, Ali was not called by the prosecution; one wonders why.

So the brothers settled into their prison existence. Arthur spent some time in the high-security unit at Leicester Prison, where his skills as a tailor came in handy altering prison apparel for luminaries such as Eddie Richardson of the 'Torture Trial' fame.

In November 1987, his case was considered by the Parole Board; it was refused, but it was decided that it would be considered once more in February 1993. During the intervening period, Arthur's mental health deteriorated and he was transferred to Ashworth Hospital, Liverpool. The Home Secretary refused his application for a review by the Parole Board on 2 September 1994.

Arthur therefore petitioned the European Commission of Human Rights on the grounds that had the Parole Board reviewed his case after twenty years, it could have ordered his release. The Commission sat in private on 28 February 1996, but the President, Mr C. L. Rozakis, and thirteen members of the committee unanimously rejected the application as being 'manifestly ill-founded'.

He died in Ashworth hospital in 2009, aged seventy-three.

After twenty years' imprisonment, Nizam was released in February 1990 and deported to Trinidad. He lives there today, married to a human rights activist.

Rooks Farm had not quite done with killing. In 19 September 1972, the new owner, Tony Wyatt, was holding a wedding reception there for his sister-in-law when there was an altercation with an uninvited guest named John Scott. It was not merely that Tony Wyatt and the other male guests were wearing grey morning suits and John Scott was dressed in a striped T-shirt; he was also drunk, belligerent and threatened Wyatt with a champagne bottle. Wyatt picked up 'something' which turned out to be a grass sickle and stabbed Scott in the heart, severing an artery.

The body was dressed in fresh clothes and driven to Leytonstone, where it was found in Scott's van, the following Monday. Charged with murder, Wyatt was convicted of manslaughter at the Old Bailey on 9 March 1971 and sentenced to three years' imprisonment.

The farm was put up for auction on 15 June 1973 and a client of Edward Watson & Sons – described as 'a mystery buyer' – purchased it for £46,500.

The farm appears to have been peaceful since then.

Chapter 23

Post Mortem

The investigation, which had cost almost £100,000, was over. The matters contained in correspondence CR201/70/39 were tidied up, a closing report was submitted and it was sent off to the Yard's General Registry. The enquiry's index cards, messages, pro formas, actions and exhibit books were put away, and the incident room was handed back to its original occupiers. The officers on the enquiry – including those who had sat for weeks in a freezing cold nondescript observation van in Arthur Road, to see if M3 and his associates were monitoring the movements of the police and/or the McKay family – dispersed.

No one doubted their commitment or that the investigation had taken its toll on Bill Smith (whose cigarette consumption, already high, was said to have risen to a hundred a day) and John Minors, both of whom, in the opinion of their subordinates, had aged ten years.

Jim Parker remained on 'V' Division for another five years before being promoted to detective inspector and posted to the Anti-Terrorist Squad, but only for ten months. He received a sideways move to the Serious Crime Squad, where his expertise was much needed, to replicate his success as office manager with a massive investigation into the 'Hungarian Circle'. Jim's proficiency meant that not one of the 5,000 surveillance photographs or any of the documents contained in a pile 9ft tall went astray, and the outcome was another commendation to be presented by the commissioner, the Trial Judge and the Director of Public Prosecutions.[1] After a year, following his well-earned promotion to detective chief inspector, Jim accepted a well-deserved retirement.

Tony Stevens was promoted to detective inspector and continued his glittering career with the Flying Squad, achieving a

1 For further details about this remarkable case, see *You're Nicked!* Robinson, 2007

considerable success during the investigation into the 1975 Bank of America robbery.[2]

Jack Quarrie did not lose his taste for adventure; following the Hosein case, he was one of a team who went to Northern Ireland and was commended by the commissioner for his part in the arrest of two men for murder in 'a dangerous and complicated case'. In retirement, for several years he acted as the police adviser who brought absolute authenticity to what became the highly successful television series, *The Sweeney*. The youngest ever Regimental Sergeant Major of No.9 Commando died on New Year's Day 2007, just two weeks after the death of his beloved wife, Irene. The members of 9 Commando's Old Comrades Group, 'The Black Hackle Society', mourned the loss of the man who had been their honorary secretary.

John Bland rose to the rank of detective superintendent. On 28 April 1978, a small black cloud appeared over New Scotland Yard; John left under it.[3]

* * *

Afterwards, there were recriminations on all sides regarding the handling of the case. The family blamed the police, as did the press; the police blamed both the family and the press.

The family first: one can only feel the greatest sympathy for them, especially Alick McKay. Right from the start, he *knew* Muriel had not left the house by her own volition. When the first ransom call came at 1.15 the following morning, he *knew* she had been kidnapped and he was understandably frantic. And yet he felt he was being treated as a suspect by the police – the very people he wanted to find her and return her safely.

His first mistake was to involve the press; as a newspaperman himself, he knew the value of advertising, but unfortunately it also attracted unwelcome and time-wasting publicity. The family's next mistake was to inform the public that, having consulted one spiritualist, they were going to call upon the services of another. It is easy to appreciate the agonies experienced by the family;

---

2 For further details of this robbery, see *The Sweeney: The First Sixty Years of Scotland Yard's Crimebusting Flying Squad, 1919–1978*, Pen & Sword Books, 2011 and also *Scotland Yard's Flying Squad: 100 Years of Crime Fighting*, Pen & Sword Books, 2019

3 For more details regarding Bland's demise, see *Scotland Yard's Gangbuster: Bert Wickstead's Most Celebrated Cases*, Pen & Sword Books, 2018

all they wanted was their mother back and they were clutching at whatever crumbs of comfort these charlatans could offer them, but the immense amount of time-wasting rubbish that came pouring in was catastrophic for the investigation, slowing it to a snail's pace. So that – plus begging with the kidnappers, promising them anything within reason – put huge obstacles in the way of the enquiry.

Next, the press. To publish details of Mrs McKay's letter and the ransom demand was an act of gross irresponsibility – even though it is accepted that those details were furnished by a police officer. It appeared that every newspaper wanted to outdo its rivals to boost sales, and it was not considered necessary to publish the facts; many of the stories which appeared in print were pure invention.

So do those foregoing matters let the police off the hook? Not a bit of it.

It has already been said – and it'll stand a repeat – that this enquiry was unprecedented in the annals of the British police. From the time that Alick McKay telephoned the police – at 8 o'clock on the evening of 29 December – until 5¼ hours later when the first telephone call was made by M3, it could be said that valuable time was lost, and it was. But no one had seen Mrs McKay being abducted and there was deep scepticism that she had been; it's difficult to apportion blame there.

However, with that 1.15 am telephone call matters should have changed dramatically, but they did not. This is not said with the benefit of hindsight; it is said with the benefit of experience. As soon as that phone call came in, a major enquiry should have got underway, because if there was any evidence to be found, it had to be found straight away; if not, it might never be. That's why in other murder investigations the enquiry team would initially work flat-out, taking 20–24 hours without rest, to establish that the basics had been covered.

And if, with such an enquiry underway, Mrs McKay had suddenly walked back in through the front door of 20 Arthur Road 24 hours later, saying she had 'wanted some time to herself', so what? The officer ordering the enquiry might have been censured by a higher authority – he would certainly have attracted derisory comments as well as a red face – but that would have been all.

No. With faster action, Mona Lydiatt would have been seen quicker, to impart her vital information of seeing a dark saloon parked on the driveway of St Mary House; and impressions of that vehicle's tyres might have been recovered.

Next, a 'stop' notice should have been sent to the editors of all the national newspapers, requesting that no details of the case be released. There was a precedent from seven years earlier; when senior officers at the Yard had published photographs in the press of the men wanted for the Great Train Robbery, the officer in charge, Tommy Butler, had protested furiously. He had wanted to trace the robbers using his own methods and his own informants and he told the management that publishing their photographs would drive them underground or abroad – and he was right. It took Butler years to finally catch all the men involved.

A telephone line with a unique number should have been immediately supplied to 20 Arthur Road, the number only to be imparted to M3. And an officer should have been posted to the house to impersonate Alick McKay and answer all incoming calls on that line. I fully appreciate that at that time there were no trained hostage negotiators in the British police, but despite the fact that there was not then a department to train undercover officers, police had utilized the skills of such people for years to carry out clandestine and undercover work. In those days there was a wealth of such ad hoc talent.

The ludicrous plan of having a dragged-up officer attend a ransom demand and the overkill of the first ransom drop have been dealt with in detail and are best passed over; but the fact remains that the officers concerned acted with great courage, especially after M3 was fully aware of the police presence on the first ransom drop and stated on the second that he and his gang had 'high-powered rifles with telescopic sights'. It took real gallantry to press ahead on that night.

So, it all begs the question, could Muriel McKay have been saved? The answer is no, almost certainly not. The general consensus of opinion is that having written those heart-rending messages, she was dead, probably within 48 hours of her abduction. The wrong woman had been seized and she was an encumbrance; plus, of course, that within days, Elsa and the children were due back from Germany.

Was she at Rooks Farm? The telephone was not answered until 10.30 on the night of the kidnap and that was when Liley Mohammed called, only for Arthur to tell her that Nizam was not there. It was two days later when she came to visit the farm, and by that time Muriel McKay must surely have been murdered.

From what Elsa Hosein later said (although not for the benefit of the jury) regarding the state of the bedroom and the piece of lady's apparel which was burnt in the fire, yes, it appears Mrs McKay was at the farm; and it was there that she met her end. There had been the sound of a gunshot round about that time, the Leopard Dog with the acute sense of smell, the odour of a crematorium, the blunt hacksaw blade and billhook, the discharged, sawn-off shotgun.

Were Muriel McKay's remains fed to the pigs? Almost certainly. But it leaves one question mark, an enormous one, hanging over the whole case, and it is this.

If one accepts that despite one of the brothers having an ungovernable temper and the other, a vicious streak, neither were professional criminals. Although they had attempted to extort one million pounds, they were staggeringly inept. On both ransom drops they used a car which was registered to their address; Arthur left his finger- and palm-prints on five different incriminating items; and Nizam made seven damning admissions in court which inexorably tied him into the case.

But the question mark referred to is this. In spite of all their combined incompetence, they left not one forensic clue at the farm which would point to Muriel McKay ever having been there. Not one.

And was anybody else involved in the kidnap? Quite possibly. Nizam, as we know, visited another brother and his cousin on the evening of the kidnap; but of course, they were eliminated from the enquiry. Was Arthur able to control Mrs McKay by himself? Not necessarily, if we accept the evidence of the torn curtains in the Hoseins' bedroom. All very baffling.

Of course, there's always Nizam, isn't there? Stretched out on some Trinidadian beach, he could throw quite a lot of light on all of these matters, couldn't he?

Providing, of course, that he doesn't feel too frightened.

Bibliography

Brown, Antony M.	*Death of an Actress*	Mirror Books, 2018
Clark, Geoffrey (ed.)	*Trial of James Camb*	William Hodge & Co., 1949
Cooper, William	*Shall We Ever Know? The Trial of the Hosein Brothers for the Murder of Mrs McKay*	Hutchinson, 1971
Davidson, Earl	*Joey Pyle*	Virgin, 2003
Deeley, Peter and Walker, Christopher	*Murder in the 4th Estate: An Investigation into the roles of Press and Police in the McKay Case*	Gollancz, 1971
Du Rose, John	*Murder was my Business*	W.H. Allen, 1971
Frasier, David K.	*Murder Cases of the Twentieth Century*	McFarland & Co. Inc., 1996
Honeycombe, Gordon	*The Complete Murders of the Black Museum*	Leopard Books, 1995
Hoskins, Percy	*No Hiding Place!*	Daily Express Publications, 1951
Howe, Sir Ronald	*The Pursuit of Crime*	Arthur Barker, 1961
Kirby, Dick	*You're Nicked!*	Robinson, 2007
Kirby, Dick	*The Guv'nors: Ten of Scotland Yard's Greatest Detectives*	Pen & Sword, 2010
Kirby, Dick	*The Brave Blue Line: 100 Years of Metropolitan Police Gallantry*	Pen & Sword, 2011

Kirby, Dick	*The Sweeney: The First Sixty Years of Scotland Yard's Crimebusting Flying Squad, 1919–1978*	Pen & Sword, 2011
Kirby, Dick	*Death on the Beat*	Pen & Sword, 2012
Kirby, Dick	*Scotland Yard's Gangbuster: Bert Wickstead's Most Celebrated Cases*	Pen & Sword, 2018
Kirby, Dick	*Scotland Yard's Flying Squad: 100 Years of Crime Fighting*	Pen & Sword, 2019
Kirby, Dick	*Scotland Yard's Murder Squad*	Pen & Sword, 2020
Kirby, Dick	*Scotland Yard's Casebook of Serious Crimes: 75 Years of No-Nonsense Policing*	Pen & Sword, 2021
Lisners, John	*The Rise and Fall of the Murdoch Empire*	John Blake, 2013
Morton, James	*East End Gangland*	Time Warner, 2001
Napley, Sir David	*Not Without Prejudice*	Harrap, 1982
O'Flaherty, Michael	*Have you Seen this Woman?*	Corgi, 1971
Rawlings, William	*A Case for the Yard*	John Long, 1961
Richardson, Eddie	*The Last Word*	Headline, 2005
Scott, Sir Harold	*Scotland Yard*	André Deutsch, 1954
Simpson, Professor Keith	*Forty Years of Murder*	Harrap, 1978
Thomas, Donald	*An Underworld at War*	John Murray, 2003
Thomas, Donald	*Villains' Paradise*	John Murray, 2005

Tullett, Tom	*Strictly Murder: Famous Cases of Scotland Yard's Murder Squad*	Bodley Head, 1979

Index